Strategy for Law Firms

Strategy for Law Firms

After the Legal Services Act

Nick Jarrett-Kerr

The Law Society

© The Law Society 2009

ISBN–13: 978–1–85328–758–9

Published in 2009 by the Law Society
113 Chancery Lane, London WC2A 1PL

Typeset by IDSUK (DataConnection Ltd)
Printed by TJ International Ltd, Padstow, Cornwall

FSC
Mixed Sources
Product group from well-managed forests and other controlled sources
Cert no. SGS-COC-2482
www.fsc.org
© 1996 Forest Stewardship Council

The paper used for the text pages of this book is FSC certified. FSC (the Forest Stewardship Council) is an international network to promote responsible management of the world's forests.

Contents

Acknowledgements

A number of people have helped me greatly in writing this book. First, Michael Roch kindly contributed Chapter 9 on law firm valuation. We originally planned to write this book together but pressure of work meant that he was unable to contribute beyond this chapter; he did, however, assist greatly in the early design of the book's structure. My colleague Harriet Hall has helped throughout the project, with ideas, research and the identification of key issues as well as proof-reading. My sincere thanks go to both of them.

Thanks also go to my colleague and friend Ed Wesemann, who got me started and worked with me on the road to discovering strategy; to Patrick McKenna and Gerry Riskin, who helped me in my early career as a strategy consultant; and to Alan Hodgart, who has always shared his ideas with me so openly. My friend Robert Millard has also stimulated many ideas. Friedrich Blase introduced me to Edvinsson's concepts of intellectual capital, and Peder Hofman-Bang of Intellectual Capital Sweden AB helped to develop my knowledge. More recently, Denise Crawford at Nottingham Law School has helped me a great deal in pointing me to new areas of reading and more sources, both for the book and for my leading the strategy module on the Law School MBA. My thanks to all of them and all others who have assisted my thinking over the years.

Last, but very much not least, I would also like from the bottom of my heart to thank Sarah, my long-suffering wife, who has stoically put up with my general grouchiness throughout the project as well as the cancellation of a holiday so that I could get the book finished.

Nick Jarrett-Kerr
November 2009

Abbreviations

ABS	alternative business structure
CEO	chief executive officer
CFO	chief finance officer
CHRO	chief human resources officer
CIO	chief information officer
CLSO	chief legal services officer
CMO	chief marketing officer
COO	chief operations officer
DTI	Department of Trade and Industry
HOFA	head of finance and administration
HOLP	head of legal practice
IPO	initial public offering
LBO	leveraged buy-out
LDP	legal disciplinary practice
LLP	limited liability partnership
LSA	Legal Services Act 2007
LSB	Legal Services Board
MBO	management buy-out
MDP	multi-disciplinary practice
NFP	not for profit
PEP	profit per equity partner
REL	registered European lawyer
RFL	registered foreign lawyer
SRA	Solicitors Regulation Authority
WACC	weighted average cost of capital

The new world

KEY POINTS _____

- Introduction: consolidation and segmentation, the need for a sensible strategy, competitive forces, the effect of the internet
- The Legal Services Act 2007: the Legal Services Board, the need for increased investment, types of investor, opportunities and challenges for law firms, successful structuring
- The importance of strategic planning

Introductory themes

The next decade is likely to be an exciting time for law firms, as they face a future of change, upheaval and new horizons. The legal profession has already entered a time of huge change and transformation right across the world. In the midst of challenge and uncertainty, however, there are some huge opportunities for entrepreneurial law firms which manage to get their strategies right and to implement them effectively.

Many of us dislike change or are frightened by it and lawyers are no exception. It would be easy to paint the new challenges for law firms in entirely negative language, and many have already chosen a doomsday approach. Richard Susskind's latest book is provocatively titled *The End of Lawyers?* (Susskind, 2008), whilst other commentators[1] have talked about the legal profession – in the UK at least – facing a dramatic upheaval somewhat similar to the Big Bang which completely transformed London's financial services industry in 1986.

Lawyers form an easy target, and attacking an unpopular profession by jokes, jibes and criticism has proved to be a popular national and/or even global sport for many generations.

In the United Kingdom, it seems that the government has had it in for lawyers for some years now. After all, the Legal Services Act 2007 (LSA) was brought in to introduce, amongst other things, further competition at much the same time as reforms to the litigation and courts systems have reduced volumes of litigation, and budgets for publicly funded work have contracted. The burden of compliance and the cost of professional indemnity cover also continue to rise and threaten the survival of smaller or more chaotically run firms. Firms are indeed telling us – not just in the UK – that they are finding that the regulatory authorities are becoming much more rigorous in their enforcement and monitoring activities than before. Clients also continue to demand more for less, and are shopping around for a wider range of services than ever before, both inside the profession and amongst other organisations seeking to provide legal services. And then came the 2007 recession, accompanied by a dramatic reduction in the volume of work for the profession as a whole. Few firms have escaped rounds of redundancies or financial and cash flow pressures.

All this comes at a time when we are also witnessing great changes within the profession as firms seek to improve their market shares at the expense of rivals. Put bluntly, dog is developing an increasing appetite to eat dog.

Consolidation and segmentation

We should remember that the legal profession has often been described as the last of the cottage industries. In England and Wales alone, there are nearly 11,000 law firms, over 85 per cent of which are small firms with four partners or fewer. Yet more than 40 per cent of all solicitors are now working in the small percentage of firms with more than 26 partners and this percentage goes up every year.

Lawyer numbers have also gone up, but most of this growth – from around 66,000 in private practice as solicitors in 2000 to more than 80,000 now – has been concentrated in the larger firms. We are witnessing the market becoming steadily more dominated by larger firms, with the medium and smaller firms facing increasing pressures. In addition, there are roughly 15,000 barristers, and a further 12,000 or so people engaged as legal executives, licensed conveyancers, patent and trade mark attorneys, notaries and law costs draftsmen.

According to the Office for National Statistics (2006), the legal services sector now generates some £23.25 billion which equates to around 1.8 per cent of national GDP and employs well over 300,000 people in all (UK Treasury, 2009).

The shape of the legal profession is also changing, with an increasing vertical division of the profession into two separate business sectors – the large national and international law firms on the one hand and the domestic firms on the other hand acting for both consumers and commercial firms in the small and medium size category. Firms which I describe in Chapter 4 as market rulers, together with firms competing for similar work, dominate the top of the market for both clients and lawyers.

BOX 1.1

Segmentation of commercial work

The marketing for commercial work divides into four main segments:

- **Top tier** work that goes automatically to London: complex transactions, financings, litigation, etc. (upper end London market work) – the *icing*.
- **High end** work that could be directed to mid market London or leading regional/national firms: big but standard transactions and matters for big and medium clients – the *marzipan*.
- **Mid tier** work, where clients want a competitive supplier: could be leading regional/national or mid market regional – the *cake*.
- **Lower tier** work, for medium to small enterprises and private clients. Includes bread-and-butter work for large companies – the *cake base*.

Top end segments of work – however defined – for both corporate and rich individuals are increasingly becoming the natural domain of the top end law firms.

We often use the analogy of a cake to describe how work divides into layers or segments. The cake is the legal market. Segmentation – which divides law firms into groups serving the different types of potential clients with broadly similar needs and perceptions of value – describes the layers of the cake, from the thin layer of top level work (the icing) for mainly corporate clients and the super wealthy at the top of the cake, down to the cake base and crumbs at the bottom of the cake. Segmentation affects work types as well as client types, with complex matters falling within the higher layers of the segmentation cake and standardised work being done at a lower level.

Segmentation differs from consolidation. Consolidation describes how any market over time become less fragmented and increasingly dominated by smaller numbers of larger organisations. In a consolidating industry, strong firms will gain market share at the expense of the weak. In describing the way market share is apportioned, consolidation therefore describes the vertical slices of the cake – the way in which the various shares of the market are divided.

At present, we are seeing both segmentation taking place and also a certain amount of consolidation.

The segmentation phenomenon is seen at the two ends of the legal market – the big commercial work end and the bulk commoditised end.

In the arena of commercial work, the success of the bigger firms has been in exploiting the desire of commercial clients to see critical mass in key practice areas. The result has been that to be a full range commercial law firm, with in-depth major commercial practice areas, generally requires a size of around 400 fee-earners or more. Such scale enables strong teams of specialists to service large transactions (see p. 30). One strategy is to be proactive in only one or a very few practice areas and to remain small; hence the advent of small niche firms specialising in areas such as intellectual property, employment and construction law. At the commoditised end, there is also a concentration of work into larger 'factory' style law firms which are rapidly sewing up panel appointments, whether those are with chains of estate agents, insurance companies, mortgage providers or unions.

The result is that the larger firms are increasingly taking bigger and bigger slices of the available legal cake and the slices of the cake available to the smaller firms are decreasing. I would therefore expect to see over the next five to ten years a growing consolidation in the medium and smaller ranges of law firms, leading to a smaller number of somewhat larger, medium size firms. This is likely to be brought about by many firms under 26 partners in size seeking to grow by acquisition of firms and teams and through merger. This trend will also accelerate as sole practitioners reach retirement age or become absorbed into other firms.

The need for a sensible strategy and well-run businesses

As we face the current economic downturn and in the light of market and external pressures, law firms usually fall into three broad categories. In the first category, some firms may feel that their survival strategy is best served by going for further growth or by becoming part of a bigger enterprise where the advantages of scale, critical mass, economies of scale and deep teams will allow them to maintain or improve their financial and competitive positions. The second category of firm may elect to follow a strategy that allows it to avoid all the disadvantages of growth and to remain niche (or at least small), by competing in a restricted set of markets or services and specialisations, and by occupying specific strategic positions relative to competitor firms in terms of quality, or cost, or client focus. This strategy is not as easy as it sounds as it may require the firm to discard irrelevant or unprofitable offices, departments and partners. The third category of firm seeks to batten down the hatches and survive the recessional storms in whatever way it can.

Whatever strategic choices a firm decides to make, there is one simple truth for all three categories of firms and indeed the profession as a whole. The message is that firms need to be more focused than ever before in managing themselves rigorously as well-coordinated and professionally run businesses. This means a bit more than a 'back to basics' approach, although it is vital to keep a tight control on cash, overheads, working capital and all the key financial drivers. What seems to me to be necessary – and is already noticeable in many well-run firms – is to start to work more as a team than just as loose groups of individuals. Many firms are now making at least some efforts to develop a one-firm approach where consistently applied and agreed methodologies and processes are brought to bear upon clients' matters. Clients want to see firms deliver a consistent and not a patchy service, and to some extent these trends are client driven. The imperative, therefore, is for a firm to be run as an efficient business with well-designed systems and processes. Additionally, every firm needs to find ways of streamlining its services wherever possible. Clients do not usually want to pay for the wheel to be reinvented. They prefer to see the experience of the firm, garnered from previous similar engagements, put to use in their matter in a cost effective manner.

Sound management practices are necessary in order to achieve consistency of service and to enable the firm to be run as an efficient business. This means five things. In the first place the firm must take time to agree management roles, to select the right people and then to allow those people to get on with the job of managing. In the second place partners need to understand that they cannot be involved in every decision and that those who have been chosen to manage the firm should be allowed to do so without undue interference. This leads to the third point, that partners do have to be supportive of their management, to accept necessary disciplines and should avoid, wherever they can, opposition and undermining of decision-making. Fourth, partners have to be accountable for their actions and decisions and ultimately they have to be responsible for their own autonomy in areas where they have to maintain independence. Finally, and perhaps most important, the firm must constantly try to work towards a high performance culture in which there is no room for passengers and underperformers.

The brutal truth is that there is not much fun in store for many law firms over the next five years, but it is surely better to impose some management rigour and essential disciplines now and thereby to survive and prosper, than to do nothing in the vague hope that the current pressures and difficulties will soon pass.

Competitive forces

The new statutory provisions affecting the United Kingdom represent both a set of opportunities and a host of threats.

Thirty years ago, a Harvard Business School professor, Michael Porter, identified some structural determining factors which influence competition in most industries (Porter, 1980). The Five Forces Framework which he developed still holds true and Figure 1.1 illustrates the five competitive forces which affect the legal profession. First and foremost is the internal competition in the form of other law firms in each locality or performing

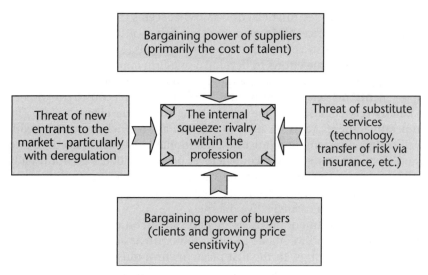

Figure 1.1   Competitive forces

similar services. As Figure 1.1 shows, there are three horizontal sources of competitive pressure forces increasingly coming into play in the shape of new entrants to the legal services market, the threat of substitute services (technology, the internet, transfer of risk via insurance) as well as competition from established rivals within the profession. There are two sources of vertical pressure in the form of the bargaining power both of suppliers (mainly the cost of hiring and retaining talented lawyers) and of clients and users of legal services.

The effect of the internet on legal services

It has needed neither deregulation nor the full advent of the LSA for the existence of the internet to start to have a profound effect on law firms. A recent research survey of over 1,000 consumers found that, after direct recommendations and word of mouth, the internet is now the most important source for those looking for a law firm for the first time (LegallyBetter.com, 2008). Many lawyers rely heavily on emails via BlackBerries and similar devices and cannot now imagine a working life without a computer. Yet, according to the same survey, around one-third of all law firms still do not have a website. New comparison and matching sites are proliferating to augment the traditional law firm directories. Virtual law firms and firms providing an overall umbrella of marketing and support services (see Chapter 6 for a description of umbrella firms) have been formed and more will come. We have also seen the growth of referral firms and agencies, all keen to introduce potential clients to law firms in return for a commission. Clients are also finding it somewhat easier to cut out the use of law firms altogether by the use of document assembly sites and open-source software which enables free access to legal research and knowledge through search engines. More is to come. As Richard Susskind (2008, p. 22) says: 'I believe that what lawyers have enjoyed so far is little more than improved plumbing. The infrastructure (the global network) is in place now but the really exciting developments that will penetrate to the very heart of legal service and our legal systems are coming in the next decade.' He goes on to identify nine 'disruptive' technologies that will redefine the legal market-place and the practice of law – automated document assembly, relentless communications and connectivity, the electronic market-place, e-learning, online legal guidance, legal open-sourcing (the legal equivalent of Wikipedia), closed legal communities, workflow and project management advances, and embedded legal knowledge.

What is also clear is that the next generation of web design and development, known as Web 2, is rapidly creating new ways for lawyers to communicate through social, collaborative and participative services. Information sharing, webinars, podcasts, video technologies and the use of blogs and social networks are all changing the way that lawyers can interact with their clients, hold conversations with them, build rapport and introduce new services. Lawyers have got used to producing and transmitting documents electronically without the need to clutter up the post room, and now have to adjust to new methods of web-based document sharing which reduce the need for heavy email traffic and multiple document versions. This in turn means that lawyers sitting in Mumbai can converse as easily with clients in the UK as can a lawyer sitting in a UK office, except those who have the benefits of very local access to clients.

Internet connectivity also eases the way for outsourcing of both back and middle office functions to cheaper areas of the world. Firms such as Clifford Chance are saving tens of millions of pounds in this way. In addition, the advent of legal process outsourcing provides further competitive pressures. These facilities mean that lawyers, primarily in India and the Philippines but also in more cost effective areas of the UK, regularly supply services such as document review and production, discovery, legal research and writing, and their services extend also to the drafting of pleadings and briefs and the provision of patent services.

The Legal Services Act 2007 and the removal of special protection for lawyers

The LSA is not just a peculiarly British phenomenon. Whilst the Act affects only law firms in England and Wales, similar legislation is either predicted or has already taken place in many other jurisdictions (for instance, Australia). The Act had a gestation period of approximately five years until it received the Royal Assent in late 2007 and it will take at least another four years from enactment until all its provisions are in force.

There were three main concerns which led to the considerable review and enactment process. First, there was a concern that the regulatory framework governing the provision of legal services in England and Wales had become outdated, inflexible, over-complex and insufficiently accountable or transparent. The piecemeal arrangements for at least six front line regulatory bodies (for solicitors, licensed conveyancers, barristers, notaries public, legal executives, patent and trademark agents, and law costs draftsmen) made for a regulatory maze with no clear objectives and principles. The second substantive concern was the handling of complaints and in particular the question whether a system of complaints against lawyers, run by lawyers themselves, could ever gain consumer confidence. The third – and perhaps the most famous – issue was what the government saw as the very restrictive nature of the business structures under which legal services were arranged. Not only did the government oppose restrictive practices, it also perceived that modern market forces – both from consumers and from the commercial market – demanded both greater competition and different and more modern methods of delivering legal services. The changing nature of business practices also required from lawyers different and wider skills and business structures where different types of lawyers, as well as other professionals, could work together on an equal footing.

The first two concerns – the updating of the regulatory framework and the handling of complaints – found their way into mandatory provisions and regulations, the detail and regulatory complexity of which are largely outside the scope of this book. The changes have involved the introduction of the Legal Services Board which will supervise the regulation of legal services by all approved regulators including the Solicitors Regulation Authority (SRA), the Bar Standards Board and the Council for Licensed Conveyancers. It also creates the Office for Legal Complaints, a new independent ombudsman service to deal with all consumer complaints about legal services. This body will deal with redress rather than regulation.

The third concern forms one of the main subjects of this book. This is the government's desire to promote greater competition and to permit different economic units, and the objectives were addressed by facilitative provisions which are likely to change the provision of legal services in England and Wales radically and to affect legal services materially throughout the world. The first change has already happened. In March 2009, legal disciplinary practices (LDPs) became permissible under which non-lawyers and different types of lawyers can now become principals of legal practices, provided that at least 75 per cent of the principals remain regulated lawyers. However, outside participation by non-lawyers who are not managers of the firm is not yet permissible under these LDP regimes. Non-lawyers who intend to become managers will be subject to approval by the appropriate regulatory body (which in the case of solicitors is the SRA) to ensure they are fit and proper, and the SRA then regulates all managers and employees in the firms under its regulatory umbrella. The remaining changes are being introduced incrementally so that eventually new structures will be permitted which allow two main things. First, the traditional law firm will be allowed to continue to practise either as before, or with different types of lawyers (and some non-lawyers) through operating entities co-owned with other lawyers as well as non-lawyers, but under their traditional 'approved' regulator such as the SRA or the Bar Council. Second, the new regime will permit entirely new types of law firms (from about 2012), such as a firm with more than 25 per cent non-lawyer managers, or a company taken over by a non-lawyer enterprise, or a company floated on the stock exchange, or a firm which provides both legal and non-legal services. These entirely new types of business structures, known as alternative business structures (ABSs), are expected to be regulated by a body licensed by the Legal Services Board (LSB) under the LSA's arrangements for ABSs.

There are also international ramifications. It is currently possible for European qualified lawyers to register as registered European lawyers (RELs) and for lawyers from other jurisdictions to register as registered foreign lawyers (RFLs) and then practise in a law firm regulated by (for example) the SRA. These arrangements will be relaxed with the introduction of LDPs as overseas lawyers who do not qualify or wish to register under the present arrangements have the additional option of applying to be a non-lawyer manager of a LDP.

Special provisions apply for in-house lawyers. At present a solicitor employed by a non-solicitor employer (in commerce or industry, in central or local government, in the not for profit (NFP) sector, or in a trade union or other association) acts only for the employer, subject to limited exceptions which allow, for instance, a law centre solicitor to act for members of the public. Purely in-house work, where the solicitor is not working for the public or a section of the public, is not affected by the Act. However, most organisations whose solicitors currently act for sections of the public – such as law centres or insurance companies – will eventually need to be licensed as ABSs under the Act.

The Legal Services Board

The Legal Services Board (LSB) was appointed in 2008 following the passing of the LSA. It becomes fully operational in 2010. The aim of the Act in legislating for the LSB was to create a new system of oversight regulation with the LSB being responsible for ensuring (amongst other things) that consumers and the public at large receive the best possible deal. The LSA recognised the strong history of professional self-regulation and the position of the various regulatory bodies that have so far been responsible for regulating the legal profession. The LSB will therefore work to oversee the existing regulators to build and deliver a higher standard of consistent regulatory excellence. The LSA commits both the LSB and approved regulators to undertake their various activities in ways which are transparent, accountable, proportionate, consistent and targeted only at cases in which action is needed.

To quote the first LSB business plan (LSB, 2009a): 'This does not mean that regulation should be necessarily "light touch" or that every piece of regulation should be the subject of some kind of "zero budget" test on the assumption that a regulatory requirement can never be more than a necessary evil.' It does mean however that both the LSB and the approved regulators are obliged to ensure that their regulatory interventions are swift enough and appropriately targeted to reflect the changes of a fast, ever changing and ever developing market-place both globally and in the high street.

In preparing its first business plan the LSB developed a vision of the way in which it wants to see the legal services market deliver its regulatory objectives. The Act sets out eight regulatory objectives for the LSB and approved regulators together with five professional principles. The regulatory objectives are to:

- protect and promote the public interest;
- support the constitutional principle of the rule of law;
- improve access to justice;
- protect and promote the interest of consumers;
- promote competition in the provision of legal services;
- encourage an independent, diverse and effective legal profession;
- increase public understanding of the citizen's legal rights and duties;
- promote and remain adherent to the professional principles.

These professional principles are further defined as:

- acting with independence and integrity;
- maintaining proper standards of work;
- acting in the best interests of clients;
- complying with the practitioner's duty to the court to act with independence in the interests of justice; and
- keeping clients' affairs confidential.

The goal of widening access to the legal market is a key part of the LSA rationale and the LSB is tasked with the development of the licensing regime for ABSs. The development of the ABS structures will be carried on by the LSB in conjunction with the various approved regulators of legal services. It is clearly going to take some time for these regulators and the LSB to get the right regulatory framework in place. The LSB hopes, by the end of 2009/2010, to have issued a policy statement outlining the approach to ABS, including its thoughts on potential risks to consumers and ways to manage them. The LSB also plans to establish the process for approved regulators to seek designation as licensing authorities and there will also be proposals to deal with professional boundary disputes between the various types of professionals involved in the legal services market. At the same time the LSB hopes to agree a timeline for the full roll-out of the ABS regime.

The need for increased investment capacity to meet new challenges

The larger and better resourced law firms have historically found it relatively easy to raise the necessary funds to finance the development and growth of the firm. Historically, the two main types of investors in law firms have been partners and banks – the partners investing by the introduction of capital and the banks by lending to firms. Until around 2007, banks were usually willing and keen to lend in what they saw as being a low risk environment. In addition, both new and existing partners could usually be persuaded to introduce or build up the necessary working capital reserves within the firm. By the early part of this century, some frustrations were beginning to surface. Larger firms were engaged in a sustained growth period, adding people, offices and equipment at an impressive pace. Firms of all sizes tried to latch on to one of the well-known pieces of economic logic of law firms – that the leverage structure contributes to profitability by allowing equity partners to take the profit generated by non-partners. Whilst the larger firms have been able to resource their growth from partners' capital and bank borrowings, the smaller firms have lagged behind through their own lack of investment capabilities. Growth strategies, however, have caused four main difficulties for law firms. In the first place, it takes both time and working capital to generate sufficient new work and fee income in order to cover the extra staff costs and the rise in other overheads. Whilst larger firms may have been able to swallow hard and invest the necessary working capital, smaller firms have simply not been able to take on additional levels of overheads which materially adversely affect their short-term profits. Equally, many lawyers simply do not have the confidence in their own business generation activities to hire new lawyers ahead of client demand. Secondly, the so-called war for talent has meant both an increase in the market value of decent lawyers and difficulties in attracting and retaining them. Thirdly, it does not take many years before developing lawyers are knocking on the partnership door; admitting them to partnership status just starts the whole leverage cycle off again. The fourth problem has been the tendency of larger law firms both to focus on short-term performance and to benchmark their success by reference primarily to their levels of profit per equity partner comparative to other firms. Whilst many firms, therefore, have perhaps been prepared to invest a modest part of this year's income to see their firms grow, their preparedness to invest has been somewhat restrained by shorter term considerations.

The ability to attract external investment to fuel further and more ambitious growth is therefore appealing to many firms, both as part of an offensive strategy to outstrip existing competitors and as a defensive strategy to position themselves to withstand attack from new entrants to the market.

Who is likely to invest in a law firm?

Apart from the traditional law firm investors – partners and banks – there are four possible types of investors in a law firm. The first and most obvious category is formed by competitor law firms which may be prepared to invest in other law firms by taking over the firm as a whole or by acquiring a team. Usually dressed up as a merger, the advantage to the smaller law firm is to find a partner who has the financial resources and capabilities to help them to expand further. Equally, some larger law firms find that they have department sole practice areas which are no longer core to their future and may be prepared to transfer such departments or practice groups to more specialised law firms. In both cases, the acquiring law firm is attractive to its merger partner because of its investment capability and additional resources. As law firms are not yet listed on stock markets – at least in the UK – the problem of hostile takeovers does not yet arise. However, teams and partners can be enticed to leave against the wishes of their firm.

Secondly, with the advent of the LSA, it is entirely possible that other professional service firms, such as accountants and surveyors, might see some advantages in 'purchasing' a law firm. Whether or not such firms will be prepared to invest in a law firm by way of a minority stake is less certain. The third type of investor is more informal and attuned to smaller firms. It may be possible to look to family and friends to provide much needed finance against an agreed return on investment. Equally, there are a number of business angels and private investors who are always attracted to start-up companies and to helping smaller organisations to grow in their geographical area. Finally, there are the larger institutions and bodies such as private equity houses which have already expressed an interest in investing. This final group of investor types gives rise to some obvious issues. For them, the main requirement is the firm's ability to demonstrate some factors which will make that firm attractive to external investors either for partial stakes or for outright purchase. Investors of all sorts will want to see both an eventual return on an investment and some capital growth. In order to achieve this, firms will need to demonstrate some strategies and plans which will show a solid prospect of fast growth. They will also need to show that they have an experience and track record of managing a firm which is growing. Furthermore, for a firm to be attractive to investors, it will need to embrace the structure and culture of capable, efficient and progressive management.

There are some key points about raising capital. The first is that raising capital by way of an investment in a firm is likely to be more expensive than borrowing. The investor will want a dividend and a return. There has to be enough profit to enable partners to retain a realistic salary after the capital has been raised and to give credit to the investor for dividends. The issue is that selling the crown jewels leaves partners as long-term employees and shareholders, and experience in other professional firms shows that this is not an attractive prospect. Institutional investors will probably not be interested in investments below £25 million, which limits the raising of significant amounts – especially by way of minority stake – to very large firms. A partial sale of, say, a 25 per cent stake of firms with turnovers of less than £100 million is, therefore, unlikely to be of much interest to the market. Equally, many private equity houses are saying that they would only be prepared to invest in a law firm in return for achieving a majority stake, as otherwise they would not perceive that they would have the necessary strategic and management control.

Opportunities and challenges for law firms to embrace new business models

Law firms can, of course, themselves become acquisitive as a strategic purchaser or investor. They can buy out smaller firms in order to build scale and focus. They can acquire teams and even caseloads of work and could also invest as business angels in other law firms. There is also the opportunity to sell off or hive off non-strategic parts of the firm. As overseas examples have made clear, it is also possible for firms to enter into mergers in order to create scale for eventual flotation. Finally, there is the opportunity for firms to raise finance at the right level provided that they understand the needs of investors for hands-on involvement in the business and ongoing income in return for directors' fees, etc. Firms also need to understand that most investors will have very firmly in mind a 'harvesting' return which will entail an exit from the business by way of sale of the investor's share or, ultimately, a trade sale of the firm itself.

Whatever a law firm's strategy – including strategies of complete independence and strategies to become an ABS or which involve being acquired in whole or in part – it is clear that law firms of all types must do their best to structure themselves in such a way as to attract internal and external participators.

Structuring to be successful

The options for both defence and attack are similar. In the first place there is a need for a clear and valid strategy whether a firm is intending to preserve an established market position or to push forward in a new direction. The strategy should include some clear and attainable strategic goals allied to a valid vision for the future. It should make the best use of the firm's tangible and intangible resources and capabilities. It should thoroughly understand the competitive environment in which the law firm is situated and be designed to place the firm at the best possible competitive advantage as against rivals. Allied to this must be a clear and achievable business plan and budget for a sustained growth in profitability. Not only must profitability be considered but funding arrangements and the balance sheet also become important parts of the structuring equation. The firm must also be increasingly better managed so as to be a cohesive, well-run and disciplined organisation. Thought must be given to governance and the composition of boards. The firm's structural capital must be developed in such a way as to maximise management effectiveness. In short, the firm must consider a conversion from the old loose partnership model to a more disciplined corporate model, at least in terms of its cultures and behaviours. Partner performance and the behaviour of partners must be aligned both to the firm's strategy and to its implementation. Above all firms should strive for a 'one firm' approach. Consistency is becoming increasingly important to clients. Reinventing the wheel is always inefficient, and well-thought-out precedents, processes and templates can save time and improve quality and consistency. It is immensely powerful if clients can see both consistency and harmony in working methods and approaches at all levels of the firm. Clients also appreciate the benefits of consistently applied and agreed methodologies and approaches. How the firm delivers its services is becoming of as much importance to clients as what the firm delivers. In addition, well-designed systems and processes can help to get the work done at the right level and can achieve stunning performance levels. A well-designed institutional feel and culture lessens the ransom risk, i.e. of partners leaving and taking valuable and unshared knowledge with them.

The imperatives to undertake strategic planning

The strategic choices any firm makes are critically important, especially in difficult times. This is because strategy is essentially all about choices – how a firm decides to be different from competitors in some meaningful way; to compete in one set of markets but not in others; to select and reject services, activities and specialisations; and to occupy a specific strategic position relative to competitor firms in terms of quality, or cost, or location, or client focus. We were stunned to hear a commentator on the professions say to us recently that law firms are not interested in strategy in the middle of a recession, they are just focused on survival. The assurance of survival is exactly why firms should look at their competitive strategy. It is clear that the LSA provides particular challenges for UK law firms which bring urgency to the need for firms of all sizes to clarify future plans to remain or become competitive and profitable. The urgency and turning points facing the UK legal profession are not, however, unique to England and Wales. The profession throughout the world faces similar competitive challenges and pressures and the need for strategic planning is a worldwide imperative.

Hence, this book is useful for all law firms throughout the world and outlines much more than answers to the local legislation in England and Wales. We guide law firms through the whole range of strategic analysis, strategic planning, competitive positioning, diversification both generally and through the use of ABSs, as well as planning for funding, for succession, for acquisitions and disposals and for mergers.

But above all, this book is about strategic thinking.

The importance of strategic thinking

Strategic thinking should be externally focused on markets and clients and not internally focused on questions of technology, compensation, morale, training and similar issues. It directs the firm towards the future not the past and encourages aspiration and ambition as well as a down-to-earth appraisal of both the challenges which face the firm and the practical restraints and realistic practicalities. Strategic thinking should also avoid four pitfalls. The first mistake is to believe that it is not necessary to change and that the firm can continue to rely on some sense of already achieved impetus to guide it roughly in the right direction. Like a rocket sent into space, this works well if it has been sent in the right direction but not if it is off track. The past is not always a good guide to the future and, as we shall see, the legal profession in the UK is facing some difficult and new challenges which will require traditional and historical strategies to be revisited. The second pitfall is slavishly to follow an industry recipe or a business book formula. Law firms are context specific and books, such as this one, can only help firms run through the right processes and ask the right questions, but cannot provide generic shrink-wrapped solutions for individual law firms. Thirdly, whilst firms can obviously learn a huge amount from competitors, imitating a competitor simply makes you a copycat and will hardly ever place you in a better competitive position than the firm you are trying to copy. The fourth pitfall is to produce an aspirational plan that is not grounded in reality and is unlikely to be achievable. It is vital to be clear and realistic about what can be achieved bearing in mind the firm's resources and capabilities and its current position in the competitive market-place.

BOX 1.2

False notions of strategy

Strategy is *not* the following (although they may be part of the execution of strategy):

- implementing best practice;
- organisational restructuring;
- changing remuneration schemes;
- creating an agile, flexible organisation;
- encouraging innovation;
- forming mergers/alliances.

Strategy is by nature *divergent* – it leads us in a different direction from competitors. Execution is by nature *convergent* – most firms are trying to do roughly the same things in terms of improving and achieving high quality, working on client service and client satisfaction, managing people well and striving for hygienic finances and good profitability.

Strategy is also inherently risky. As Phil Rosenweig (2007) points out, strategy always involves risk because we have little or no idea how our choices will turn out. Uncertain client demands, capricious economic conditions, unpredictable competitors, and changing technology all combine to make life difficult. Rosenweig offers a solution (2007, p. 150): 'The task of strategic leadership is to gather appropriate information and evaluate it thoroughly, then make choices that, while risky, provide the best chances for success in a competitive industry setting.'

Most law firms do nothing like enough to review their strategies on a regular, frequent and consistent basis. In many cases, firms seem to have no real idea of where they are heading next. Indeed, if you ask the average partner of even quite a large firm what he thinks the firm's strategic plan is, the answers you will get are often muddled, differ between partners of the same firm, and at times are limited to the individual partner's sense of where his own career is heading. What is more, there is typically confusion between strategy and various other elements – such as marketing, systems, and structure – which may form part of the strategy, but are not in fact strategy themselves. Some firms also show a marked aversion even to think about and discuss their strategic plans. One partner I spoke to said: 'Please not another strategic review; I thought we had banned the "S" word in our organisation.' I have some sympathy with his view; especially as the old style of ponderous strategic review (particularly those which attempt a five-year plan) has an awful habit of repeating the obvious and of failing to address anything new. What is worrying is that things are moving so fast that firms ought to be reviewing their strategies more often than in the past, not less often. And that statement presupposes that the firms in question know roughly their purpose and destiny. This is a bigger assumption than may be thought; most firms answer quite strongly that they know exactly where they are going and how they are going to get there, but the evidence often points to the contrary.

I have also been constantly surprised by the number of even quite large law firms where the leading partners (or in some cases departments) are each following their own quite separate strategies in relation to their own practice areas without a unified plan holding the whole enterprise together. It may be that a sort of working accommodation has emerged over the years with historically few problems. But like a yacht with no single guiding hand on the tiller, it is, in those cases, entirely a matter of luck and tradition as to whether the firm's overall direction and purpose is both consistent and competitive. Indeed, many such firms have severe fault lines which are either ignored or suppressed.

The fact is that most merged firms remain, at least in part, a product of their own separate histories. Partners have to become used to working together, sometimes in situations which, given an entirely clean sheet of paper, they would never contemplate. There are, for example, still some law firms around who have traditionally acted for both claimants and defendant insurers in personal injury cases. In other firms, such a possibility would not for a moment be contemplated, either because the insurance clients would oppose such a practice, or for internal reasons such as the clash in culture and working practices. For the same reason, it is rare to find employment practices in highly successful law firms which are focused on advising both employers and employees. It is usually one or the other. But some firms persist in trying to be all things to all men: general practices attempting to offer legal services across the complete range. For such 'utility practices', the adage 'we have always done it that way' is sometimes the justification. The problem is that fault lines can exist, sometimes for many years, without too much apparent problem. But underneath, fault-line firms have two strategic disabilities. First, and invariably, the existence of the fault line commands internal attention and energy on an ongoing basis; energy and time which will accordingly not be available for moving the firm forwards. Second, and more difficult to prove, the firm will fail to achieve its long-term potential even in its strongest areas. In short, I believe the firm will underperform in all its chosen markets. This may sound like a strong claim, but I find it hard to identify any law firms with underlying fault lines which have done better than they would have done with a focused and consistent strategy. Like a yacht with more than one hand on the tiller, which can never be sailed tightly and efficiently, such a firm is hampered by its tradition and history.

Sadly, many firms choose to ignore such fault lines and limp on through the problems. The more honest and ultimately more sensible route is to address such fault lines sooner rather than later, even if this means dumping a practice area or demerging part or all of the firm.

Endnote

1 For instance, Alan Hodgart writing in *The Lawyer* in June 2008 said, 'the shake-up is coming and it will be huge' and Tony Williams writing in *Legal Week* in October 2008 expressed the view that 'the smaller firms that manage to survive the economic downturn risk being swept aside by the tsunami of new and invigorated competition unleashed by the Legal Services Act'.

2

Understanding your assets
and resources

KEY POINTS

- A firm's assets and resources: tangible and intangible; intellectual capital (people, know-how, clients and the brand)
- How an appraisal of a firm's resources and capabilities can help guide strategy formulation
- Summary

A firm's assets and resources

Those involved in law firm management have always entered into debates about what makes up the assets of a law firm. What is clear is that the assets which appear on the balance sheet – office equipment, cash assets and creditors, and (sometimes) cars or premises – all give a very limited insight into the real worth of any firm. The firm's annual accounts often bear very little relation to everyday activities and give few clues as to the firm's current state of health or its future prosperity or fate. Even when you look at the firm's monthly management accounts – for the most part a historical record – the overall future health of the company can remain murky. The brutal truth is that the present and future success of a law firm simply cannot be understood solely by looking at traditional financial data, but requires a better understanding of all the firm's tangible and intangible assets and resources. In this context, it is universally accepted that one of any firm's main non-financial assets is its people. Indeed, when you ask the average law firm partner about this subject, the response is that the firm's people are its only *real* assets. Additionally, however, one also hears law firm managers at times talking about the value of their firm's brand and client relationships. All this, whilst correct, is far from the full picture.

Tangible assets and resources

The tangible assets of a law firm seem obvious enough. A firm's financial resources, premises, equipment and furniture are all items which regularly appear on its balance sheet. In addition, the working capital and cash flow requirements of a law firm are capable of being measured and quantified in terms of creditors, debtors, work in progress and the predicted availability of cash to pay the fixed and variable costs of the firm as and when they arise. In this context, there is a slight difference between a tangible asset shown on the balance sheet and a tangible resource which is available for a firm to use but is not necessarily shown on the balance sheet. To use an obvious example, the historic valuation of items on the firm's balance sheet often provides little indication either of an asset's market value or of its potential importance to a firm's ability to do business and compete. As another example, the level of a firm's overdraft at the end of a financial accounting period is reflected in the assets and liabilities of the firm on its balance sheet. The actual overdraft facility, however, is a resource. Hence, the firm's ability to raise borrowings, inject further capital and enter into leases and hiring agreements all form part of the firm's tangible resources which are not necessarily shown on the firm's balance sheet but which can be brought to bear in helping the firm develop and maintain its competitive position in the market-place.

The problem for the smaller law firms – those described in Chapter 4 as utility players and minor league firms – is that they rarely have the financial resources either to compete adequately or to fuel expansion and growth. They typically find it hard to hire, retain and promote good people ahead of client demand, and it becomes hard for them to invest in leverage via the employment of lawyers below partner level. Such firms find it difficult to invest in the infrastructure, equipment and systems necessary to compete with better resourced firms and they do not have the financial clout to compete with the marketing power of the bulk suppliers.

The advent of the LSA presents further significant threats and creates a stark and bleak picture for firms which are under-resourced in tangible terms. A constant theme of the next decade will be the increased competitive pressures brought to bear by law firms and new market entrants with pockets deepened by external investment and by new and well-resourced ABSs.

Intangible resources

A firm's intangible resources are those which can never be shown on a balance sheet, and are difficult to replicate just by the use of a cheque book. These resources are critically important in terms of a law firm's ability to compete. These are the resources which are critical for future growth and profitability. These assets are not only important for current performance, they also form the vital determinant of future earnings potential. They can be broken down into three groups, which link with a fourth. The four groups constitute every firm's 'intellectual capital' (Edvinsson and Malone, 1997) and are shown in Figure 2.1.

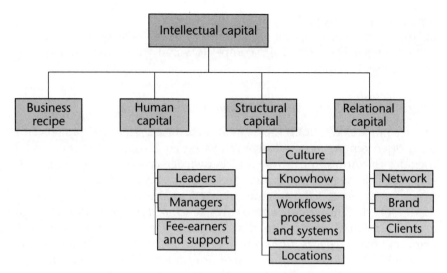

Figure 2.1   The firm's intangible assets – its intellectual capital

Intellectual capital

Human capital – the people and their handling

The first group is the firm's human capital. At a glib and superficial level, every firm will be aware that its workforce of partners, managers, fee-earners and support staff form the life-force of the firm. Any firm analysing its strengths will always count its people as its greatest asset. Clearly the competence, motivation, loyalty and incentives of the firm's partners, associates and other professionals doing legal work are critical to superior performance. In addition, firms rely heavily for success on the qualities, abilities and management methods of the firm's leaders, including the firm's management board, senior non-lawyer managers and leaders of the firm's various practice areas and industry sectors. But there is much more to it than a superficial understanding of the importance of human capital. One of the keys to competitive performance is to understand precisely how the elements of human capital can be developed, organised and applied to enable the firm to win against its rivals and to secure a profitable future. Table 2.1 shows some of the deeper resources and capabilities which are included within the human capital grouping for a typical department or practice area. It can immediately be seen from this somewhat generic table that some factors may or may not be relevant and important depending on the context of any department or practice group. For instance, the expertise of large numbers of guru lawyers will not be relevant to bulk suppliers, whilst a huge team of paralegals will not be of much benefit to a specialist department of tax lawyers. As with the other groupings, it is helpful to understand a firm's human capital needs by reference to the firm's core organisational capabilities. Put another way, a firm needs to know the distinctive competencies and capabilities which give the firm the capacity to perform well relative to its competitors and which make a valuable contribution to its success.

Structural capital – the know-how and systems

The second area of intellectual capital is the firm's structural capital. This is an often ignored area of a law firm's resource base. Structural capital includes the firm's know-how and knowledge management systems. It also includes the processes, workflows and systems which are used by the firm as part of its infrastructure, as well as the customised solutions, methodologies and pricing approaches developed for delivering value to clients. Structural capital also takes account of the extent to which the firm can reach clients from the location of its various offices – the geographical boundaries which extend or limit the firm's ability to serve distant clients. Structural capital furthermore embraces the firm's organisational culture. Sometimes known as 'the way things are done round here', this part of the firm's structural capital takes into account the firm's values, behaviours and accepted norms. It is quite interesting to note how few firms have an in-depth understanding of their own culture and in particular those cultural traits and behaviours which should be nurtured in order to increase the firm's effectiveness in the market-place. When we ask managing partners to describe their firm's culture, we very often get similar responses (a popular one is 'we are collegiate'). The brutal truth, however, is that much of a firm's ability to compete comes from the way in which its structural capital has developed or, in some cases, failed to develop. The firm's values, traditions, routines, working methods and work ethic, are all vital determinants of future success, as is the value which the firm attributes to efforts to marshal its knowledge management. If these elements remain disorganised, outdated and under-developed, the firm will rapidly become uncompetitive.

Relational capital – the clients and the brand

The third area of intellectual capital is the firm's relational capital. The core of relational capital is the firm's client base, its brand and the networks which assist the firm to develop. As most firms are aware, work from existing clients for most practice areas outweighs new work from new clients. In some firms as much as 80 to 90 per cent of each year's revenue emanates from existing clients. Hence, the quality of the firm's client base is a key factor in any firm's continuing success, along with the potential of clients to increase the firm's business and the ability of the firm's clients to increase the value of the firm's brand. A focus on certain client types and industry sectors is also a material part of a firm's relational capital and can help to distinguish the firm from competitors. Firms are also aware of the need to develop their networks that give access to relevant contacts within existing or potential target clients. Such contacts are normally referrers such as banks, accountants, insurance companies, estate agents and the like, but can of course also include other important networks. Networks within relational capital also include those which give access to clients, the media, professional associations, unions, administrative institutions, courts and tribunals, which can be beneficial to the firm for recruitment, public relations or the obtaining of cutting-edge knowledge. Many firms allow these networks to remain fragmented and unamalgamated – isolated in the ownership of individual partners. We know of one medium sized firm which identified over 300 different network relationships with overseas law firms which partners had individually built up and which were not coordinated. Some firms are better at concentrating and coordinating their efforts and relationship building on a few selected referrers, and find a competitive edge as a result. The final part of a firm's relational capital is its brand and reputation – the recognition and reputation of the firm as an institution, linked with its overall proposition and assurance of quality in the market-place.

The extent to which the firm is able to harness these three groups or resources and manage the mix between them is dictated by a blend of the firm's vision, its strategy, its business ideas and its competitive position in the market-place. This is known collectively as the firm's 'business recipe'.

Harnessing intellectual capital through the firm's business recipe

What is clear is that for every law firm, its intangible assets – its intellectual capital – form its greatest strengths. The tangible assets, such as the building, the bank accounts and the equipment, are of little use without the brain power of the human resources. The effective application of the firm's intellectual capital can confer sustainable competitive advantage for a firm if harnessed in an organised way correctly. What is more, a thorough analysis of a firm's intellectual capital can assist as a basis for formulating strategies which exploit the firm's internal strengths. As a further benefit, the strength of any law firm's intellectual capital forms one of the biggest barriers to entry for new competitors under the LSA who, however deep their pockets in terms of tangible resources, have to build from the ground up in terms of intangible assets.

For many firms, however, their intellectual capital – however strong or weak – is often badly coordinated and applied. Take, for example, a firm's human resources, namely the expertise and effort offered by partners and employees, which are clearly critically important to success. Law firms are, after all, essentially people businesses and heavily reliant on partners and staff to manage engagements, satisfy the needs of clients and produce results and outcomes which are worth paying for. If, however, the firm remains a loose collection of individuals, it will not be making the best use of its assets. The firm's individual sets of resources are not fully productive on their own. If resources are seen as the productive assets owned or used by the firm, capabilities are what the firm can do with those resources when harnessed together. The resources of individuals do not, of themselves, confer much competitive advantage – they must work together within the firm's business recipe to create organisational capability and it is organisational capability which is the essence of superior performance. The problem is that in many firms the relationship between the skills of individual lawyers or departments and the overall performance of the firm is a weak one. Like some very famous football clubs, firms may often fail to punch the weight which they appear to have when viewing their expert partners individually.

Table 2.1   Sample identification of capabilities in a typical law firm department

Area of IC	Organisational capability

Human capital	• Technical expertise
	• Depth of experience of departmental practitioners
	• Depth of team
	• Size of department
	• Areas of specialism
	• Services offered
	• Quality and effectiveness of client service
	• Responsiveness to emerging and growing areas of client demand
	• Departmental management ability
	  – The ability to delegate and manage work at the right level
	  – The ability to manage multi fee-earner matters
	  – Training and mentoring
	  – Maximising productivity
	  – Obtaining consistency
	  – Project management

Relational capital	• The strength of the existing client base and its potential for continuing to produce a stream of work • The ability to mine the client base effectively • The capability to serve different types of client

Structural capital	• Experience within certain industry sectors • Relationships with referrers • Relationships in other networks • Reputation, brand and name recognition • Effectiveness of business development • Processing, case management and systems • Knowledge management and research capability • The creation, use and deployment of precedents • Cohesiveness and teamwork within the department • Organisation culture • Work ethic • Effective use of office space and facilities • The ability to price and process work profitably

It is not necessarily the size of the firm's resource base, the numbers of its people, its network of offices or the depth of its pocket which is the primary determinant of its capability. It is the firm's business recipe which brings together all items of the firm's intellectual capital and moulds them into the firm's overall market proposition. Indeed, the larger the law firm, the more difficult it is to harness a spirit of collaborative cooperation.

This can give the smaller firms a useful starting point in trying to address their competitive capability in relation to larger firms. The smaller firm can often prove both more flexible and more collaborative than its larger competitors in organising resources into competitive organisational capabilities.

How an appraisal of a firm's resources and capabilities can help guide strategy formulation

In appraising resources and capabilities to guide strategy formulation, there are four key steps. First, the key resources and capabilities have to be identified. Second, they have to be appraised both for their strategic importance, and then, third, for their comparative strength in relation to competitors. Finally, strategic implications – how these capabilities can drive value – have to be developed.

Step 1 – identifying key resources and capabilities

The first step is to identify the firm's key resources and capabilities and this should be done both from the client end (what the clients need) and the firm's supply end (what the firm can offer). Sources of identification of key resources and capabilities include the usual analysis and review factors. These will include an overall look at the practice, some investigation of client needs, industry and sector analysis, financial analysis, market intelligence, partner interviews and practice group discussions. Much of this work can be done at practice area level. The key is to work out the elements of the overall practice mix which help make the firm successful. Clearly the elements of intellectual capital listed earlier in the chapter are the starting point for this identification. It is relatively easy to identify the particular skills and experiences of each practice area, the types of engagements and matters in which the firm is experienced and the client types and industry sector in which it normally operates. What lawyers, however, find difficult is identifying their relevant sets of expertise and experience in terms which are compelling to clients. Equally problematic is to be brutally honest in testing the strategic importance of the firm's capabilities. The first step is for the firm to compile an inventory. Table 2.1 gives examples of the sort of capabilities which a practice area list might contain. The capabilities at firm level might of course appear somewhat different.

Step 2 – assessing the strategic importance of the firm's resources and capabilities

Once each practice area has fully identified all the resources and capabilities available to it, the second step is to appraise the strategic importance of the items in the list. The principle here is to assess how vital (or unimportant) it is for the firm or a department to have certain capabilities in order successfully to pursue its strategic objectives. A volume conveyancing department would clearly place great importance on systems and efficiency, whereas a specialised tax department might rate technical expertise as extremely important. A useful plan here is to look at the list of resources and capabilities established in Step 1 and to work out which items established and potential clients are likely both to seek from their lawyers and to value most, as these are likely to drive future profitability.

Some clients are, for example, likely to value a personal approach whilst others will value efficiency above all other value drivers. Various authors have tried to list some generic value drivers for law firms, depending on what sort of law firm is involved, the segments in which they are positioned, the types of clients for whom they generally act and the sort of work done for those clients.

Stephen Mayson, for example, lists nine value propositions in his latest book (Mayson, 2007, p. 129):

- personal relationships;
- location;
- local knowledge;
- high specialisations;
- coordinated services;
- 'deep' resources;
- reputation;
- processing ability;
- legal information engineering (the repackaging of know-how).

David Maister (1993, pp. 23–6), distinguishes between efficiency practices, experience-based practices and expertise practices. Surveys also show that clients value the quality and effectiveness of client service including good project management, partner accessibility, cost-effectiveness, commerciality of approach, the ability to communicate, proactivity, and the avoidance of duplicative efforts and over-lawyering. This topic is dealt with at greater length in Chapter 4; the important issue here is for partners to stand in the clients' shoes and work out what it is that they require of their lawyers. Clearly, the truth is that no list is complete and that there is no substitute for individuals within firms to try to work out what they see to be the important dimensions of their clients' needs and the value points which existing and potential clients seek.

The true test of strategic importance is to assess the extent to which the resources and capabilities of the firm actually give the firm a sustainable competitive advantage against its rivals. In this context it has to be remembered that many law firms have practice areas and offerings which, however strong, are irrelevant or superfluous to their competitive position, unless they provide strong support to a core group. Another example is the formation of industry sector groups mentioned under Step 1. The firm may have identified an industry sector in which it would like to focus but if the clients in that sector currently provide only a small level of fees or marginal profitability, it is hard to see the strategic importance of that sector unless there is a business case for investing in a new or emerging area. It also has to be borne in mind that some resources and capabilities are necessary merely to give the firm the chance of playing in its competitive league rather than winning it. In his excellent book, *Contemporary Strategy Analysis* Robert Grant (2008) suggests that in any assessment of the strategic importance of resources and capabilities for profit earning potential, there are three other key criteria. The first is to assess the potential for establishing competitive advantage, the second is the potential for sustaining competitive advantage, and the third is the extent to which competitive advantage can be regarded as belonging or 'appropriated' to the firm. These criteria take into account issues such as scarcity, relevance, durability, transferability and replicability. The enduring problem for law firms – along with many other areas of professional service – is that some of the firm's expertise and capabilities remain in the heads of key people and can be easily transported with them when they leave. Institutionalising key capabilities is an important strategic challenge.

First, the firm should be thinking how it can establish competitive advantage by effective deployment of its resources and capabilities. Two main features apply here, scarcity and relevance. The first is scarcity. If a resource or a capability is widely available it will not usually be a sufficient basis for giving a firm a competitive edge over its rivals. Such capabilities may be needed in order to play in certain markets but they are not usually sufficient in order to become the winning firm in those markets. The resource or the capability must also be relevant to the factors which make for critical successes in the market-place. Here firms should be considering what it is that their clients want, and how the firm survives and beats its competition. The second appraisal of the strategic importance of resources and capabilities towards the profit-earning potential is to work out if and how the competitive advantage, once established, can be sustained. How long-term and durable are the resources and capabilities and can those resources and capabilities be imitated over time by copycat strategies or the loss of vital fee-earners?

The question of durability of resources in a law firm is a difficult one. Where most of the resources are based upon human resources, the life spans of the people in the firm are finite. As we point out in Chapter 4, it is often not possible for a law firm to sustain its competitive advantage in the long term but, instead, it has to rely upon continuously repeating temporary competitive advantages through deployment of new skills and new ways of servicing clients. The durability and the life span of resources and capabilities can, however, be enhanced and buttressed by succession planning and fee-earner development.

This is where the larger firms score well in that they always seem to have a cadre of staff and employees who are learning fast from their superiors. If it takes 10 years to become an overnight success (as the saying goes), then it certainly helps to be in a team where the lawyers can be practising on high-level clients and difficult complex matters. It is also important here for law firms, in recycling their resources and capabilities into new areas of emerging and growing work, to take into account industry and legal trends in trying to stay ahead of the game.

There is a risk of other firms employing copycat strategies in the sustaining of competitive advantage. If capabilities can be transferred to another firm by partner or team defections, an opportunity can quickly arise to give competitors and rivals the chance to catch up and overtake the law firm. Teams can be highly firm- or client-specific and the dependence on the firm's network of relationships, brand and culture can often assist to ensure that, even if key fee-earners leave, they do not leave taking clients or knowledge with them.

Replicability enables copycat strategies. Most legal services and innovations are highly copyable and replicable. It seems that as soon as a firm or an individual has researched and developed a new idea or way of doing things, the temptation becomes irresistible to write a book or give speeches and seminars on the subject. Charismatic individuals are, however, difficult to copy and capabilities built on complex organisational routines are also hard to mimic.

The extent to which competitive advantage belongs to the firm – Grant's third test of appropriability – is always a difficult one in law firms where partners can leave and in which it is difficult to protect knowledge, systems and processes by establishing intellectual property rights. No firm can own that which is inside the brain of an individual defecting partner, but the right to act for clients of the old firm can still be restricted for a while and to an extent by properly framed restrictive covenants. Furthermore, the firm can take positive steps to ensure partner retention and also to see that, as far as possible, the capabilities of the firm (that is the way in which individual resources are coordinated and exploited) remain embedded in the firm itself. The more deeply entrenched individual skills and knowledge can be made within organisational routines, and the more they depend upon the firm's system's reputation and client relationships, the weaker the partner becomes relative to the firm. Conversely, the closer the organisational capability becomes identified with individual expertise then the greater is the individual bargaining power in relation to the firm.

Step 3 – assessing relative strength

At Step 3, the firm or the practice area should assess how its resources and capabilities match up with those of rivals. Resources and capabilities need to be assessed for relative strength compared with those firms identified as competitors. It is important for this exercise to be carried out in each department or practice area, as competitor firms will vary in different parts of the firm. Here the firm should be wary of internal hype – past glories, hope for the future and wishful thinking. Most firms also find it difficult to know how they compare with rival firms – insights into the strengths and weaknesses of other firms tend to be anecdotal. Nevertheless, the collection of publicly available data about rival firms is essential, because no strategy to achieve a competitive advantage can really work unless the firm has a profound understanding of the competitive environment in which the firm operates. A thorough competitor analysis – considering the likely strategies of competitors, their overall objectives, their resources and capabilities, their positioning in the markets, their specialist strengths, the sorts of clients and sectors they serve, their pricing, service levels and profitability – helps to establish ways in which the firm can successfully compete. In addition to publicly held information, it is usually also possible to gain feedback on rivals from joint clients, referrers and staff who have joined the firm from a competitor. There are two other key matters to consider in an analysis of relative strength. The first is the size question. A larger firm is not necessarily a more profitable firm, but it may mean that the firm is able to field deeper teams of experts and it may also mean that the firm has greater financial resources to support its development. 'Depth' describes two things: the scale of firms which allows them to field strong teams of specialists able to service large matters and engagements (sometimes known as 'bench strength') with an appropriate number of lawyers; and the capacity to deal with complex issues which require not just a broad understanding of principles but a deep and profound expertise. The second question is the matter of comparative branding and name recognition. The firm needs to identify if rival firms enjoy benefits from being better known, having a higher profile and enjoying the fame of leading individuals.

In its review of comparative strength of resources and capabilities, the firm should also look out for stagnating capabilities and declining competitiveness. Where relevant, benchmarking and other analytical methods should be used to move analysis from subjective to objective.

Step 4 – bringing it all together

These capabilities can then be brought together in accordance with Figure 2.2 (adapted from Grant, 2008, p. 147) and strategic implications can be developed. Capabilities and resources which are relatively strong but are not seen as significantly important from a strategic point of view will be shown in the top left box. Capabilities and resources where the firm is weak but the issues are of little strategic importance will appear in the

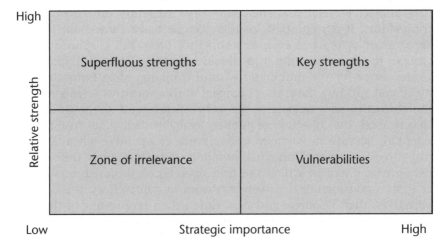

Figure 2.2   Resources and capabilities as a basis for competitive advantage

bottom right box. Capabilities and resources which are both important and where the firm is comparatively strong will appear in the top right box and those which are important but where the firm is relatively weak will appear in the bottom right box. The key is to focus on the two right quadrants. How does the firm exploit its key strengths more effectively and what should the firm do about its vulnerabilities, either to correct them or reduce the firm's exposure to them? On the two left quadrants, the firm should consider whether superfluous strengths are a possible distraction and therefore should be dropped or alternatively deployed to greater effect. An example of just such a superfluous strength for some firms is personal injury work. For years, this work may have been an extremely profitable area for many firms, and has provided them with high level experience and reputation. However, such practices are notoriously hungry for working capital due to the long-running nature of cases, and may therefore utilise resources of the firm which could be better used elsewhere. In the face of increasing competition from well-organised and well-resourced bulk suppliers, many firms are deciding to abandon such practices. Another obvious example is publicly funded work. However expert a firm in areas where public funding applies, the relative lack of profitability of such work may mean that the strength of the firm in such areas is not material for future profit-making potential.

The next step, therefore, is to develop some strategic implications so as to exploit strengths more effectively and so as to address weaknesses by correction development, outsourcing or acquisition of further resources.

Industry sectors and client types as key capability

We find many firms investigating and exploiting the advantages of employing a sector-based approach. Indeed, a sector-based approach is an ideal way of approaching the identification and harnessing of key capabilities right across the firm rather than just in individual pockets or departments. Industry sectors are identified in which the firm has experience and these are refined to assess the benefits of increasing focus on certain sectors and forming industry or sector groups across the firm. Often firms will consider emerging and growing sectors and those where the firm can create some level of differentiation by becoming known for its expertise and offering to certain groups of clients.

The identification of suitable industry sectors or client types has two main advantages. First and foremost, commercial clients value law firms who understand their industry sector and their business. Private clients value law firms who understand deeply their context and situation. New clients often choose law firms on the basis of their experience and therefore take great comfort from the firm's credibility and reputation. They are reassured if the firm understands their business, has a good track record of dealing with similar issues and problems for broadly similar clients and enjoys a good reputation (and even influence) in their sector. Firms therefore which can demonstrate that they have good experience, a deep understanding and an extreme client focus on certain types of clients or sectors of business are often able to build a competitive capability which is both strategically important and a relative strength in the market. The second advantage of a sector approach is that it concentrates on cross-firm effort rather than departmental effort. By examining both the sorts of work done and areas where there are gaps in groups of clients and industries, sector initiatives become powerful aids to cross-selling and integrated services. Analysing the client base by sector rather than by department often reveals a capability which the firm had not previously exploited to the full.

The vital strategic issue is then to refine the list of sectors down to those which are strategically important. One way of doing this is to identify the current and anticipated levels of both activity and profitability for such sectors and then to prioritise the list to just a few. I have seen many firms trying to create too many industry groups and the same lawyers can then find themselves falling into several such groups, and have insufficient time and energy to devote to them all. Once the groups have been refined down to only those where there is a strategic imperative, the firm's relative strength in the sector has to be understood. Where the strength of the capability is strong compared with competitors, the strategy may be to achieve not just strength but dominance. Where the capability is relatively weak, the challenge will be to develop better strength by skills development, recruitment and internal sector focus under which individual lawyers agree to devote effort to become a sector expert. In many cases, there is very little required to establish a sector-based strategy by way of expense or effort. All that is sometimes required is the identification and creation of an industry group, membership in a trade association, subscriptions to trade journals and several lawyers willing to develop some knowledge about and contacts in the industry.

Summary

In my work, I find that only a very few firms are able effectively to manage beyond today's profit per equity partner, accompanied by a slowly growing focus on the firm's people. The theory goes like this: 'If we manage today's income and have good people with enough experience and a decent client list, we will be successful.' This approach, however, will not establish an institution; at worst the firm will remain a loose association of sole practitioners – a 'motel for lawyers' with very little value in itself. We believe that the main driver for the long-term financial success of the firm is the extent to which a law firm manages all areas of its underlying intangible assets.

Until about 2007, law firms had been operating for more than a decade in benign conditions (except for government funded and other lower end work). It was relatively easy to be successful. But things are changing quite rapidly, due to a combination of recessional market conditions, client pressures and rapidly increasing competition. As the UK and Europe get ready for the implications of possible outside investment in law firms, those using this additional capital will need to demonstrate an increase in the value of the business.

At the same time, client and market pressures are squeezing levels of profitability. The centre of economic gravity is shifting. The easy fixes to increasing profitability are becoming exhausted. For the last decade or more, law firms have been able to make huge progress by increasing rates, investing in leverage, squeezing overheads and increasing productivity. Many firms are now experiencing increasing pricing sensitivities, recruiting and retention problems, and are reaching a ceiling on both productivity and overheads management. A shift is needed to regard the cultivation and leverage of the firm's tangible and intangible resources – and in particular its intellectual capital – as the most significant act of value creation.

Effectively executing the firm's strategy (or, indeed, of a firm's practice group) therefore means managing the mix of the firm's resources in light of the firm's overall strategy. The goal is for the firm's partners and associates to work to improve the firm's components of intellectual capital in a way that drives the firm's strategy. What makes a difference is the firm's ability to leverage its capabilities and its resources in a number of ways.

The first important area is that the firm should concentrate and focus its resources on a few, clearly defined and consistent organisational goals. The firm should avoid, if at all possible, the retention or development of lone wolves operating under the umbrella of what has often been described as a 'motel for lawyers'. A second imperative is for the firm to focus the efforts of its practice groups on their specific priorities including their markets, their specialised services, their efforts to beat competitors and their endeavours to serve clients better than any other firm. It is also important for the firm to target activities which have the biggest impact on the perceived value of the firm which clients may hold.

Finally, the firm should accumulate resources by mining industry experience and borrowing experience and expertise from other firms and organisations through alliances, best friend relationships, and outsourcing arrangements.

3

Harnessing intellectual capital – strategies for optimal law firm infrastructures

KEY POINTS

- The importance of systems and consistency
- Professional and talent management
- Encouraging marketing best practice throughout the firm
- Strategic branding for a distinctive profile
- Nurturing all the levels of a firm's culture to improve performance
- Financial management for the long term

Introduction

Law firms are operating in a knowledge-intensive sector. It is their thought processes, their know-how, their sources of experience and their tried and trusted formulae that lawyers apply to find solutions, to solve problems and to transact matters for their clients. At a wholly superficial level, it might appear that the ability of law firms to make a profit out of their knowledge will decrease as free access to knowledge grows through the use of the internet and open-source technology and as many of today's expert legal services become copied tomorrow and commoditised the day after. The opposite, however, is the case for any law firms which are able to con-vert their knowledge into wisdom and insight and to create a competitive edge by leveraging the economic value of the firm's capabilities and intan-gible assets. See, for example, Ridderstrale and Nordstromm (2004) and particularly pp. 143–151 which set out how organisations need to leverage their key resources.

The problem is that in many law firms, the wisdom and 'thoughtware' of the individual practitioners remain largely in their own heads and in the islands of their own offices and are not joined up into any sets of institutionalised or firm-specific capabilities. For this reason, the con-cept of examining a firm's 'intellectual capital', which was introduced in Chapter 2, is a helpful architecture to organise and harness the intangible and knowledge-based assets of the firm. A firm's intellectual capital is made up of its human capital – its partners, managers, lawyers and support staff – its structural capital – its culture, know-how, workflows, processes and systems and its locations – and its relational capital – its networks, brand, referrers and client base. These are all linked to the firm's tangible assets (its financial assets, premises and equipment) and the firm's strategy and business recipe.

It is easy for a law firm to take these intangible assets for granted or to operate on a level of 'unconscious competence'[1] in which the lawyer's work becomes 'second nature' and can be performed easily and often without concentrating too deeply. It is helpful, therefore, to visualise starting a new law firm and to consider how all the facets of intellectual capital could be constructed or acquired. This process enables firms both to identify the entry barriers which might impede a new competitor, and at the same time to think of ways in which the firm can act to marshal and exploit its assets and capabilities more effectively. If, on analysis, the entry barriers to new competitors seem too low, then this is a sure sign that the established firm's competitive position is in danger. In most cases, however, an examination of any firm's intellectual capital discloses and demonstrates a rich array of competences, skills, talents, relationships and ways of doing things which can be developed and utilised to the firm's advantage.

This chapter examines possible strategies for firms, whether or not they intend to embrace an ABS structure as described in Chapter 6, to consider in relation to a number of aspects of their intellectual capital – systems, talent management, clients and marketing, strategic branding, culture, financial management and technology.

The importance of systems: structuring to obtain consistency

Even in the case of the most specialised services, much can be learned from those who are supplying high volume commoditised professional services – the bulk suppliers (see Chapter 4). What the bulk suppliers have done is to respond to the pricing challenge and low margins by standardising the processes so as both to reduce the time involved in each step and to enable delegation to less costly staff, by clarifying the level and extent of necessary intervention by skilled professionals into each piece of work and by organising the work into well-managed teams.

As one senior partner of a bulk supplier law firm told me: 'This is not rocket science. In most cases it is just common sense.' Yet, as I go round law firms, I am struck by the cottage industry atmosphere and general air of disorganisation which still pervades many partnership corridors. Partners are still insisting on the freedom to practise law in their own way, with their own styles and formats, and their own tailored precedents. The way clients are dealt with may well vary considerably from one room or work station to another, and junior members of staff are expected to react flexibly to differing working practices and procedures, depending on their supervisor for guidance. As an example, we have frequently elicited widely differing answers within the same firm when asking how long the same standard step takes in a transaction or litigation matter. More worryingly, some partners have no idea of the answer! What is clear is that, for the bulk suppliers, the old cottage industry model has completely disappeared in favour of something far more organised, efficient and commercial. It seems to me equally clear that the old, inefficient working practices are steadily becoming unsustainable even for firms which pride themselves on being at the high value end of the positioning diamond (see Chapter 4).

Systems make for consistency and the consistent firm will almost always succeed better than firms which show patchy service and uneven quality. To achieve better organisation, optimal systems and greater consistency, firms need to embrace or answer seven potential challenges.

First, the old partnership model has to be redefined. I am not arguing here for firms to become entirely corporate in structure as indeed there is much about the partnership and limited liability partnership (LLP) structure which is commendable in strategic and structural terms. What, however, has to be redefined is the old 'motel for lawyers' or chambers mentality in which partners continue to practise in their old ways more or less as individual sole practitioners. We have lost count of the number of times that both new entrants to a firm and clients report on how differently things are done in different parts of the same firm. Even within the same practice group or the same department we still hear reports of many partners whose working methods, systems, precedents and approaches are entirely different from those of the partner in the next door room doing similar work for similar clients. This has to change. It has to change because clients do not like it and it has to change in order to attract new partners and new investors. In addition, the partnership model has to be refocused into a business model which encourages swift decision-making and active management of matters and people. Partner behaviours have to be adapted and harmonised. Management roles and responsibilities need to be defined and those with management responsibilities need to be accountable. All firms need to consider introducing some form of performance management system whether entirely formal or partly formal and informal.

The second important challenge is to ensure that a compliance regime is in place. This should be designed not just for the avoidance and management of risk but also in order to manage quality and service efficiency. Again, the formality and definition of an appropriate compliance regime will vary from firm to firm in terms of regimentation or informality, but every firm needs to sense and answer how it can address matters both of regulatory importance and of risk in this uncertain future.

The third consistency challenge is to develop efficient management of time and money. Tight financial management and discipline is necessary in all firms, not just in firms doing low margin work where every penny and every hour counts. This means that amongst the systems and processes which need to be introduced or strengthened, the systems for financial accountability and performance management are critically important. External investors will place a great deal of importance on the twin attributes of strong financial management and stable cash flow. Leaders of divisions, department and practice groups have to be responsible for the financial performance of their group. This responsibility should not just relate to revenue generation, productivity, recovery and pricing but extend to margin control as well – leaders should be responsible for managing their own direct costs. Partners should be responsible for their own performance and that of their team.

The fourth challenge is for firms to take much more seriously than ever before the nurturing of their referrer and key client relationships. This has become a crucial responsibility for partners who tended in the past to spend too much time focusing on chargeable client work and arguably too little time on the nurturing of relationships.

The fifth challenge is to spend time and effort on training and development of people. Law firms are people businesses and it is the brain power of the individuals in law firms which provides much of the firm's competitive advantage. People do not learn just by watching what other partners do. There is no doubt at all that training, both to induct new people and to foster career development, assists in retention and also helps lawyers more quickly to develop skills and competences which clients find valuable.

The sixth area is that firms must find ways of consistently and persistently tracking trends. A deep understanding of the market-place is vital for firms to be able both to compete and to offer solutions to the issues which are keeping their clients awake at night. It is vital to establish work areas which are emerging or growing, as well as those that are maturing and fading. It is also important to track and embrace technology developments and the ability of both competitors and the clients themselves to be able to harness the power of the internet and technology to provide their own solutions.

Finally the seventh consistency challenge is to spend as much time as possible streamlining all areas of work. In every law firm, processes need to be re-engineered to take the cost out of work wherever possible. We are increasingly seeing a tendency for clients to expect efficient measures in firms doing high level work at high rates. Clients are increasingly demanding that their firms process and leverage parts of their work wherever possible and synthesise recurring work into processes, methodologies and templates.

In order to streamline work effectively, I believe there are some principles of conscious and systematic improvement which need adequately to be applied at file and lawyer level. These principles (adapted from those set out in *A Manager's Guide to Leadership* by Pedler, Burgoyne and Boydell, 2004) are as follows.

- **Step 1.** Define what is to be improved; select the work-type process to be worked on, identify its clients and what they require of it.
- **Step 2.** Measure and examine the performance of the chosen work-type – how well and efficiently files and matters are run compared with what clients would like.
- **Step 3.** Analyse the data and causes of problems in actual file management compared with the ideal.
- **Step 4.** Improve the process and remove the causes of the problems.
- **Step 5.** Control and manage the new processes, making sure that old customs and working habits do not creep back in.

Any firm which is struggling to complete its roll-out of case and matter management, or which simply desires to work more efficiently, would do well to review its work processes by planning and implementing (or, in some cases reimplementing) these steps stage by stage. For this purpose, a project team with appropriate departmental representation should be assembled, preferably steered by one of the firm's leaders.

Define the opportunity for improvement

Too often, it is assumed that only repetitive commodity work (like residential property work or personal injury litigation) is in need of process

---

BOX 3.1

File review

Analyse and review files to find examples of:

- waiting time between steps;
- incidences of delay;
- iterations and unnecessary work;
- poor matter strategy;
- use of the wrong level of lawyer;
- poor/inadequate delegation;
- inefficient use of secretaries;
- poor client reporting;
- failure to use standard forms and precedents.

improvement. In fact, most clients would like to see standard forms, templates and matter management systems introduced in all areas of legal work. As an example, the British Venture Capital Association has for some time been seeking feedback on proposals to introduce model documents to venture capital deals. There is a strong argument that 90 per cent of deals are a well-trodden path and come down to the same points.

Examine your current performance

The key here is the collection of specific data from at least three areas, from clients, from internal file and systems data, and from the firm's people.

1. Client data

We know that clients want speed and efficiency and do not like to pay for the cost of unnecessary work, such as documents dictated from first principles instead of using a template or standard form. But it goes deeper than those generic lessons. What are the clients actually saying about our service? What are the main sources and types of negative comments or even complaints? How do they rate us in comparison with our competitors?

2. Internal data file analysis

This is an often overlooked area, dealing only with issues of compliance. Useful data can, however, be collected to reveal processes and working methods which can be improved. Other internal data can reveal productivity per lawyer, average costs per case, recovery rates, inefficient levels of infrequently turned-over work in progress, and effective billing rates.

3. Internal staff data feedback

This feedback from your staff is enormously helpful, both in terms of those parts of the systems which do not work well and also in relation to individuals who are not facing up to new working methods. By what (or sometimes by whom) are your staff irritated? What dissatisfies them and what would they like to change?

Analyse the data

It is not enough just to pick the letters, forms and precedents commonly in use and make them part of the case management system. What is vital is to work out systematically what is inefficient about current methods of working files – including matter strategies, processes, file management, workflow and resolving problems. To achieve this, all the information and data which is collected needs to be systematically considered and the root causes of any problem areas identified. Inefficient processes will need to be uncovered, but it is often the case that the root cause of any problem is the failure or reluctance on the part of lawyers to get to grips with changed ways of doing things.

Improve the process

Redesigning work processes can then take place against a vision of what the project team feels can be achieved by way of streamlined service. This step needs to be taken innovatively and with a streamlining mindset which constantly challenges and questions. Key questions at this stage are:

- How can we do this differently?
- What documents and steps in this line of work can be systemised into precedents and templates?
- Can we run files in a simpler fashion?
- Where can we make efficiencies?
- What steps, formerly carried out by secretaries, can lawyers carry out cost-effectively?
- What steps, formerly done by lawyers, can be commoditised and carried out by secretaries, juniors, paralegals or technology?
- How can we get more for less?
- Which are the areas for development and where are the cuts and efficiencies to be made?
- What changes do we expect to see in the next five years?

During this stage, there needs to be a great deal of work with the whole constituency of lawyers to ensure that buy-in is obtained.

Control and manage the new processes

This is perhaps the most difficult step of all. The main problem is that new working practices take time to become familiar – more time in the first instance for a busy practitioner than his or her old working practices. In addition, busy lawyers will be reluctant to spend time (which they may feel they can ill afford) training and learning new ways. Some partners, particularly those who have been in practice for a number of years, may even feel exempt from new working practices. But if the project team has managed to work through all the steps, with full feedback from and communication with the lawyer teams, then the chances are considerably increased that real beneficial changes in working practice can be implemented and stay implemented.

Professional and talent management – structuring for a committed and developing workforce

It seems almost platitudinous to repeat the point that law firms are very much people businesses, that people form any law firm's greatest assets (and headaches) and that the challenge of attracting, retaining and motivating a law firm's human capital forms one of the most vital objectives which any firm can have.

The main challenge for any start-up firm will be to identify, attract and recruit the right staff. Established law firms that have a stable and loyal workforce hold a vital competitive advantage in this area over new entrants to the market which will have to start from scratch. Human capital strategy is accordingly a vital element in the firm's overall strategic mix.

Even the legal sector's market rulers find they have to focus a great deal of energy and attention on attracting and retaining good lawyers and warding off their competitors. Lower down the positioning diamond, utility players and minor league players (for which see Chapter 4) find it extremely difficult to hire good people and to persuade young lawyers to come into partnership. The whole dynamics of employee commitment and long-term security have also changed rapidly. Long-term partnership in a law firm no longer defines success, as young lawyers seek new opportunities, exciting projects and novel experiences at the same time as developing a growing requirement for excitement, danger, travel and leisure time. Lack of job security engendered by an economic downturn could rapidly disrupt the employee need for flexibility and a variable career structure.

For much of the last two decades, the so-called 'war for talent' has been a constant theme. Only with the advent of the recession in 2007 was a temporary truce called, as the battle for recruitment and retention of the best people gave way to mass redundancies and lay-offs. The laws of supply and demand dictate that there will virtually always be an imbalance between the availability of staff and the desire of law firms to recruit. During a benign economic period, the strongest firms find it easiest to hire, and during a downturn firms which are in a position to invest have access to a pool of talent which would not previously have been available to them.

The war for talent will, however, be waged once more and law firms need to invest time and money in working out strategies to win the necessary battles in that war. Better positioning, as discussed in Chapter 4, carries with it the reward of gaining access to talent which would not otherwise have been available. Simply becoming bigger – as part of a merger or consolidation plan – can make hiring easier. Internally, however, there are two strategic areas where firms can work to establish and develop long-term career structures and retention ability in their lawyers.

The first strategic area is to plan for and work towards the provision of ample opportunities for staff to do work of high quality; the second is to promote teamwork and a sense of cohesion amongst employees. In the first of these areas, many studies have pointed to the desire of young lawyers throughout the world to gain satisfaction and motivation from the best possible work for high quality clients. The Harvard Business School professor, Rosabeth Moss Kanter, points to the generic desire which people have for mastery – the need for satisfaction and success coupled with increasing opportunities to achieve success in the future (Moss Kanter, 2001). As she puts it (p. 206): 'Challenging work, training and the chance to learn, paths to greater success, and a stake in the future are all components of mastery.' She adds: 'The "stickiest" work settings (the ones people leave less frequently and more reluctantly) involve opportunity and empowerment. Cutting-edge work with the best tools for the best customers is important in the present because it promises even greater responsibility and rewards in the future. Knowledge workers want to build their human capital – their individual package of skills and accomplishments – as much as their financial capital.'

A lawyer's earnings can therefore be seen as a return on his or her investment in his or her own human capital, but he or she can generally only realise that return on investment by working within a law firm, and by specialising to increase that human capital over time (see, e.g., Gilson and Mnookin, 1985). This area therefore holds the promise of a virtuous cycle, in which any firm which has in its strategy a set of goals and objectives to improve its work quality and client base will find resonance in its employees' desire to improve their lot as well. But in badly run firms, there is also the probability of a vicious cycle in which the loss of competitive capability coupled with increasing levels of commoditisation and price sensitivity result in decreasing profitability and the ultimate exit of the firm's best talent.

The second strategic area is for firms to work on the promoting of teamwork and a sense of cohesion and belonging amongst the firm's people. All law firms, whether large or small, share at least one thing in common: generally speaking, the groups which work closely together are broken down in size usually to no more than 12 to 15 people, and very often fewer than that. A partnership of four partners, for instance, is a ready-made team, as is an office made up of a sole practitioner who may have an assistant, a legal executive, and some secretaries. At the other end of the scale, the organisation of a large firm is almost invariably broken down into departments, usually with small teams within them. In addition there is often a broad range and variety of boards, committees, and project teams all contributing to the hopefully smooth running of the firm. And yet, in general, many law firms fail to make the most of their teams. Specifically, the importance of teamwork is constantly underrated, and insufficient time and resource is spent in establishing, maintaining, nurturing and developing teams. Both experience and research show that working with and in teams is by no means easy and nowhere is this more true than in a law firm, where past traditions and working practices have all emphasised individual working rather than teamwork. Working together with other people is never easy. Truly effective teams are quite hard to find in law firms.

Traditionally, lawyers have worked largely alone – developing their own client bases and operating in their own way, at their own speed and with their own idiosyncrasies. Even in large firms, we still hear complaints about partners exhibiting poor project management skills, lacklustre delegation ability and insufficient coaching, mentoring and feedback. Additionally, in law firms where teams have developed, a combination of poor team leadership, lack of trust between team members and poor planning have all contributed to an undistinguished team success rate. The failure rate is perhaps not surprising, given the general unwillingness of lawyers to modify outdated working practices or to appreciate the benefits of working together in a team, and given also the confusion over team goals and objectives that typically exists.

The main starting point in addressing any firm's strategy for human capital is to place people at the centre of the law firm's efforts to gain sustained competitive advantage (see Gratton, 2000) by developing a workforce that feels it is an integral part of the general needs and aspirations of the firm and whose members direct all talents and energies to the firm. One very important feature of an effective strategy for a law firm is that there should be a clear line of sight for every partner and lawyer between his or her day-to-day operations and the firm's overall strategic goals. In short, the firm's lawyers must be capable of identifying how their work, career aspirations, specialisations and capabilities fit in with and contribute to the firm's overall strategy. It is difficult to achieve this line of sight when the firm's stated but vague objective is just to get bigger, to become generally famous, or to improve its profitability.

Clients and marketing – structuring for better work

There are three main reasons why lawyers find it difficult to change lifetime habits when it comes to winning new clients.

The first reason is that for decades, even centuries, lawyers have been able to restrict their marketing strategies and activities to previously successful formulae, unconsciously applied. Successful businesses were built up on the back of the firm's goodwill and a database of existing clients developed slowly over many years by dint of instinctive marketing, opportunistic activities and haphazard relationship building. In the past, and (for some lucky firms) even now, there has been little need to do anything different, despite the fast-moving and increasingly competitive age in which the legal services industry now finds itself.

The second reason is that the behavioural patterns endemic in most law firms conflict with a methodical marketing ethos. These behaviours result both from the technical attributes and traits which characterise the good lawyer and from the chargeable hours culture which has developed in law firms in recent years.

After all, most lawyers became lawyers in order to practise law, and doing and concluding a piece of legal work is what they find most interesting. By virtue of both training and inclination, lawyers can be or become introspective and focused on precedent. And for those who developed their client bases in the dim and distant past, there can sometimes seem to be little incentive to go out and 'do some marketing'. What is more, the cerebral and analytical traits expected of lawyers can militate against taking an entrepreneurial and wider view of life. In short, lawyers are amongst the worst in the business world at picking up the phone and making a cold call, or in following up an identified prospect. Furthermore, if lawyers are rewarded and valued mainly for client work and profitability, the pressure is inexorably applied to the achievement of short-term chargeable targets and objectives, rather than long-term, non-chargeable business development activities.

There is a third reason for the lawyer's difficulty in embracing the principles of sound marketing. Successful marketing depends, at least in part, on being able to demonstrate that the services on offer are sufficiently attractive to dislodge the competition. The problem is that the services of one law firm, or indeed an individual lawyer, are relatively difficult to differentiate from the services of another.

Most law firms will fail to reach their true potential in the future unless they embrace a clear marketing strategy and an organised marketing process.

Anchoring marketing best practice in a law firm has a number of elements. Clearly, the whole area of marketing and business development needs to take its proper strategic place on the management agenda, with the need to develop business embedded in every aspect of the lawyer's life and training – at appraisals, in partner reward systems, in the recruitment process, and in training and development programmes. Equally, the leaders of the law firm must ensure that the marketing department (if there is one), and its staff, are fully integrated into the strategy and operations of the firm, and that the department supports and is aligned to the needs of the lawyers. But, at the end of the day, every lawyer has a responsibility to develop his or her own career, and, either individually or by proper teamwork, to build a client base or contribute to the firm's efforts in this connection.

Strategic branding – structuring for a distinctive profile

A firm's brand is much more than the firm's name, its logo and its website. As Tom Peters (2003, p. 155) has observed: 'Effective branding is in fact more *internal* than *external*.' The firm's brand sums up the way in which the law firm identifies itself and distinguishes itself from its competitors in ways which clients find compelling and meaningful. The firm's reputation and the quality of its service both demonstrate the standing and importance of the firm, carrying with them a guarantee or assurance of the firm's quality and certainty of service. As such, the firm's quality assurance is a vital part of its brand proposition. The firm's positioning on the diamond matrix (see Chapter 4) also both informs and is assisted by the firm's brand image. Not only does a strong brand carry a promise of value, quality and reliability, it also conjures up a personality – such as safe and comfortable, or aggressive and detail-oriented (see Kotler and others, 2002). It is vital, however, that the words used in any brand proposition should match the music being played in the firm. Branding cannot be faked. Every aspect of how a firm and its lawyers behave must harmonise with the image that is being presented. How things are done within the firm, how the firm communicates, the attitudes and commitment of the lawyers and even the firm's extracurricular activities all must be consistent (see Forsyth, 2003). Solid brand awareness can help in recruitment, attracting important referrer organisations, gaining good clients and facilitating media attention.

In one sense, therefore, a project to research, validate and establish a law firm brand needs the same careful attention as is needed to establish the firm's strategy and such a project can naturally be carried out as part of a full strategy review. If the branding project is carried out separately, internal and external research is vital. Internal research will help to verify the firm's actual values and expected behaviours, from the way telephones are answered to the manner in which the largest projects are handled. Internal research can also look at the internal environment, office layouts, house styles, dress codes and all the other artefacts from which clients and staff take their cues and form their opinions of the firm. External research of former and current clients, referrers and opinion formers is vital both to establish the extent of the world's familiarity with the firm, and perceptions of what the firm stands for, as well as feedback on service levels, experience and expertise. Only when this research has been carried out and analysed, can the firm start to consider a consistent and impactful brand design which is compatible with the firm's strategy and competitive positioning, which harmonises with the firm's internal ecology and culture, and which helps to distinguish the firm from its competitors.

Then the hard work begins, because no brand works without a commitment to excellence and the discipline to enforce the values and behaviours which the brand promises.

Culture – nurturing the cultural traits which increase the firm's effectiveness

Over-simplistically described as 'the way things are done round here', a firm's culture is generally defined in three ways. It is first defined by the firm's rituals – the way work is organised, authority exercised and how the firm's structures and processes are constructed. Second, it is identified by the firm's values – the way people in the firm relate to each other and to the firm itself, and how people are rewarded, empowered and controlled. In this context, it is also determined by the way the firm adapts to its clients and the outside world, the firm's history and experiences and the way the firm sees its values, direction and strategy. There is a third and deeper level which is the firm's shared and tacit beliefs, perceptions, thoughts and feelings (see Schein, 1999). It is quite interesting to note how few law firms have an in-depth understanding of their own culture and in particular those cultural traits which should be nurtured in order to increase the firm's effectiveness in the market-place. When I ask firms to describe their culture, I very often get similar responses (a popular one is 'we are a caring organisation'). I am often left with the impression that many managing partners tend to believe their own publicity and rely on their own perspective without necessarily asking the right questions in the deeper subterranean layers of the firm. In addition, the culture in many firms is quite heterogeneous rather than homogeneous, with almost as many mini-cultures as there are partners. In some firms different offices and different departments display quite different cultural traits.

What is also clear is that people in any organisation will take their cues from what they see or feel is going on, more than what they hear. If, for example, the managing partner says – with all the sincerity in the world – that the firm is committed to learning and development, but no training resources are allocated, the view will quickly form that the managing partner's fine words are not matched by reality. Table 3.1 sets out some typical examples where the firm espouses certain values which are not matched by the behaviours of firm members.

We believe it is vital to gain an intimate knowledge of the levels of culture, the sub-cultures and the behavioural traits which are evident throughout the firm. In order to take any subject seriously, partners must engage with this process but this is easier said than done. There is an array of management issues and subjects which make the eyes of the average partner glaze over. High on any such list would be the linked areas of culture, values and behaviour, subjects on which it has proved generally difficult to gain the attention of outcome-oriented partners, obsessed as they are with the short-term delivery of results and profits. In general, partners will usually wake up and take notice if they perceive there is something in it for them. That is why it is so interesting to note the vast body of evidence which now links culture and effective performance. This can make it possible to use these links to get partners thinking more about the impacts, both positive and negative, which cultural and behavioural issues have on the business and its underlying profitability. There are, of course, other ways of grabbing partners' attention. One is to consider with them how the firm ought to present itself to the market-place. A

Table 3.1   Examples of misalignment between espoused values and actual behaviours

Values espoused	Behaviours exhibited
• We have high values	• We tolerate transgressions by prima donnas
• We are open and honest	• We talk about people behind their backs
• We have an open-door policy	• Doors are often closed
• We have a flat structure	• Many firms are still hierarchical
• We believe in cooperation and teamwork	• We build walls around our clients
• We believe in promoting quality	• We still tend to reward quantity
• All partners have keyboard and computer skills	• Many partners still insist on a one-to-one secretary
• We promote an external client focus	• Most of our value measures are internal
• We encourage training and development	• We do not give staff enough 'down time' from chargeable hours for training purposes
• We encourage our staff	• We are good at criticising our staff
• We want to be commercial and business-like towards our clients	• We want our clients to like us
• We respond well to the challenges which we face	• We hate change
• We value satisfying our clients completely	• This often cannot be reconciled with working within targets
• We value those who are good at managing people and teams	• We respect high personal billing achievement
• We believe in proper delegation	• We hog work which could be delegated, in order to enhance personal billings
• We want to enforce proper disciplines	• We want to be liked and to avoid confrontation
• We are good at cross-departmental integration and coordination	• Departments are often independent islands with their own sub-cultures

discussion about 'brand values' is often more fruitful than trying to engage partners in a debate about culture per se. Another method is to highlight the effect of the current state of the firm on the attrition of talent which often results from poor working conditions and a negative climate.

Financial management – structuring for long-term performance

Law firms have traditionally been obsessed by short-term profitability considerations to the detriment of long-term investment. Law firms are different from most other mature commercial sectors in two material respects. First, law firms, unlike other commercial organisations, distribute or allocate the entire profit of their firm to shareholders every year. Second, most commercial organisations in other sectors judge their performance, at least in part, on the concept of 'shareholder value', whereas in most law firms partners' capital is fixed, with retiring and outgoing partners taking away with them only the amounts originally invested by them without any capital appreciation. While this historical model will continue to find favour with traditional law firms, it will not suit many of the ABS models discussed in Chapter 6; where external investment is needed, external investors will be looking for a return on their investment in the form of an increasing income as the firm grows and a capital return in due course.

Investing for growth can be expensive. Even in the best run law firm, the extra working capital required in an expanding firm can be approximately one-third of the expected fee revenue growth from new work. This is because the investment in new fee-earners, as well as the work in progress and the amount of bills delivered but unpaid, all have to be funded. In poorly managed firms this 'lock-up' of work done but not yet paid can be painfully high. This in turn has a knock-on effect on the firm's borrowing need, which therefore tends to increase as the business expands. There is clearly a limit, however, to the extent to which law firms can or should borrow money. The best way of keeping borrowing under control in an expanding, or even static, business is to generate more cash internally.

Box 3.2 illustrates some essential points to watch for in controlling and building the firm's working capital. These points illustrate the need for efficiency, discipline and performance management in the financial

---

BOX 3.2

Generating cash within the firm – essential points

- In an expanding firm, ensure that the breakeven point rises at a slower rate than the increase in fee income.
- Improve fee rates wherever possible.
- Dump unprofitable work.
- Improve billing cycles and cash collection.
- Look for financial efficiencies.
- Apply performance management.
- Manage the expectations of partners for cash draw-downs so that there are sufficient retained profits in the business to improve the gearing.

affairs of the law firm. Many smaller firms nevertheless find themselves caught in a financial vice caused by the competitive forces discussed in earlier chapters – suffering declining profits, unable to invest for growth or defence, and at the limits of their borrowing capacity. Financial efficiencies and discipline can only help such firms to a limited extent. More firms are entering voluntary arrangements, merging or simply going out of business and we see this trend growing. The key is to understand that sound financial management is not just about the numbers alone but all the non-financial elements of intellectual capital that affect how those numbers move and change. Indeed, good financial management can only be performed if good overall management is in place. This is why the firm's long-term future financial performance and profitability is an important and integral part of the firm's strategy for survival and prosperity. The implementation of any strategy ultimately depends not only on the firm's commitment to implementation but its financial and non-financial resources and capabilities to fund and support the firm's objectives and goals.

Technology – structuring to improve service and to gain competitive advantage

Technology presents both threats and opportunities. Online automated tools and open sources of legal knowledge will help some clients to do their legal work themselves. Internet suppliers of legal services will compete with more traditional law firms. Even social networks will become competitors to the traditional legal adviser. In addition, new forms of ABS will rely heavily on large investments in technology. External investors in legal services and larger law firms will work to eliminate the outdated working practices and tribal customs of so many traditional practitioners, and are already investing heavily in standardisation, commoditisation and technological solutions.

To counter this, law firms need to redouble their efforts to change both their mindsets and their competitive capabilities. Technological solutions should play a critical part in this. In many law firms, the technology departments have traditionally been seen as a support function, low in the hierarchical pecking order, with limited respect accorded to them. What is becoming clear, however, is that the more go-ahead firms, where such departments are seen as a proactive and trusted part of the strategic function of the firm, are not only thriving, but are also finding that they are well able to respond to the challenges of an increasingly competitive market-place. An integrated technology strategy ought to focus on the reduction of internal costs and the improvement of efficiency. Automated document assembly, case management, standardisation and the application of knowledge management, workflow and process management all call for a technological approach. And there is a human side to it as well, as technology can be used to take the brunt of the humdrum – via time-recording and desktop activities, for instance – and can enhance team-working and communication. Technology can also play a key role in any risk management strategy, and enhance or provide training and e-learning.

It has, however, to be recognised that technological advances will radically alter the business recipe and profitability of many law firms. Instead of firms employing more and more lawyers in an endless cycle of leverage and pyramid building, outsourcing and computerisation can replace at least some of the work done by junior lawyers. As Richard Susskind suggests (2008, p. 278): 'This will not finish law firms but will necessitate major structural change in the long-run. For example, it may lead very large firms to give up routine work (or multi-source it) and to build instead a much narrower pyramid with a lower proportion of junior lawyers to partners.'

Technology does, however, give firms the opportunity to become more efficient, to bring about greater consistency and higher quality standards (through enforcement of standardised workflows and documentation), and to become better law firms through knowledge building and sharing, e-learning and enhanced methods of constant communication in an electronic market-place. In short, technology needs to be considered at the start of the strategic review process[2] for its possible impact on the firm's competitive position, its business recipe and its capabilities to deliver future services to clients profitably and efficiently. Technology also becomes an essential part of the firm's implementation and investment strategy as it moves forward.

Endnotes

1 There are four levels of competence. (a) Unconscious incompetence, where the individual neither understands nor knows how to do something, nor recognises the deficit, nor has a desire to address it. (b) Conscious incompetence, where although the individual does not understand or know how to do something, he or she does recognise his inability. (c) Conscious competence where the individual understands or knows how to do something, but demonstrating the skill or knowledge requires a great deal of consciousness or concentration. (d) Finally, unconscious competence where the individual uses his knowledge without thinking about it.
2 For example, by a PEST analysis which scans the macro-environment in which the firm operates to assess the likely effect of Political factors, Economic trends, Social factors and Technological influences.

4

Understanding differentiation, market positioning, and competitive advantage

KEY POINTS

- Differentiation: distinguishing features of a firm's capabilities
- The nature of market positioning in the legal profession
- Typical means of competing
- Repositioning and gravitational pull: how to improve a competitive position

Differentiation

Even though the legal profession is consolidating, it remains a fragmented profession with a bewildering choice of possible legal advisers facing every client. In some businesses the main way of competing consists of developing and marketing unique products or services; for such businesses true differentiation means being or becoming the only show in town. Professional service firms find it almost impossible to differentiate in this fashion. As Mark C. Scott (1998, p. 23) puts it: 'Differentiation means the quality of the intellectual capital of the firm – the collective ability of the senior people, embodied in its brand reputation.' It is vital to note that a firm must not just be different from its competitors; it must also be capable of being distinguished from them in ways which clients and markets find valuable and meaningful.

Differentiation has to be distinguished from segmentation. Segmentation is concerned with where a firm competes in terms of groups of clients, localities and services. As Robert Grant (2008, p. 243) explains:

> Whereas segmentation is a feature of market structure, differentiation is a strategic choice by a firm. A segmented market is one that can be partitioned according to the characteristics of customers and their demand. Differentiation is concerned with a firm's positioning within a market (or market segment) in relation to the product, service and image characteristics that influence customer choice. By locating within a segment, a firm does not necessarily differentiate itself from its competitors within the same segment.

The extent to which a firm can differentiate itself is an important element in achieving competitive advantage. A set of key differentiation questions faced by every firm are:

- How do we stand out from the crowd?
- Why would clients choose us?
- What do we do which is different, cheaper or better than our competitors?
- How can we demonstrate added value to our existing and future clients?

As can be seen from this set of questions, the firm's differentiation is largely client oriented and externally focused. If the clients can see no added benefit or advantage from the firm, then the firm is not likely to progress and prosper.

As the firm reviews its competitive position, it should be careful to recognise that we are not living in a world of constancy where the competition stands still. A stunning year, a key new hire or a merger may well have given the firm a temporary advantage in that it may have leapfrogged other similar firms in the eyes of clients, but other firms will be progressing their strategies as well. What is more, it is extremely difficult for a law firm to achieve true differentiation. The new legal landscape faced by any firm will undoubtedly display a surplus of similar firms, employing similar people, with similar educational backgrounds, coming up with similar ideas, producing similar services, with similar prices and similar quality. Most firms may think they are different from other competitors, but this does not mean that they are differentiated in the eyes of potential clients who are perhaps choosing between a number of alternative firms to solve their particular legal problems.

The point I am trying to make is that the particular make-up of the firm may well be entirely unique, but it does not necessarily enable the firm to obtain a particular feature distinguishing it from its competition in any of its main practice areas, and any distinguishing features which it does have may very well differ depending upon the type of target client and its industry sector.

What is clear is that the firm must decide how it wants to be seen in its market-place, what position in this market it wishes to occupy and what type of client will provide its core business as it goes forward. It needs to consider its resources and capabilities in order to service the clients for whom it aspires to act, and the required depth in each practice area.

In short, the firm needs to decide and define how it is going to compete and what it wishes clients to perceive as its competitive edge.

In a number of surveys which my colleagues and I have conducted for clients in recent years, we asked the clients how they perceived their law firm's competitive advantage, value and edge. The most common answer was that the differentiating factor was the power of the relationships between the law firm partners and its clients. Hence the power of relationships remains a huge source of competitive advantage for any firm. This is or should be no surprise as the high reliance on the quality of the firm's human capital, allied to the quality of its client relationships, has been a long held assumption in most law firms.

Competitive differentiation factors tend therefore to be frequently intangible and do not bear direct comparison with competitors. They also tend to be capability based; in other words differentiation factors are highly dependent on the ability of the law firm to meet the specific business and individual needs of clients fully. They are also focused on value propositions in terms of service, process and value for price.

Differentiation also depends on the sort of firm that the law firm is or is trying to be. Bulk suppliers rely on high volumes with good leverage, but the work is price sensitive and the margins are low. Differentiation for the bulk supplier concentrates on systems, processes and efficiency to produce fast and streamlined services. These qualities are emphasised in marketing, and the building of relationships with those who want commoditised services. There is also a particular emphasis on the development of referrer networks. Niche or boutique firms rely on distinctive offerings – for example, extreme and focused specialisms or industry sector expertise – for their competitive edge. What they are emphasising is their skill, knowledge and experience in their chosen niches. The dangerous position is to hover somewhere in between these two extremes – it is not differentiated to be offering all things to all men as your offering is probably similar to that of many other similar firms. Only the large and dominant firms can really pursue this option with any success.

A firm's strategy in relation to the pricing of its services should both reflect the firm's positioning in its market-place and also influence it. If the firm is choosing to practise at the lower or commoditised end of the market, then its pricing will reflect that choice. Rates and prices for such firms will always be sensitive and under downwards pressure, but the profit is to be made by increasing volumes of work at the same time as decreasing the cost (to the firm) of doing the work via leverage and systems. If the firm is choosing to practise at the higher end of the market (high net worth individuals and commercial organisations), then the price ought to reflect the partner intensive nature of the work and the rarity factor associated with extreme expertise.

The nature of market positioning in the legal profession

Put at its very simplest, strategic choices can be distilled into two basic parts. The first is the firm's choice as to where it should compete (positioning) and the second is the firm's strategies to address how it should compete (gaining and sustaining competitive advantage).

A law firm derives its ability to compete from a number of different factors – its tradition and history, the market-place it is trying to serve in terms of both geography and client types, where it fits into that market-place, what services it is offering and in what industry and market sectors, and its credibility in offering those services. To a large extent, a firm's market position – where the firm chooses to compete – is the result both of choices made by its partners many years before and evolution since then, as opposed to a recent decision to make a radical shift in strategic choices. In assessing a firm's ongoing strategy, it important to understand where it is now and what realistic decisions the firm can make to address a profitable future. Radical changes to a firm's current market position can only be made with enormous effort and large-scale investment. A firm's positioning also is aligned with its approach to market segmentation – the groups or segments of clients and potential clients who have broadly similar needs and perceptions of value

At the same time, we are beginning to see a number of generic market positions arising in the legal profession both nationally and throughout the world. Although most firms will fall into one of nine generic types shown in Figure 4.1, an important point must immediately be made. This is that every firm has its own unique history, tradition and culture and

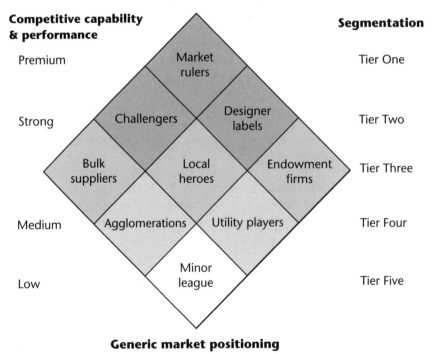

Generic market positioning

Figure 4.1   Competitive capability and performance

may well enjoy features from more than one generic type. The figure – or diamond matrix – is therefore offered as a diagnostic planning guide rather than a set of prescriptive 'pigeonholes'. The figure's nine different generic types of market position are also divided vertically into five segments of client demand. The description of each generic type and its unique features helps to explain where firms might stand and how firms can develop their strategic choices.

Figure 4.1 is contextual and applies to the relevant market for any firm, which will usually mean the domestic market within which the firm is practising. Whilst Figure 4.1 can also be used to consider the global marketplace, it is perhaps immediately most relevant to think of it in terms of the market in England and Wales – the market to which the LSA will immediately or imminently apply. The diamond shows five different layers or divisions of law firms working from top to bottom. The first layer – market rulers – contains the premier division of law firms. The second layer contains two types of firms which we have described as challengers and designer labels and forms the first division just behind the premier division. The third layer or division is made up of three different generic types of law firms – bulk suppliers, local heroes, and firms which we have described as endowment firms. The fourth layer contains agglomerations and utility players, whilst the fifth division contains a large number of minor league firms. The typical profile of each generic type demonstrates their positions in terms of sustainable competitive capability, dominance characteristics (if any), as well as comparative performance and profitability.

These five layers or divisions more or less match the segmentation of the legal profession discussed in Chapter 1, with the top tier work (complex transactions, financings, etc.) going mainly to market rulers and the top end firms in tier two, and the purely local and low grade work going to the lower tiers of the firm.

Each segment in the diamond describes a typical market position for a law firm. The diamond does not, however, seek to define the number of law firms in each segment, nor their relative sizes. There will, for example, be very few market rulers and it is likely that they will all be very large law firms. There will also be large numbers of minor league firms but they will all be small in size. There will also be large numbers of utility players of varying sizes.

Market rulers

Market rulers are the major national and global players. They are often to be found as magic circle players in most capital cities and amongst the global leaders. These firms apply the laws of dominance to attain huge critical mass. This means that they can field deep teams (see Chapter 2, p. 30) across all or the majority of the heavy-lifting areas of corporate and commercial work and can resource major transactions and matters at a moment's notice. It also means that they can provide leverage to all their transactions and matters by producing expert teams led by highly competent and leading specialists. They also have a strong brand and name in their jurisdictions which command respect and credibility. They tend to get the high profile mandates from an impressive list of top clients. They also tend to be the pricing leaders in any area and they often have clout in government relationships and the corridors of judicial and regulatory power. Because of their resources and their investment capability they are often at the leading edge of unique new flexible capabilities. Hence they are able to ward off or defend against attack by always being one step ahead. Market rulers are also pre-eminent in terms of superior profitability and performance. Their profitability is based on three main profit drivers. First, they tend to be involved with the high value deals and the 'bet the farm' issues where premium pricing can be applied. Second, they tend to be efficient in the management both of overheads, where they gain huge economies of scale, and the maximisation of productivity. Third, the application of leverage through the building of deep teams helps build and sustain an enviable profit model.

They obtain a level of uniqueness and sustainable competitive capability in at least five different ways:

1. Because of the strength of their client base and the high value of the engagements in which they are often involved, they have developed cutting edge technical expertise and experiential knowledge which puts them into a different category from the next segment of law firms.
2. They have built an infrastructure which enables them to be market leaders in process and technology and the use of outsourcing.
3. They have developed structural capital in the form of systems, processes and knowledge management which smaller firms cannot rival.
4. In understanding the dynamics of their markets, they can derive a continuing position of dominance though developing a constant stream of services, changing over time, which give them a position of repetitive competitive advantage.

    As Stephen Mayson (2007, p. 123) puts it, 'the sustainability of competitive advantage is therefore not based on a continuing dominant market position but is rather derived from a continuously achieved series of temporary competitive advantages'.
5. Competitive advantage is achieved through a truly global reach. Here, there is room for contention and controversy in placing global capability as a prerequisite for market ruler status. In some countries, there are 'magic circle' firms like, say, Slaughter and May in London, which are single office firms and therefore are based in only one country. Whilst these firms might argue that they have truly global reach, it is

also arguable that these firms do not demonstrate all the features of true market rulers and fall into one of the two next segments – niche players or challengers.

Challengers and designer labels

The second layer is made up of what we have described as designer labels and challengers. Whilst these firms differ widely from each other, they do share some common characteristics with each other and the market rulers.

Designer labels

This describes three distinctive types of firms which have some broadly similar positioning and competitive characteristics. Two of these types are described by Mayson as focus firms and portfolio firms. The focus firms – also and perhaps better known as niche firms – are usually highly differentiated with narrow scope. They tend to specialise in one or a few particular areas of law or in carefully defined sectors of client types or industries. Stephen Mayson (2007, p. 102) calls these firms 'focused firms' and defines them as ones where at least 50 per cent of the firm's revenue derives from one practice area or sector, or where at least 75 per cent is derived from two such sectors or practice areas. In relation to a niche firm's chosen markets, they share many of the same features as demonstrated by market rulers and may indeed be market rulers in their areas of fame. They do not, however, offer the same spread of services, or serve the variety of sectors, as market leaders do, nor do they usually have the same global geographical reach.

The third type of designer label firm describes firms which may offer a relatively full service but which exploit some other distinctive characteristic which appeals to certain types of clients – such as a range of unusual but strategically placed locations or an accentuated brand image – which helps to define them and give them a competitive edge.

Designer labels are usually extremely profitable and their specialist core focus makes them highly competitive. They often have an impressive base of clients who value their extreme efficiency and their sector knowledge. Niche firms with a client sector based approach include firms specialising in the public sector, media, shipping, aeronautics, and pharmaceuticals. Examples of firms with specialist areas of law include firms focusing on such areas as employment law, IT, tax, white collar crime and personal injury. Within the overall definition of designer firms, portfolio firms share some of the characteristics of niche firms although they will not usually have such a narrow focus. Again, Steven Mayson offers a helpful definition. According to him, a firm is a portfolio firm if at least 80 per cent of its fee income derives from no more than four practice areas or market sectors. This seems too restrictive a view but Mayson also has a category of 'general firm' which he defines as one providing a wider range of services to a wider range of clients than either a niche firm or portfolio firm. The point here is that a designer label firm will have decided to limit its choices in relation to the sort of clients it serves or the sort of legal services which it offers. These firms have made a distinctive choice to avoid the temptation to become a full service jack of all trades but master of none. They will seek instead their own areas of fame within some specifically defined areas. Within those areas designer label firms share some of the characteristics of market rulers. The question becomes whether or not their competitive capabilities are sustainable over a long period of time. The problem is that in legal firms no competitive capability can ever be permanent. The more a firm restricts its services or its sectors, the less chance of adaptability, diversification and innovation it has.

Challengers

Challengers are firms which traditionally have been a bit behind the market rulers but which are making a strong bid to climb into the elite club of law firms. In short they are firms which are seeking to attack the position of the dominating firms by a combination of smart strategies, huge investment and driven leadership. Often firms such as these operate from a traditional position of strength, as they are usually highly profitable and frequently enjoy excellent client bases and heavy-hitting business development capability. DLA Piper falls into this category. Firms such as Eversheds and Berwin Leighton Paisner are also firms which would like to see themselves as challenging for membership of the elite club. Challengers also enjoy a lot of the same features as market rulers but their brands do not carry the same level of client assurance and credibility. Their areas of core competence may also be similar but the experience base is often not as strong, and the development of experts with deep 'guru' status is not as pronounced. Alternatively, a firm falls into this category if it is dominant in its own national market but, whilst having some international offices, cannot be described as a true global heavyweight. Challenger firms are often also the first movers in trying to 'break the mould' so as to be at the leading edge of new law, new service methodologies and new trends. Pioneering firms therefore include firms which are using innovation and new methods of service delivery (the outsourcing of back office IT and accountancy processes) as ways of breaking new ground. Challenger firms can also be pioneers in developing services in emerging or growing areas and in time these developments can lead to the gaining of a strong or dominant market position.

Firms in the challenger category are likely to include a number of organisations which would be keen to use the possibilities of the LSA to obtain external funding in order to fuel expansion and development.

Bulk suppliers, local heroes, endowment firms

On this view of positioning, Figure 4.1 then descends to a third layer, comprising three generic types of law firms.

Bulk suppliers

The bulk supplier is a fairly new phenomenon in the legal services sector. The only way of making large amounts of profit out of commoditised work in the legal professions is to pile it high and sell it cheap, making use of technology and low cost employees. In order to achieve a high volume, low margin, profitable position, such firms have to grow quickly to become big and to obtain much of their work by large investment in marketing and sales in individual markets within one or more jurisdictions. Thus the profit drivers of such firms are systems and leverage to take advantage of high volumes albeit at low margins. The differentiating features of such firms are their overall propositions for pricing, efficiency and branding. The problem with using pricing as a differentiator is twofold. First, it is difficult to sustain a position of being the cheapest in a sector in which somebody else will always try to undercut you. There can be only one cost leader at any time in any profession or industry. The second issue is that most buyers of legal services tend in the long term to purchase on value rather than price.

It also has to be remembered that the power of advertising and branding has only become evident in the legal profession in England and Wales within the last 25 years, and due to the large number of law firms in existence and the relative fragmentation of the profession, we have not yet seen the sort of branding power experienced in other sectors of professional services such the financial services sector. In the short term, however, the advent of a small number of heavily marketed bulk suppliers has already proved to be a massive challenge for the high street practices and these challenges are likely to grow stronger and to threaten to a more worrying extent.

The advent of the LSA will affect the market in two ways. First, deregulation could well see non-legal organisations, such as Tesco and the Co-op, making a bid for volume work by establishing their own law firms. These firms have no particular uniqueness in their sales proposition and relay on their assurances to clients that they can do the job quicker, cheaper and with the minimum of fuss. Hence, they rely on efficiency, systems and processes to enable them to take cost out of each matter. The second threat is from the existing leading bulk supplier law firms. In the field of personal injury litigation, a number of firms such as Irwin Mitchell, Russell Jones and Walker, and Lyons Davidson have grown enormously and, by implementing systems, processes and the features of commercially run businesses, have begun to erode the ability of the utility players and minor league firms to compete. Yet none of these firms seems to have more than a 10 per cent share of the available market for such work. The advent of the LSA will enable these firms to introduce external finance in order to build market share dramatically and to dominate the market further for personal injury services.

Local heroes

Almost every county, city and town has a firm which has achieved national, regional or local fame and even dominance. Examples of such commercially oriented local heroes in the UK include Wragges in Birmingham, Walker Morris in Leeds and Burges Salmon in Bristol.

Local heroes share many of the features of market rulers. Indeed, they are usually market rulers in their own fiefdoms. Their client bases are strong and the depths of their teams and strength of their specialised core competences is usually huge. Their profitability is also good, although not as high as the market rulers because of their inability to charge premium rates.

The drivers of profitability for these firms usually include a combination of factors which place them in a strong position of profitability relative to their local competitors. Thus pricing (though lower than the premium pricing obtainable by market rulers) and leverage can be applied to their strong local client bases. Whilst these firms might not be able to aspire to the very top tier of complex global transactions, they nevertheless enjoy a good selection of high value work. Some local heroes also have designer label status in such areas as private client and public sector, and some have niches to rival higher tier firms in corporate law, commercial property and commercial litigation.

Local heroes, however, suffer from their lack of geographic reach. They will not usually have offices in more than one jurisdiction and indeed, within the United Kingdom, are very often to be found in only one major city. This can hamper their efforts to attract and retain clients in other geographical areas who may appoint firms in different localities. The question for these firms in terms of their own positioning is where they go next. The options for them are to stay as they are or to try to challenge for the premier league by becoming a challenger firm or even designer label firm.

Endowment firms

The final type of firm in this third tier of firms is what we have described as the endowment firm. Whilst almost every law firm depends to a greater or lesser extent on the client bases and traditions which it has inherited from the past, the generic endowment firm type relies predominantly or exclusively on history and inheritance for its competitive position and profitability. They are often yesterday's market rulers. Whilst their position remains strong, it is in danger of waning. The strategy of the endowment firm is largely to continue doing what it has always done. Such firms rely on the loyalty and inertia of their established client base. Although it can be relatively easy and inexpensive to switch suppliers of legal services, clients will often continue to tolerate their existing lawyers rather than go to the trouble and risk of changing to a new firm. Much of their client base includes 'old money' individual clients and old-established corporate clients. Endowment firms are often slow to move and averse to change. The culture and routines of the endowment firm tend to be hierarchical, bureaucratic and risk averse, making such firms slow to react to market changes. Innovations are largely client driven, and the development of new services, new clients and new markets tends therefore to be reactive rather than proactive. Such firms tend to be pillars of the establishment which helps them to be listened to in the corridors of power and to retain premier tier clients and partners. Hence their competitive positions are based on their status as known quantities, and client perceptions that they continue to be thoroughly safe hands. Reliance on past glories and historical fame places endowment firms at great risk of further erosion of their competitive position.

Utility players

Every geographical market contains a host of small and medium sized and even quite large firms which are general practices offering a broad range of services to a broad range of clients. These firms have few differentiating features except for their relationships with their clients and convenience of location. Utility players have also been described as 'vanilla firms' to describe somewhat ordinary firms which are simply part of the pack. Utility players rely on 'me-too', copycat strategies to ensure they do not fall too far behind their competitors in terms of specialisms, services and processes. Profitability is largely based on maintaining high productivity and efficiency with a carefully controlled overheads base. The existence of a few loyal star partners and staff often helps to carve out a niche or degree of fame and expertise in particular sectors or specialisms. Utility players share some of the characteristics of the next tier up. They will often have a department or niche dealing with bulk commoditised services, or they may have some niche specialisms which are characteristic of designer label firms. In their particular locality, they may be one of the firms challenging for local hero status.

Agglomerations

Agglomerations tend to be consolidations of firms nationally or regionally whose strategy is based upon the creation of bulk and critical mass in order to challenge for new market positions. Such firms are often created by unrelated acquisitions and consolidations and spend significant periods of time trying to shed old inefficiencies, such as over-partnering and inefficient working practices. Hence their profitability is often unremarkable and their specialist areas can often be wide rather than deep. Many agglomerate firms remain large but mediocre and rather amorphous. Bulking up, as such, is not a strategy as it is based on the theory that you have to be big to be credible, and that by getting bigger, the firm will be able to compete better. As David Maister (1997, p. 147) points out:

> It cannot be denied that size helps in marketing. However, it is a poor substitute for it. Market credibility, and being invited to propose with great frequency, are goals that can be achieved through effective marketing. Merging to achieve market credibility is like using a sledge hammer to crack a nut. Firms that are interested in bulk mergers are, in effect, saying, 'We don't know how to get better, so we'll get bigger because size helps – a little'. Of course, increasing size does not necessarily lead to greater profitability for professional firms. Few of the things that determine a firm's success – client service, innovation, productivity enhancements, collaboration – are critically dependent on size.

These firms will usually make their way into one of the other higher profitability brackets.

Minor league players

Minor league players form the majority of small and medium sized firms throughout the country which are struggling both to provide something unique to the market and to provide profitable performance. The competitive characteristics of a minor league firm tend therefore to become factors like convenience (locality of office), local knowledge and price. The competitive disadvantages are, however, formidable – lack of investment capacity, low profitability, succession issues and competitive pressures from above. The minor league firm cannot compete on price with the bulk suppliers, nor does it often enjoy the specialised experiences and resources of the local heroes with whom it is usually trying to compete for the better value work. For the minor league player the positioning opportunities are restricted. It is not easy on any part of the diamond to move directly or diagonally up. Exploiting any particular strengths the firm may have may enable the firm to become a utility player, but whilst this might improve the firm's position a bit in terms of performance and profitability, the firm is still exposed to an uncertain existence in an increasingly competitive market. In the face of these issues, it is not surprising that many minor league firms are taking refuge by becoming subsumed – where they can – into larger firms.

Repositioning and gravitational pull

It is important to appreciate that a firm can dramatically improve its performance and competitive position within the positioning segment that it already occupies. The increase of competitive pressures in no way requires a firm to change its basic positioning or to become a very different type of law firm. However, whilst it is difficult to move upwards in the diamond, gravitational forces will tend to pull a firm down by an increase in competition, or by the firm's own default and incompetence. All positions of competitive advantage should be treated as temporary, eroding over time unless continually renewed and reinforced. This gravitational pull is usually into one of the three boxes on the south-eastern side of the diamond at Figure 4.1 – the endowment, utility and minor league boxes. Hence a market ruler can lose its dominance and become an endowment firm through complacency. The utility player, long enjoying medium profitability and competitive capability, can find itself elbowed into the minor league box by bulk suppliers, local heroes and even by agglomerations.

Here, again, the advent of the LSA produces an extra area of threat through the arrival of new competitors and the increase of competitive resources of existing firms through external investment capacity. The strategic response to such competitive responses must be for firms not only to improve performance within their overall existing market positioning, but to consider whether repositioning might be part of their ongoing strategy and aspiration. Table 4.1 helps to identify the profitability and performance drivers in each part of the segment together with the main value drivers and pricing models for each. All these factors will need detailed analysis if any firm wants to try to change its market position. Thus a utility player may well build a strategy to become a local hero, or to try to become a bulk supplier and will need a different business recipe in each case. A local hero might choose by one means or another to become a designer label, or to challenge the national elite by trying to take up the position of challenger. There are at least four steps a firm has to consider in order to address the improvement of its competitive position, either by repositioning or by becoming more competitive or differentiated within an existing competitive positioning.

Step 1 – understanding the importance (or irrelevance) of geography, location and size

The diamond matrix has some geographical overtones. The market rulers at the top of the diamond will certainly be nationally elite and will usually also have international or global capability and profile. At the other extreme, the minor league firms at the bottom of the diamond will be primarily reliant on their local client bases and markets. There seems to be an increasing number of firms describing themselves as 'regional' or even 'national' and whilst the diamond does not factor in the number of offices, the location of the firm or its size, certain competitive characteristics of so-called 'regional' and 'national' firms will usually bracket them

Table 4.1 Diamond segment characteristics

Segment	Profit and performance drivers	Main value drivers	Perceived pricing
Market rulers	Rates, leverage	Expertise in highly complex work across all heavy-lifting areas Deep resources Reputation for quality	Super-premium
Challengers	Rates, leverage, productivity	Innovation and drive Leading edge pioneering Expertise in pockets of fame Reputation as rising star Flexibility and speed of response	Premium with super-premium elements at times
Designer labels	Rates, leverage	Specialised expertise and experience in services, markets, geographies Designer brand and reputation	Super-premium in some areas/premium in others
Bulk suppliers	Volume, systems, margin and leverage	Efficiency Branding and marketing Processing ability	Cost leaders/commodity prices
Local heroes	Rates, leverage, productivity, margin	Regional/local excellence and expertise Local knowledge Location Local hero reputation Quality and effectiveness of client service	Discounted premium
Endowment firms	Rates	Historical client base and brand Firm-specific processes and solutions	Client reactive pricing

Segment	Profit and performance drivers	Main value drivers	Perceived pricing
Agglomerations	Economies of scale and financial hygiene	Brand building Critical mass Coordinated services	Conformity pricing
Utility players	Financial hygiene	Client/partner relationships	Local market driven
Minor league	Financial hygiene	Local convenience Capability for lower tier work	Price sensitive

into one of the diamond segments appropriate to their market position and segmentation of work.

A regional firm can be defined either as a firm with more than one office in a particular region or as one whose reach of services and client base extends across a whole region. Thus a 'regional' firm can be a local hero, an endowment firm, or one of the lower categories depending on its competitive capabilities. In the same way, a national firm is one with national reputation and reach. The three segments at the top of the diamond – market rulers, challengers and designer labels – will all have national characteristics. In the same way, bulk suppliers can also be national. Agglomerations often aspire to national status due perhaps to a proliferation or network of offices, but unless those networks improve their competitive capability by coordinated and integrated services and nationally organised practice areas, the danger for them is that these firms will remain agglomerations – their national geography is not necessarily meaningful to clients.

In the same way, size tends to become a consequence of strategic positioning rather than a cause of it. Market rulers, for example, will tend to be large, not least because they will have deep teams across many practice areas. In addition, the rules of dominance are predicated upon, amongst other things, an increase in market share in chosen markets. But size is far from being everything. There are some fairly modestly sized designer label firms which are extremely famous and competitively eminent. Equally, there are some very large firms which remain mediocre in terms of quality, competitiveness and performance.

Whilst, therefore, the importance of size can be overstated, scaling up the firm can provide some important advantages and can be part of a repositioning exercise. The question needs to be examined first from the clients' point of view – how important is the issue of size to a firm's chosen client types and sectors? In this context, it is certainly true that size usually means that the firm has critical mass and resources, with the possibility of large specialised teams and strength in depth. Size can also be taken by clients as a proxy for excellence and quality. An internal analysis of the size question should additionally concentrate on the building of resources and capabilities and the firm's investment capability to hire people, diversify into new markets, or improve the value of services to clients. The size question often dominates merger discussions, for example. Here the diamond can help. If the merger of two utility player firms is merely likely to lead to either a larger utility player firm or a sideways movement into the agglomeration box, then at first sight the merger can appear pointless. The rationale for such a merger would have to be that a sideways step into agglomeration forms an important stepping stone towards becoming a local hero. Equally, the merger of two local heroes merely creates a larger local hero, but may also provide a route into becoming a challenger firm.

Step 2 – aligning resources and capabilities to the firm's value drivers

At the simplest level, the job of a lawyer is to provide solutions to problems and issues which the client faces. The victim wants redress, the house buyer wants to move, the disputant wants a successful result (or at least a good compromise) and so on. The main challenge for any law firm is to satisfy its clients that it can give them the successful outcomes which they perceive that they require, at a cost which the clients feel to be value for money.

The diamond at Figure 4.1 and the segment attributes at Table 4.1 help to establish some of the drivers of value for each segment. Top tier work requires high levels of expertise and specialisation across many areas of legal service as well as deep resources, and sound reputation and credibility. A premium price becomes an inevitable concomitant. Smaller clients may require the convenience and personal attention of a utility player or minor league player with whom they feel comfortable. Conveyancing and personal injury clients may simply require the job to be done cheaply and efficiently. Hence the value–price equation for any law firm is to a large extent determined by its market positioning on the diamond and the perceptions of value formed by the client types in the relevant market segment in the context of the work which those clients require their lawyers to do.

In Chapter 2, we saw that the features, functions and processes of law firms that the clients perceive are of value to them can be developed and moulded into capabilities which can be appraised against two key criteria – strategic importance and relative strength (against competitors). The exercise of analysing resources and capabilities – carried out at practice group level – helps each department or group to work out what it is that benefits existing and potential clients and which they find useful in their lawyers. The assessment of competitive strength compared with competitors forces firms to analyse in some depth the competitive environment in which they operate. The resulting blends of organisational capabilities that are both strategically important to the firm and which place the firm at a competitive advantage become the main drivers of value for the law firm in its competitive strategy.

Step 3 – planning for action

Much of the work set out in Step 2, together with the appraisal of intellectual capital, resources and capabilities set out in Chapter 2, will have been carried out at departmental or practice group level. The outputs from this work need to be brought together to create an overall understanding of the firm's current and desired positioning and competitive advantage. By this time, the firm should be fully and sometimes brutally aware of its competitive strengths and weaknesses, the aggressively competitive market-place in which it is operating, where the firm currently stands in that market-place and the resources and capabilities (both tangible and intangible) available to it, both to defend existing positions and to attack the competition.

There are two further elements which need to be considered. The first is to establish some agreed goals and objectives. The second is to consider implementation. It might at this stage be fairly argued that an agreement over goals and even vision should be the first step in any strategy formulation. The problem is that most partners in most law firms have a very disjointed and vague idea of what a realistic, credible attractive future for the firm might be. They often seem to talk of being a top 50 law firm, or a regional law firm, or a firm pre-eminent in a certain area, or a leading commercial firm. While such thoughts may give some basic clues, they do not really aid the firm in deciding its direction and strategy in ways which will help the firm to be successful. Added to this, many partners of law firms are more focused on their personal career objectives, or the goals of their office or practice group than on the goals of the whole firm. Hence, by leaving the creation of goals until Step 3, it is possible to have a discussion which is grounded in analysis, cognitively reached insights and realistic appraisals rather than in gut reaction.

A law firm's vision is an image of the possible and desirable future state for the firm that is in some ways better than what currently exists. This vision is really a statement of aspirations and objectives to describe the end result which the firm is trying to achieve. Typically, the vision describes the firm's practice mix, positioning, areas of focus, geographic markets and any constraining features. This brief statement – short and simple – is used to develop a shared commitment by the partners to the firm's desired goals.

What is vital, however, is to achieve some goals which are simple, consistent and long term and which reflect the ambitions of the firm and its partners and reinforce the firm's values. In setting goals, it helps to be able to identify the spectrum of conditions and opportunities available to the firm, as well as the areas where the firm is best placed to focus its attention and resources in order to develop new clients, new markets and new revenue streams.

To accomplish this, the partners need to review, discuss and digest the information and then develop observations about the firm and its environment. The result will be a variety of different pathways for the firm's future which can be developed into strategic objectives.

5

Developing a value-added strategy

KEY POINTS

- The nature of strategic decisions: the need for clarity, purpose and direction, the client perspective, how to make choices
- Deliberate offensive strategies: repositioning, dominance and growth
- Diversification: resources and new practice areas, launching a volume arm, alternative services
- Defensive strategies: stability, efficiency and reliability

Strategic decisions

Introduction

Two initial questions arise when a firm decides to think about the choices which it should make about its markets, its differentiation and strategic position relative to competitor firms. Such questions often revolve around issues of quality, or cost, or location, or client focus. The first question is whether the firm needs to make any conscious deliberate choices on the one hand or whether it can simply rely on its traditional market position and its existing business recipes in order to succeed in the future. The second question is who it is in the firm who makes such strategic choices when they have to be made. Clearly, a small firm will usually rely on all its partners to address matters of strategic importance, but once a firm gets above 15 to 20 partners, it is often very difficult for all partners to have an equal contribution in strategy setting.

What is clear from studies outside the legal profession is that power is central to strategic choice (see, e.g., Finkelstein, Hambrick and Cannella, 2009). Hence, in a larger law firm it is important to identify the partners and executives with the greatest power to affect the strategic direction of the firm, and to work out the distribution of power between individuals and practice areas. The power of position will, of course, usually give the managing partner a leading role in strategy-making, although we have seen many firms where the managing partner seems to have little more than an administrative role and the real authority remains with a few 'power partners'. The partnership structure of a law firm often makes it difficult to arrive at a methodically and analytically prepared strategic plan which resonates with both the partners and the firm's clients. This is usually partly due to lack of cohesion in the firm, but often is also due to some strategic confusions which arise along the way. The aggregation of individuals and different practice groups usually results in the firm having multiple goals that sometimes conflict. Additionally, partners of law firms can get really quite muddled between what is strategy and what is a whole range of other things.

The likely increase in competitive pressures requires law firms to address three burning issues. First, if law firms fail to face up to their future with clarity of purpose and direction, they are likely to meander. Second, if firms do not have an external focus on what their likely clients may require of them and how they are going to fulfil their clients' needs with excellent service, their strategies are likely to become inward looking and irrelevant to the external market-place. Third, if firms do little or nothing to make some deliberate and perhaps radical strategic choices, their strategies are likely to remain at best as worthy improvement plans and at worst as do-nothing policies leading to inevitable decline.

The need for clarity, purpose and direction

In the first place, it is vital in the face of intensifying competition and increasing law market consolidation, that the firm is clear what it is trying to achieve in creating, developing or reviewing its strategy, and that it understands clearly the nature and extent (radical or modest) of the strategic choices which the firm should make in the current and future environment. The partners should understand the kinds of business planning which are operational or tactical, and those which amount to improvement planning as opposed to strategic planning. For example, strategy is not the same as financial management. Partnership is, as the old saying goes, carried on with a view to profit. But whilst it is true that every strategy should have long-term profitability as one of its foremost objectives, that is not all that strategy entails. If profitability were the only goal, then firms would never invest strategically. The pursuit of profit is also a convergent aim of all law firms along with client service improvements and quality initiatives.

Strategy is also not the same as structure. Many firms are internally obsessed. The recent obsession in the UK has been conversion to limited liability partnerships (LLPs), but firms are similarly preoccupied with departmental and management structures, profit-sharing debates, and IT systems. As the McKinsey 7-S framework[1] taught us, a valid strategic question for any firm is to ask how it should be best organised and structured to generate success and profit. Strategy and structure are therefore linked but the latter is subsidiary to the former.

Furthermore, strategy is not the same as marketing. Again, there is a direct link between a firm's business development plan and its strategic one. It is possible, in admittedly rare cases, to have a strategic review which has no marketing or business development consequences. But it is certainly not possible to have a marketing plan without a strategic plan. The picture does, however, become confused here. Many strategic plans in fact turn out to be no more than marketing plans or improvement plans, which do no more than set out some initiatives to win better clients or make the firm better known in the market-place. In reality, the marketing or business development plan is shaped by the overall goals of the business. Some of these goals may be financial, some may be skills-based and some may be to develop market opportunities.

Strategy is also not the same as vision. Lawyers' eyes start to glaze over when the subject of vision, mission and values comes up. They feel that talk about vision is meaningless waffle, or too soft and too 'touchy-feely'. To some extent, many would agree. A lot of firms have found that having a 'vision' or a 'mission statement' changes absolutely nothing. But behind the words are some truths. Where do you hope to take your firm (vision)? How do you plan to get there (mission)? What holds your partnership together (values)? A vision is a vital precursor to any strategy – simplistically, if you do not know where you are going, you are unlikely to get there. But it is not a strategy of itself.

Strategy is different from implementation. Strategy without implementation is clearly a complete waste of time and energy. Implementation without a guiding strategy is directionless and often futile. And yet, many strategic plans get muddled with implementation and tactics in a number of ways. In the first place, strategy documents can end up full of implementation detail of projects for best practice improvements, and organisational restructuring. They can also be very operationally focused, dealing with internal projects for technology, staff matters, training and similar issues. Conversely, strategy plans can be totally vague and lacking in action plan orientation – so full of empty phrases that they get put in a drawer and forgotten, or are simply unrealistic and unachievable.

The need to be client focused

In the second burning issue, the most important element is that the strategy should add value to clients. When thinking about strategy many firms remain very inwardly focused. A large part of partners' deliberations often concerns matters of business planning rather than strategic planning. Discussions can easily become dominated by operational matters of little interest to clients such as budgets, targets, partner remuneration, promotions, office layouts, the disposition of printers and plans for training.

Creating a value-added strategy requires thinking about adding value to clients rather than saving costs or adding immediate value to partners' pockets. After all, it is axiomatic that superior profitability is a consequence of excellent client service to satisfied clients. If the firm's primary goal is to satisfy clients, then profit will follow; the pursuit of profit as the firm's major objective does not resonate with clients and is not therefore a useful or meaningful strategic mission. Perhaps worryingly, there is now a proliferation of client survey evidence across the world all of which demonstrates that clients are not entirely happy with the service which they receive from law firms. It is therefore becoming increasingly urgent for firms to create and frame their strategies, their market positioning and their measures of competitive differentiation in ways which are meaningful and attractive to clients.

The strategic plan should not only identify the list of the firm's most important and loyal clients, its preferred client types, and work sectors, but should also be aimed firmly at the fulfilment of their latent and blatant needs, and should identify and aim to develop the necessary resources and capabilities to enable the firm to obtain the most lucrative work possible during the lifetime of the plan.

The need to make deliberate and radical strategic choices

Law firms are now starting to look back with nostalgia on a recent past which is beginning to look somewhat like a golden age and which featured a benign trading environment, in which law firms found it relatively easy to keep growing, to make profit and to find new markets for their services. In those benign times, the strategy of many firms was to keep on with a successful business formula – 'if it ain't broke, don't fix it'. In the last 20 or so years, the strategies of law firms have been largely developed in two organic ways – an emergent process and a strategy of conformity in which the strategies of many law firms look somewhat similar. The emergent process consists of actions and decisions taken one by one which converge gradually in some sort of consistency or pattern (for a discussion on emergent strategy, see Mintzberg, 1994, pp. 24–7). Most firms realise that successful strategies do not get formulated entirely in an ivory tower but generally emanate from a powerful group of leading movers and shakers in the firm who have interacted over time in an iterative process or series of processes. Big strategies tend to grow organically from small initiatives to which the firm's context, client demands and trading environment (stable or unstable) contribute in ways which can only have been assessed or measured after the event with the benefit of hindsight. The second organic strategy is that of conformity. At worst, a conformity strategy is downright imitation in which a law firm slavishly follows what it perceives to be the strategy of other firms or a particular firm it admires. Conformist strategies are not limited to copycat solutions but apply equally to industry conformity. In an environment in which many law firms look much the same, firms often use the same language when describing themselves: they depict their culture in similar terms and they use interchangeable strategic words – such as 'regional, 'full service', 'commercial' and 'pre-eminent' – to identify their service offerings or their value propositions. Hence, many law firm observers and advisers have noticed just how similar the strategy plans of law firms can appear.

In a stable and benign environment, when there is plenty of available work and exponential growth is only limited by the aspirations and investment capability of the partners, a combination of emergent and conformist strategies has served many firms well.

However, the organic, iterative and dynamic process of emergent strategies is a somewhat slow process which does not work well on its own in emergency situations or when the going gets rough. A combination of recessionary forces, coupled with the advent of the LSA, means that the stable environment to which law firms had become accustomed has become unstable, complex and increasingly competitive. In place of conformity and imitation, law firms need to think how they can represent their own uniqueness and individuality and stand out from the crowd. In addition to an emergent process in which strategy formulation and implementation are both constantly being adjusted and revised in the light of experience, learning, trial and error, there is also a need for a rational, analytical process of deliberate planning.

In the new world of the LSA, we therefore see active and deliberate strategic decision-making as replacing the old conformist business formulae in which law firms successfully invested in strategies which involved persistence, conformity, efficiency, reliability and the defence of existing strategic positions. There is also a place for the emergent process. As Robert Grant (2008) notes, it is important for strategy to be developed 'through a combination of design and emergence. At the formal, deliberate level, strategy is made in board meetings, meetings of the top management team and within the strategic planning process. At the same time, strategy is being continually enacted through decisions that are being made by every member of the organisation'.

Deliberately formulated strategies

There have proved to be many ways of categorising various types of strategies and one way is to distinguish between strategies which are attacking or offensive in nature (sometimes known as prospector strategies) and those which are more defensive. Offensive strategies tend to involve growth, the aggressive pursuit of dominance, innovation, repositioning and the search for new opportunities. Defensive strategies involve cost control, stability, conformity and efficiency, as well as maintaining the strength of the firm's client base and client relationships.

Offensive or 'prospector' strategies

Deliberate repositioning

In Chapter 4, we examined the nature of market positioning in the legal profession. We noted that strategic choices can, at a simple level, be distilled into two basic parts. The first is the firm's choices as to where it should compete (positioning) and the second is the firm's strategies to address how it should compete (gaining and sustaining competitive advantage). We also noted that radical changes to a firm's current market position can only be made with enormous effort and large-scale investment. However, firms such as DLA Piper have demonstrated how it is possible for a firm which started its UK identity as a local firm in the North of England to expand to become one of the largest legal providers in the world. The deliberate repositioning of many of the large international firms has mainly involved growth of huge proportions, but repositioning can also take place by remaining relatively small (as a designer label), or by ruthless specialisation or skills building (to move from utility player to local hero status), or by the aggressive adoption of industrial models to pursue a business based on volume and commoditisation. There have been many examples of similar positioning moves.

Dominance, prominence and growth

BOX 5.1

The laws of dominance

- The 'rule of three' in consolidated markets:

    - the leading player gets 40 per cent;
    - number two gets 20 per cent;
    - number three gets 10 per cent;
    - the rest share the remaining 30 per cent.

    Example: Google gets 45 per cent of search engine hits, Yahoo more than 20 per cent and MSN just over 10 per cent.

- Dominance in even a small niche of the market-place leads to huge advantages.
- Dominance can be:

    - geographical;
    - by specialisation;
    - industry dominance.

Law firms have been through very much of a growth phase during which many firms have predicated many of their strategies merely on a desire to grow. Every firm needs a rational growth policy, even if it is a restricted growth policy grounded in a desire to remain much the same size. The question that needs to be answered is, what is the minimum amount of growth necessary for the firm both to retain its existing market position and to keep its strength and ability to perform or survive? As has been noted in Chapter 4, all firms need to have a viable market standing. In a consolidating market, most firms therefore need a high minimum growth rate in order merely to stand still, survive or maintain existing competitive advantage. The critical question then becomes whether the pursuit of growth is consistent with the search for profitability. Certainly, most firms who are seeking to compete in commercial areas of work need a minimum size in each of the main heavy-lifting departments in order to compete.

The ultimate symbol of strategic success is to become the market leader. As Edward Wesemann (2005) explains: 'Dominance is an integral aspect of strategy. Strategy, whether in war, sports or business is about how one can place [oneself] in a competitive position that gives . . . an advantage over competitors. If that position can be made so overwhelming by one competitor that others are effectively taken out of effective competition, that competitor is dominant. Dominance wins. The game is over. Everyone else is playing for second place or lower'. Under the dominance 'rule of three' the leading firm in a mature or consolidated market will typically have a 40 per cent share of the market, the second placed firm will have 20 per cent, the third placed firm will have a 10 per cent share and the remaining firms must fight over the remaining 30 per cent of available work. The global legal market-place – and for that matter the UK legal market-place – is highly fragmented in the sense that there are no firms with anything approaching a dominant share. However, the legal market-place is made up of many smaller markets involving localities, client types, industry sectors and specialisations. It is therefore entirely possible for a firm to establish some level of dominance in a small niche or in a region.

Size and growth, therefore, do have a bearing on any firm's ability to compete and will matter even more as the effects of the LSA start to bite. Law firm strategy is being driven as never before by client-led demands, as well as intensifying competitive pressures within the profession. As an example, one of greatest challenges for law firms is the client-led requirement for better service at less cost. This means that a standing-still strategy is likely to lead to a long-term profitability decline unless ways can be found of improving rates, making pricing methodologies more sophisticated, or using technology iteratively to decrease the cost of service delivery. Additionally, clients of all professional service firms are becoming more sophisticated. Whether they require commercial or personal services, they increasingly demand greater depth in three dimensions, all of which tend towards increases in scale in all but the most specialised niche firms.

First, and perhaps most obviously, clients require depth of expertise. The day of the broad generalist practitioner is largely over in the sense that most generalists have at least one area of practice where they can be regarded as a specialist. Whilst clients appreciate broad experience, they on the whole do not trust or value dabblers. For generalist legal advisers, a certain amount of knowledge is often a dangerous thing. We are only too aware that many client complaints and examples of mistakes come where partners stray from their core expertise into relatively unfamiliar territory. In addition, specialists often construct tried and tested wheels, rather than reinventing new ones. Hence, they tend to do their work quicker, more efficiently and more cost effectively (even at higher hourly rates) than their generalist counterparts. In this dimension it is the typical high street firm that has most to fear. Small general practices with skin-deep expertise are most exposed to the client-driven demand for greater specialisation and deeper levels of expertise.

The second dimension of depth required by clients is depth of service. The increasing complexity of legal work has over the years been exacerbated by a tide of new domestic and EU-driven legislation. The demands of a more elaborate and instantaneous society are multiplying. Apart perhaps from bulk providers, most law firms now report that they are conducting smaller volumes of larger transactions and matters. Teamwork is becoming more common, and there is less room in the majority of firms for sole practitioners. For their part, clients expect to see their matters being moved forward during holidays and sickness. Access is needed to team members at times when their main contact is otherwise engaged. Larger matters must be progressed quickly and efficiently with the work being done as a team effort and at the right level. This brings both cost and status implications. To compare professions, we all expect to have minor dental work done by hygienists and dental nurses rather than highly qualified dentists. In legal services, clients now tend to expect the law firm partner to perform only partner level work. Additionally, they value different specialists for different problems – horses for courses.

Third, clients increasingly require depth of resource. They expect their advisers to have the investment capacity and management capability to introduce and maintain a supportive infrastructure. Clients assume their firms to have case and knowledge management systems, and up-to-date libraries. Clients also want to see consistency of service throughout well-organised firms. They would, frankly, be horrified if they saw the current lack of investment their law firms make in terms of workflow processes, know-how collation, and precedent and template building. They also expect their advisers to be up to date with professional development, to provide their law firm staff with congenial working conditions in a diverse and ethical environment and to be able to communicate and process information with neural efficiency.

There are other factors driving law firms towards a strategic model in which firms scale up rather than down over time. Competitive pressures are unrelenting from other providers both within and outside the legal profession. Unless you are one of a handful of prominent firms, it is often not difficult to find law firms in every region with stronger and deeper teams across a broader portfolio of specialised services than your own firm. Why, for example, would a commercial client entrust its intellectual property or corporate tax work to a firm with only one specialist rather than a firm employing a whole department of specialists? Excellence of client relationships may save the day in the short to medium term, but in the long term all relationships tend to atrophy. It is here that the financial investments permitted by the LSA will count in the drive to acquire depth and strength.

Some smaller niche firms remain confident of their ability to occupy a deep and narrow niche and thereby to compete with leading firms. They will no doubt continue to thrive but will increasingly become the exception rather than the rule. However, even they must frequently review their offering, growth and geographic coverage in light of their individual markets. For the remaining bulk of law firms, profitable growth must be part of the strategy. Scaling up may well enable them both to meet the demands of their clients for greater depth and also to position themselves to meet the competitive pressures facing all providers of legal services. The availability of external finance following the LSA will enable forward thinking firms to make the right investments and is certain to redefine the UK legal market in the years to come. The dominance and growth option, therefore, is to drive the business rigorously and enthusiastically in order to beat the competitors. Many firms are looking at the liberalisation of investment to their advantage in order to drive their business model. The possibility of new blood and new resources, both financial and in terms of new partners and principals for the firm, can be an exciting prospect. These could maximise the opportunity of a change in the environment. At least, initially, it does require some painful choices. The business model has to change. The firm and its partners have to start behaving in way in which they might not have done previously in order to show a disciplined and commercial way of doing things.

Related diversification

There are four main reasons for a firm wishing to diversify. In the first place, the firm may wish to grow and realises that it can only grow to a limited extent in its basic core business. Hence, in order to grow further it either has to expand outside its existing geographical markets, or it has to add new services or new types of clients in order to continue to move forward. The second motive for diversification is the desire to spread risk and to balance the portfolio of services, industry sectors and client types. Firms operating for instance in the recession have quickly discovered that it is a great asset to have, amongst their service offerings, some counter-cyclical services which are much in demand during periods of credit squeeze. Equally, firms which feel somewhat trapped in one particular type of client or industry sector often feel the need to diversify in order to spread their risk. Firms that are niche firms sometimes feel that they need to become more general in their offerings in order to cut down their expo-sure to one or two restricted types of work. The third reason for diversifi-cation is to attempt to move market positioning. This is discussed in Chapter 4. The fourth reason for diversification is to move into more prof-itable areas – areas of growth or areas where high rates still persist.

One thing has to be clearly borne in mind in any diversification strat-egy which is that it makes no sense at all to diversify unless to do so adds value to the firm or the firm thereby adds value to its clients. Diversification can therefore be seen as something which is directly related to the firm's existing core business – a consequential development – or can be entirely unrelated, for example the addition of entirely new services, new industry sectors or client types or expanding geographically into areas where there is no immediate synergy with the firm's existing core locations.

In order to consider any form of diversification the firm will need to scan the external environment both for early warning signs and for areas of new and emerging opportunities. The challenge for the firm is to iden-tify the most important trends capable of impacting, both positively and

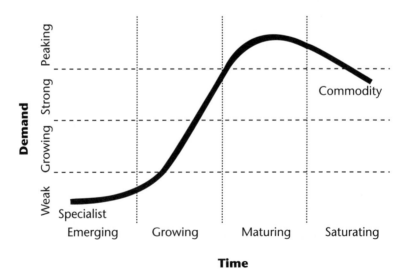

Figure 5.1   Emerging, growing and mature services – the S-curve of demand

negatively, on the overall profession in the firm's operations over the next few years. In this context it is also beneficial to attempt to exploit the S-curve of demand. The S-curve was primarily designed for products but can equally well be applied to services. The horizontal axis of the S-curve shows a spectrum of demand over time and the vertical axis shows the growing and waning strength of the demand. All services start with an emerging phase and move through a growth phase into a mature and saturating phase. When a new need for legal services emerges, demand for it is weak. It has not yet been recognised by many practitioners or their clients. Some of these demands peter out at this stage. Some demands, however, grow from this emerging phase into a growth phase, before entering a mature phase and then a phase when demand tails off. The important points for law firms relate both to business recipe and to positioning. During the emergent and growth phases the demand for services may be weak, but there are no dominant suppliers and the services are viewed by clients as being expert led and therefore the price is high with low volumes and low leverage. By the time the service or client type has reached a mature phase, many firms are offering similar services and the price tends to peak. As the service enters a saturated phase, the volume of suppliers will outstrip the demand and the price will fall at the same time as the service becomes commoditised. On the right hand side of the curve, therefore, price is more sensitive and on the left hand side of the curve the prices are premium prices.

Specialisations and resources

A further related diversification option is increasingly to specialise in existing areas of practice. Under this option, a firm would identify its core strengths and would continue to build and reinvent its niche and position in these areas. Diversification here would involve the addition of services or sector-based offerings which support the existing areas of specialisation. Again, there are some hard choices. In order to pursue such an option, the firm has to realise that there are some areas of the firm which might be ancillary and which, therefore, whilst not being necessarily abandoned, might not be allowed the same level of investment in the future. The problem here is that no partner likes to feel that he or she is in a non-core area. Every partner of a law firm wishes to feel that they have some value which can be added to their firm and that they have a real contribution to make. As soon a partner is told that the firm is not really focusing on his or her area any more, that partner will get restive and the self-fulfilling prophecy comes about as people drift off.

This ruthless specialisation option, therefore, requires disciplined focus and some hard choices. It also requires the partners to be focused upon specialising more, becoming more famous and performing at higher levels than before. The problem, of course, is that it can split the firm. One of the big dilemmas facing the small to medium sized firms in the regional and provincial market in the UK is that such firms are doing both commercial work for business clients and private client work for individuals. The balance is sometimes uneven. We have seen many firms where the commercial services departments make up less than 30 per cent of the revenue of the firm. Yet firms are very reluctant to give up their commercial lines in order to focus on private client lines. Equally, there are some large and medium sized commercial firms where private client work forms a relatively low percentage of their business. To abandon such work, either directly or by steady attrition over the years, is not an appealing prospect. This option, therefore, is probably only available to firms which are relatively niche already. In other words, firms for which the vast majority of their work is made up of one particular client type or one particular service. I know of many firms which specialise in areas such as intellectual property, employment, white collar crime, housing authority work, commercial litigation, personal injury litigation, union work and the like. For those firms the concept of ruthless specialisation has already taken root and can be pressed even further. This equation becomes less easy, however, for the general practice offering many types of services for a diverse range of clients.

Unrelated diversification

Over the years, businesses of all kinds have found it hard to diversify from their core areas into unrelated areas where they have little experience, no track record and few customers or clients. As the old sales adage goes, it is easiest to sell existing services to existing clients, followed by existing services to new clients. Selling new services to existing clients is then only slightly easier than selling new services to new clients, which is the hardest challenge of all. In the context of legal services, firms have variously tried diversifying into completely different areas such as estate agency, financial services and human resources consultancy with mixed results. Firms have also tried to diversify into other segments of legal services for which they were not previously well known. This kind of diversification is still tricky – for example, from an essentially private client firm into a firm offering commercial services, or from a firm with a mainly public sector client base into one offering private sector services.

The new regime heralded by the LSA will, of course, give new entrants to the market the opportunity to pursue a strategy of unrelated or partially related diversification into the legal services market, and the main strategic questions which will arise for them are the same as for legal firms seeking to diversify into unrelated areas. What if any are the synergies with what we do? What are the entry barriers? What is the likely cost of the investment and what is the likely return? How difficult will it be to acquire the people and build the systems, processes and infrastructure?

How easy will it be to build the brand and successfully take our offerings to the market?

Similar questions need to be answered for existing law firms which are considering diversifying into areas which are largely or completely unrelated to areas of existing practices.

If firms are to diversify in this way, it really helps to have an existing partner or lawyer who passionately wants to lead the development of a new area, either by specialising there himself or herself, or by leading the initiative with a sense of mission. Firms which have started new ventures such as new practice areas or new offices tend to be more successful if the project is led by a strong partner who is prepared to stake a great deal to ensure success.

New practice areas

It is not easy to start an entirely new practice area. Many new departments or groups have tended to develop out of larger departments, and deeper specialisations have tended to start from a more generalist base. For example, departments specialising in planning, construction and environmental law usually tend to be spawned from a commercial property department. In the same way, generalist commercial litigators tend to have found themselves specialising more and more in fields such as employment litigation, intellectual property or leasehold property litigation, family law and the like.

The growth of commercial work in smaller and medium sized firms is another interesting example. Traditionally, pricing pressure and increased competition has over the years driven many smaller and medium sized firms into commercial property work from their generalist base dealing with property matters for individual clients. In many firms, as their commercial property departments have grown and expanded, I have observed an increasing aspiration to specialise more in commercial work and that desire has led firms to try to set up corporate and commercial departments. A few firms have been able to achieve corporate and commercial departments by dint of generalist partners developing and retraining but, for many firms, new areas of practice have required new areas of skill which have to be sought and found outside the firm's existing resource base.

This is where difficulties arise. As has been pointed out many times, law firms are people businesses and need therefore to attract, develop and retain talented practitioners. Firms find it difficult to hire experienced specialists if their firm has little or no specialist foundation from which to work. For example, when firms are trying to hire lawyers skilled in corporate law, pensions law, tax law, or banking law to start up a department or team, they will often lose out in the 'war for talent' to a firm with a better base or foundation in the relevant practice area. There are two additional factors. First, clients need to be convinced that a firm with little previous experience in a new practice area will represent a safe pair of hands. Second, the cost of hiring specialised lawyers can be high in a firm where there is no existing volume of work to enable the newly arrived lawyer to attain early levels of useful productivity. The entry barriers for new practice areas are in many cases accordingly too high for firms to make a safe strategic choice and investment decision. Thus the utility firm (see Figure 4.1 in Chapter 4) will always find it difficult to reposition as a firm with heavyweight specialisms such as the local hero firms and the designer label firms.

Launching or developing a volume arm

The dilemma faced by many firms is that they have gradually found their market positions eroding in areas of work such as residential conveyancing and debt collection as such areas have become commodity services. In addition, areas such as personal injury work (both claimant and defendant) have formed rich pickings for organised and efficient firms successfully both to target and to build market share. Extreme price sensitivity is accompanied by the competitive pressure of bulk suppliers with a large budget to advertise, to pay referral fees and to provide the necessary working capital to fund rapid expansion.

In addition to a steady nerve, the launching of a volume arm needs three essential elements. First, there must be a leader or a coalition of leaders with a personal mission to see the venture succeed, accompanied by an entrepreneurial outlook coupled with a determination and commitment to instil or impose high levels of management and corporate discipline. Second, the firm must have (or have access to) large amounts of investment funds. Third, the venture must have a sensible, coherent and compelling business plan and business recipe based on the availability and deployment of both intellectual capital and resources and capabilities (see Chapter 2) which are fit for purpose, have profit earning potential and are capable of conferring sustainable competitive advantage. In short, the launching or development of a volume arm is not for the faint-hearted.

Alternative services

The most attractive alternative services exploited by law firms in recent years have been financial services and estate agency services. Some firms have also set up consultancies for human resources, IT, tax and accountancy, whilst personal injury firms have also considered consultancies offering medical and specialist reports. Many of the same ingredients that are set out in the previous paragraphs apply to alternative services. In addition to strong leadership, investment muscle and a coherent business recipe, the launch of an alternative services venture does need a heavy emphasis on compliance and risk management. The risk management elements alone require some of the firm's leaders to gain or develop a thorough understanding of the dynamics, structure and processes of the sector in which the venture is engaged, such that the entire partnership can be confident that line management, quality controls and compliance will all be properly and scrupulously addressed.

The big strategic questions, however, still need to be addressed. Other than the pursuit of profit (which is not a proper strategic goal on its own), the firm must have solid strategic reasons for making the investment. Diversification makes no sense unless it adds some value. The most obvious strategic reasons relate to three different types of synergy. The first is client synergy – that a significant part of the client base would readily use the additional services offered. The second synergy is with the firm's existing base of resources and capabilities – that the firm has people, cash, systems, processes and infrastructure that are under-utilised and could be deployed elsewhere. The third type of synergy is sector based – that the firm is famous in industry sectors or with types of clients where the additional services will add some natural extra power to the firm.

Establishing the firm's boundaries

The issues surrounding both related and unrelated diversification require the firm thoroughly and honestly to appraise its resources and capabilities to understand what drives the firm's business recipe and economic success. The core competence of the firm should be a huge influence in determining the sectors and activities which the firm should continue to develop and on which the firm should concentrate. As Cliff Bowman (1998, p. 176) points out: 'All companies, even the largest, have scarce resources, so it is not making the best use of those resources to direct them at activities which are not strategically significant. Very few companies make their own travel arrangements, for example: they subcontract them to a travel company who can then take advantage of scale economies and the experience curve to provide a better and cheaper service.' Instead, Bowman suggests that alliances and partnerships should be used where the firm's degree of competence (compared with the best in the industry) is only passable. The exception is where the venture is of such extreme strategic importance that there is a strong case for the firm investing in the necessary resources and skills.

Four elements are necessary for a firm to convert its strategic diversification aspiration into a realistic plan which can be implemented. First, the venture must form a logical area for market and skills diversification. Second, the venture must in some way help to leverage the firm's image, credibility and brand. Third, the venture must provide interesting and profitable work. Fourth, the necessary enhancement of skills and capabilities must be in reach of the firm or be readily attainable.

Defensive strategies

The whole thesis and thrust of this book is that it is unwise for any firm in the new environment faced by law firms to fall by default or inaction into a purely defensive strategic state. There may, however, be cases where the firm's competitive position is so advantageous and so strong that defence is the best option. In one sense, the market rulers described in Chapter 4, for example, will have defence of their existing positions at the heart of their strategies. Even they, however, must employ attack as the best form of defence by growing their market shares, developing deeper specialisations and consolidating positions of dominance.

The twin problem is that client relationships erode over time and that positions of competitive advantage are hard to sustain. The old adage is, 'if you always do what you have always done, you will always get what you have always got', but the competitive forces which we have described are getting stronger and the advent of the LSA has been described by some commentators as likely to be the equivalent of the 'Big Bang' on the London Stock Exchange in 1986.

Firms employing a strategy of defence tend to make strategic changes and choices based upon efficiency, stability and reliability. The tendency of such firms is to persist with the existing formulae and business recipes by applying the voice of experience and tried and tested solutions to groups of loyal clients who require of their law firms a portfolio of deeply experienced skills and well-established systems and processes. Strategic changes tend to be reactive to the changing environment and adaptation takes place only to the extent that it is necessary to sustain such stability, efficiency and reliability. Equally, the legal services environment tends to produce a powerful set of norms which can dominate the practice of law. To be successful any law firm must meet and master those norms and this can drive law firms over time to adopt similar structures, similar strategies and similar practices. The form of institutional isomorphism results in many firms progressively converging with each other, through imitation, into a set of undifferentiated practices.

Looking at the UK landscape of law firms, many of the 10,000 or so law firms seem broadly similar to each other and exhibit little or no discernible difference that might be meaningful to clients. Nevertheless, where firms have established, through defensive and conformist strategies, a strong market position, it is hard to criticise them if their primary strategy is to defend such a position. For instance, for many firms some 80 to 90 per cent of their workload will come from existing clients, and firms have rightly taken the view that it must be a primary and core objective to ensure that those clients remain satisfied and that the firm employs and deploys resources and capabilities which meet the developing needs of those clients.

Hence, all firms will employ and measure defensive strategy in their strategic mix. Every firm needs to consider its stability, efficiency and reliability as well as the challenges, issues and factors which will enable clients readily to make a choice between comparable firms. Having said that, the point must be emphasised that there is a difference between a strategic plan and an improvement plan. The problem with defensive improvement plans is that they result in convergence with other law firms or with the strategies of other law firms. This leads to difficulties for the firms when trying to differentiate themselves in the market-place and sustaining their differentiation. It is only by employing and deploying offensive strategies that firms can sustain or obtain and sustain competitive advantage.

Firms may consciously decide on a strategy of inaction. If the firm has a number of partners in their late middle age and in their 50s or 60s, they may be more likely to take a short-term view. Their main concern will be to ensure that the firm remains a cash vehicle for the next five years. Most of the older partners may be at retirement age by then and it would not really matter to them what happens after that. In an inaction strategy, the firm would exploit its existing market-place and do little or nothing to build for the future. Put at its worst, such a strategy can quickly become a race to the bottom. The firm would do what it has always done and the result is that profits would steadily contract. The problem is that there are a large number of firms around the world for which this strategy has become the default strategy, not by choice, but because they have put their heads in the sand.

Endnote

1 See Peters and Waterman (2004). According to this, strategy is only one of seven elements that best-managed companies exhibit. The 'hardware' of success comprises strategy, structure and systems, while the 'software' elements are style, staff, skills and shared values. The key to the model is to ensure that all elements are aligned with each other.

6

Alternative business structures as a tool to implement strategy

KEY POINTS

- The objectives of the Legal Services Act 2007
- Strategic implications of ABSs for law firms and external investors
- Types of ABS: owned by lawyers, externally owned, fringe models
- Governance requirements

The objectives of the Legal Services Act 2007: an introduction

In Chapter 5, the question of both related and unrelated diversification was considered in some depth. I listed four main reasons for a firm wishing to diversify. The first reason is to grow by expanding outside the firm's existing geographical markets or by adding new services or new types of clients. The second motive is the desire to spread risk and balance the firm's portfolio of services, industry sectors and client types. The third reason for diversification is to attempt to alter the firm's market positioning as discussed in Chapter 4. The fourth reason for diversification is to allow the firm to move into more profitable areas – areas of growth or areas where high rates still persist. I also noted that diversification can be seen both as an opportunity for firms who wish to be proactive about their strategy and as a threat to law firms generally, as organisations currently outside the legal profession may desire to benefit from the LSA and diversify into legal services.

It has, of course, always been possible for a law firm to diversify outside its core legal services market into other areas of professional services, but some of the structures and legal mechanisms which have had to be used have been unwieldy and restrictive. Particularly problematic have been the restrictions on both external investment and non-lawyer partners, which have prevented law firms from diversifying to the same extent as the accountancy profession, for instance.

The LSA now enables lawyers of all types – such as solicitors, barristers, licensed conveyancers and legal executives – to share ownership, management and control both with other types of lawyers and with non-lawyers. The first change has already been made. As from 31 March 2009, legal disciplinary practices (LDPs) of mixed types of lawyers and with up to 25 per cent of non-lawyers, have been permitted. These will be converted to alternative business structures (ABSs) when the new regulations are in force. The objective of the LSB is to get the regulatory framework in place to allow new types of providers to seek a licence to offer legal services as an ABS by the middle of 2011. This regime will also allow traditional law firms to link up with non-lawyers and non-legal firms such as insurance companies, banks and estate agents to offer integrated legal and other services. The new regime also allows external investment and ownership in law firms.

Our purpose is not to examine the very detailed regulatory structure which is already in place for LDPs and is being constructed for ABSs, but to consider the strategic implications for law firms for both attack and defence – taking advantage of the opportunities which the new regime offers as well as making preparations to cope with the threat offered by competitors both new and old.

Strategic implications for law firms of ABSs

The traditional model of law practice throughout the world has seen some features which have historically been shared in common with other traditional professional service sectors. Most firms have required relatively modest amounts of funding to provide adequate working capital and these capital requirements have usually been within the bounds of affordability of partners aided by willing banks. Also, the financial focus of firms has been relatively short term; the accent has been on this year's profitability, with most profits distributed to partners rather than being retained in the business for investment. Furthermore, since the time when goodwill was largely excluded from law firms' accounts, the partnership model has provided for outgoing partners to take with them only the amounts standing to the credit of their current and capital accounts. Unless the firm has owned an appreciating asset such as a freehold property, retiring partners have usually left with the same fixed sums which they introduced. There has been little opportunity for retiring partners to realise any element of capital growth.

In other sectors of professional services, sector consolidation has engendered or stimulated changes to the historic partnership model as rival firms compete fiercely for the business of global clients. At the same time, the power of branding has seen the advent of national organisations providing cheap and cost effective services at the commodity end. The effect of greater consolidation is to provide a fiercer competitive squeeze to existing providers which find their natural markets eroded, their pricing models under pressure and their client retention ability diminished. In both the accounting and advertising sectors, consolidation has seen more than half of the global market expenditure concentrated in the hands of small numbers of leading players. In financial services, the arrival of national providers such as Direct Line has dramatically affected the competitive viability of high street insurance agencies.

The example of opticians was given in a Department of Trade and Industry paper in 2004 (DTI, 2004; and see LSB, 2009 which refers to the DTI's 2004 paper). Deregulation of the opticians' sector in 1983 heralded a period of consolidation in what had previously been a relatively fragmented market-place. This forced a large number of small high street firms to leave the market and enabled the then leading four players to corner over 75 per cent of the market. These dominating forces included three significant new entrants: Boots, Vision Express and Specsavers. The only traditional optician in the top four was Dollond and Aitchison which was absorbed into Boots in early 2009 as the battle for domination of this market continues. The Specsavers model is, however, an interesting one as each practice within the overall firm is an independent business and is owned jointly by Specsavers and the practitioner. Specsavers offers training, support services, integrated marketing and promotion as well as a nationally known and promoted brand. For their parts, the practitioners are responsible for delivering the technical eye care service to their customers and for the day-to-day running of their businesses. This model has been hugely successful. From being the number three in 2000, Specsavers now claims to be the leading provider with over 20 per cent of the market.

In contrast, the legal services industry has remained fairly fragmented and has even been described as the last of the cottage industries. The example of the opticians' sector, however, offers an interesting insight into one of the ways in which a professional services sector can undergo radical transformation.

The trend towards consolidation through increasingly muscular competitive forces seems to be inexorable in all industry and professional sectors and the LSA is likely to provide a catalyst for faster sector consolidation than would have taken place naturally without its introduction.

Law firms are likely to consider an ABS for one or more of three strategic reasons. First, their strategy for survival and prosperity may require growth or diversification which needs funding to a greater extent than they can manage internally. Second, they may perceive the need to protect or increase their market share by being part of a bigger or better positioned brand. Third, the partners may feel that an ABS gives them a possibility of realising a capital value for their share in the law firm which they own.

Vehicle for funding growth

Law firm funding has traditionally been mainly generated from partners and bank borrowings. Mergers and acquisitions have usually been self-funding and investment in new teams and laterally hired partners has, for the large part, taken place against a short-term affordability and budgeting horizon. Firms which have grown quickly have often found it somewhat difficult to maintain appropriate levels of working capital even when new client work has been quick to pour in – lawyers have to be recruited and paid and office space and infrastructure provided at a faster rate than the client work can be turned into cash.

Whilst it is generally cheaper to borrow than to raise equity capital, the ceiling to bank lending can restrict fast growth. As the LSA starts to bite, we also expect to see a few law firms trading for value, which has not hitherto often been the case. Accordingly, acquisitions of other law firms will need extra funding as sellers start to exact an actual sale price rather than just expecting an integration of balance sheet book entries. Furthermore, as law firms consider their competitive positioning, bold moves up the positioning matrix (see Figure 4.1) may require firms to pay attractive sums to lure teams away from other firms, and to invest highly in new systems and processes.

Means of enabling financing for brand-building, advertising and marketing

I often hear law firm leaders asserting that they have excellent people, teams and services, but that they have difficulty in bringing their services to market. In their locality, they say that they are a best kept secret and that clients find their way to better known and more visible firms which provide no better service or expert capability than them, often at higher cost. Other law firms resent house purchasers instructing better known and more widely advertised brand names and complain about victims of accidents being lured by the television advertisements of claims providers. The utility players and minor league players described in Chapter 4 are in increasing danger of being marginalised by larger legal service providers which have deep pockets to invest in the building of relational capital (i.e., a firm's client base, brand and networks which assist development: see Chapter 2). What is interesting about examples like Specsavers is that similar opportunities might become available for law firms to retain their independence (at least in part) while benefiting from the visibility and advertising bulk of a nationally known brand.

Helping to realise capital values

CASE STUDY   **Purchase examples of professional services firms**

Example 1 – accountancy

Vantis plc – Acquisition of the non-audit business of McBrides in 2004 (Vantis plc press release 13 October 2003)

McBrides was a seven-partner accountancy firm based in Kent. Its 2004 turnover for non-audit business was approximately £3 million, generating a profit for the partners of around £1 million. Under the terms of the acquisition, Vantis acquired maximum net assets of £27,000 plus work in progress payable at cost as and when realised. The maximum overall consideration for the sale was expected to be around £3.8 million and was capped at £5 million. The price was satisfied by a cash payment of just under £1 million and the issue of some shares in Vantis then valued at £296,000. The balance of around £2.57 million was to be paid in shares over a two-year period dependent on performance.

Example 2 – law

Integrated Legal Holdings Ltd purchase of Argyle Partnership Lawyers in November 2008

Integrated Legal Holdings Ltd (IL) acquired the entire share capital of Australian, six-partner law firm, Argyle Partnership Lawyers, for A$2.73 million (£1.35 million). The firm had a turnover of A$6.5 million (£3.2 million). The consideration consisted of A$2.15 million (£1.06 million) in cash and the issuance of 4.14 million new ordinary IL shares valued at A$0.58 million (£0.287 million). The shares were valued based on IL's closing stock price of A$0.14 (£0.07) on October 31 2008.

The third motive for a law firm considering an ABS is the desire that partners may have to realise a capital value, either to retire or for other entrepreneurial reasons. Chapter 9 describes how a law firm might be valued and it is possible to envisage situations in which firms might be able to realise some value on sale, but the sums are unlikely to be large.

Simply paying out large sums of money to partners who can then retire is not a recipe that is likely to be attractive to external investors.

In the accountancy market, the consolidator Vantis plc is an example of an organisation which has bought a number of accountancy firms for prices partly paid in cash and partly dependent upon performance. The cash immediately available to the sellers is usually a small proportion of the total consideration (see the case study for an example). The continuing partners of acquired firms usually only gain a modest amount of cash upon sale, with the remainder of the price being paid either in shares or in cash (or a mixture) over a period of time.

The attraction of an ABS for external investors

The law firm sector's record of high profitability is likely to hold some attraction for investors, who will see opportunities to obtain both a return on their investment as well as capital growth in the share value. The traditionally high margins (comparative to other sectors) and the prospect of gaining high growth in an unstructured market are both alluring. As Jeremy Hand, Managing Partner of Lyceum Capital, a UK private equity firm, observed (in a press release in March 2000), 'the legal services market is large, fragmented and offers considerable potential for continued growth'. This thinking resonates with the view of the UK government which has made it clear that the limitations on innovation and competition caused by the tightly restrictive regulatory environment have constrained consumer choice and restrained normal market pressures from delivering efficient and effective legal services. Some investors may therefore see the opportunity to make a financial gain and to reap an investment harvest in due course. Other external entities will also see synergies with their existing businesses or opportunities to diversify into both related and unrelated sectors. Global networks may also see the possibility of leveraging their brand by introducing it to a new service sector.

Types of ABS

We have identified about 15 different models or types of ABSs which might be possible under the new legislation (see also SRA, 2009). One thing is clear: most of these models will require law firms wishing to become an ABS to move away from the traditional partnership model to a model which is much more corporate in structure. Even the limited liability partnership may prove to be an inappropriate structure for many of the ABS models, except those which include only a small proportion of non-lawyer involvement or investment. In Australia it appears that the largest firms have retained their partnership structure and that most firms which have adopted alternative structures are small or medium sized. We have broken the models down into three groups. The first comprises models where the ABS continues to be largely owned by lawyers and is attractive to law firms to exploit strengths, take advantage of opportunities, or address weaknesses and external threats. The second category contains externally owned models the majority of which are likely to threaten law firms, but some of which provide law firms with opportunities. Finally, there are some fringe models which are less likely to be popular with law firms.

Table 6.1 ABS Models

Type	Definition
Model 1 – Traditional law firm	Traditional law firm model with minimal non-lawyer involvement
Model 2 – Marketing umbrella	Independent law firms operating under a marketing brand
Model 3 – Law firm franchise	One dominant firm franchising its brand to others
Model 4 – Consolidated law firm roll-up	Aggressive law firms acquiring others
Model 5 – Virtual law firm	Law firm with low overheads and flexible resources
Model 6 – Legal MDP	One-stop shop with related disciplines but legally dominated
Model 7 – Integrated MDP	Law firms integrated into MDPs controlled by non-lawyers
Model 8 – Externally financed growth	Law firms selling minority interests to external investors to fund expansion
Model 9 – Branded conglomerate	Corporate brand owning law firms as part of wider (and maybe non-related) portfolio
Model 10 – Law firm plc	Large law firms floating as plcs
Model 11 – Integrated legal network	Network of law firms operating in a hub and spoke subsidiary structure under a holding company
Model 12 – The external consolidation roll-up	External investors acquiring law firms until entity large enough to float
Model 13 – Online firms	Internet firms offering legal documents and services via the Web
Model 14 – Not for profit firms	Charities and NFP law firms offering legal services for no/low fees
Model 15 – In-house teams	Institutions offering the services of their in-house legal departments on the open market

Mainly owned by lawyers

The traditional law firm

There is no doubt at all that the traditional law firm will continue, both as general partnerships and as limited liability partnerships (LLPs). Many firms will seek to compete with their new rivals on the basis of a competitive strategy in a firm which remains fully owned and managed by lawyers. Within this model, the legal disciplinary practice (LDP) will continue in firms where a small number of non-lawyer managers are able to add their financial and ownership contribution as partners and co-owners instead of employees. Any law firm which wishes to continue to have non-lawyers as partners will, however, have to migrate from an LDP to an ABS once the new regime comes into force. Those firms who are already registered as LDPs will be automatically transferred to the new regime, at which stage the 25 per cent limit on non-lawyer partners or members will also be lifted. This sort of ABS will be attractive only to those firms who want minimum non-lawyer involvement.

The marketing umbrella

It is already becoming popular for some law firms to practise underneath an overall umbrella in a marketing and branding operation. QualitySolicitors.com is a good example of how this might work – it offers a branding umbrella for about 100 firms nationwide which combines personal service, concern for professionalism and local knowledge under the aegis of a reliable brand. In a sense, this is a type of franchise, although limited to marketing support. It will enable firms to remain totally independent and to compete with other firms operating under the same umbrella without breach of the professional ethics or conflict rules. Most umbrellas will have some quality standards but – as with international alliances – we think that once a firm has been allowed to enter the umbrella arrangement, standards will prove difficult to enforce given the total independence of the firms. This model does not need enablement by the LSA as such, unless the umbrella has any degree of non-lawyer ownership. Other examples are Lawnet which has been around for some years as an alliance network of some 66 law firms, and the Legal Alliance which is a more recent umbrella network. MyLawyer[1] (**www.mylawyer.co.uk**) is another umbrella service through which clients can instruct solicitors online. Online matching sites (e.g., QualitySolicitors.com, TakeLegalAdvice and Connectlaw) are also proliferating to give contact details for appropriate law firms.

The law firm franchise

The pure franchise is similar to Model 2 (marketing umbrella) except that the concept here is that one law firm works to set up systems, processes, standards and structural capital which franchisees would be compelled to adopt. Unlike other sectors of professional services, there are likely to be very few firms currently (if any) whose brand and standing is sufficiently advanced or differentiated for such a model to work in the early years of deregulation. In addition, most go-ahead and progressive firms will probably be more keen to acquire firms than to franchise them.

It is easy to see this model at work in the non-professional services sector. McDonalds and Subway are good examples of the model working in the fast food industry. Every franchise looks the same, with unified products, service standards and pricing. In the professional services sector, a number of UK estate agencies such as Winkworths, Jackson-Stops & Staff, and Bairstow Eves (part of the Countrywide Estate Agency Group) are examples of professional services firms which operate under a franchise model. The firms recruit established and start-up estate agency businesses to operate under a known brand using the firms' tried, tested and proven methodologies and taking advantage of cost savings through group purchasing deals, central regulatory compliance, technical support and centralised referrals. Members are charged an initial payment and thereafter a monthly management fee based on a percentage of gross income.

The consolidation roll-up (law firm driven)

A roll-up is a technique used by investors (commonly private equity funds and venture capitalists, but also by aggressive firms in the same sector) by which a number of small firms in the same market are acquired and merged. Consolidation within the legal profession is already taking place and is likely to continue. The motives for firms merging or for larger law firms to acquire smaller firms may be entirely strategically driven so as to reposition, gain a competitive advantage, increase market share by scaling up or removing competitors, or so as to achieve significant economies of scale. Alternatively, acquisitions can be driven by the desire ultimately at least to have the option to be able to harvest a capital return by floating the firm. This model is therefore not new but, as we have seen, often results in the merged firm not immediately being able to improve its market positioning greatly. The firm moves into the agglomeration segment on the positioning matrix (see Figure 4.1) with the opportunity of repositioning from there. Traditionally, firms which have sought to consolidate by acquisitions have found it difficult to fund an extreme level of acquisitions over a short time horizon. This is in part because there are significant capital restraints for large-scale private acquisitions. Some firms may wish to look at the possibility of satisfying the capital requirements by external finance, and some of the models take this possibility into account.

The virtual law firm

The virtual law firm has few members of staff and operates as a management organisation and marketing tool only. If owned and managed by lawyers under the aegis of the SRA, it is a model which is possible under the present regime. One example is an American firm known as Axiom which started in New York as long as ago as 2000. The firm does not have partners or overheads and lawyers work as individual independent contractors. This firm attempts to provide sensible legal solutions at reasonable rates with key critical requirements of flexibility, efficiency and quality. Their clients are the big global companies but their aim is in part to provide flexible resources for in-house teams – by providing interim lawyers or locums to carry out projects for clients. There are some similar organisations in the UK such as Coco Law, Everyman Legal and Keystone Law. It is quite possible for these types of firms to continue to operate as traditional law firms with no non-lawyer involvement. It is, however, quite likely that the advantage of external finance from outsiders may prove irresistible.

The legal multi-disciplinary practice

In a multi-disciplinary practice (MDP), a one-stop shop is provided, allowing clients easy access not only to the legal profession but to other similar professionals providing legal and other services to clients. An example could be niche property practices with surveyors, architects, town planners, property managers, builders, decorators, furniture movers and property lawyers. It is possible under this model that the legal regulators (currently the SRA) would regulate only the legal services and all the other professionals would be regulated by their own regulators. Model 6 envisages an MDP which is dominated by lawyers. The legal MDP would probably therefore not have external ownership but would have available to it the buying power of the various different professionals who are partners of it. Equally, it is possible for other types of lawyers – such as barristers, legal executives and patent attorneys – to come together under this model. The point is (or should be) that lawyers should be seeking ways in which they can deliver superb value and expert legal and related services to their clients. As Richard Susskind (2008, p. 273) explains: '[S]uccessful lawyers of the future . . . will be increasingly multi-disciplinary . . . Legal Hybrids of the future will be superbly schooled and genuinely expert in these related disciplines and will be able to extend the range of services they provide in a way that adds value for their clients.'

Mainly externally owned

The integrated MDP

This is a variation of Model 6 but, unlike Model 6, the ABS may well be externally owned by a non-lawyer entity or a firm comprising a majority of non-legal professionals. Using one brand the firm could provide a number of different professional services. The rationale behind this model would be the synergies which occur between the legal services and the non-legal services. Whilst the law firm would be ring-fenced and regulated by the SRA, the parent external owner might, for example, be a financial institution or an accountancy firm or estate agency which might have an interest in cross-selling non-legal services to clients of the law firm as a component part of the legal services supplied to clients. Indeed, the external owner might be regulated by a regulator from a different sector (for example the Institute of Chartered Accountants or the Financial Services Authority). This model could prove to be a regulatory and licensing nightmare as the various regulatory bodies for the different professions involved tussle for regulatory supremacy.

Externally financed growth

This model has been discussed a great deal in the years running up to the enactment of the LSA. This is the way for a law firm to obtain partial private equity ownership in order to fund an extreme level of growth over a very short-term horizon. Unlike Model 12, the motive would be not to become publicly traded but instead for the law firm partners to retain overall control and majority ownership, having introduced a minority, externally owned shareholding. The representatives of the external investor – such as a private equity house – would become members of the law firm and the private equity company might hold shares in the firm. It seems that private equity houses may well turn out only to be interested in large firms with good management and, even in those cases, many private equity houses will not be interested in anything less than majority control.

The branded conglomerate

As a starting point, it has to be recognised that, even before the introduction of the LSA, not all legal services were necessarily provided by traditional law firms regulated by the SRA. Companies such as Peninsula give employment advice, Optima Legal Services deal with debt recovery and property services and Enact Direct Legal Solutions provide home moving and remortgaging services. Under this model, therefore, the law firm would be totally owned by a non-lawyer owner or company as one of its portfolio of either disparate or related services. Model 9 anticipates that the entity which owns the legal firm will have no interest in the supply of legal services except for a commercial interest in the financial fortunes of all companies within its portfolio. Under this model, the law firm would take advantage of its parent's corporate brand; it might, for instance, become part of a huge global organisation such as Tesco or an insurance company or other similar body. This model would involve either a start-up by the parent company or the acquisition of an existing law firm. The attraction for large corporates is their perception that this may prove to be an interesting and profitable diversification, made even more profitable by operating in partnership with alternative channels of distribution which can be cheaper, wider and closer to the customer – for example, mass markets dominated by a recognised and trusted national or international brand.

The law firm plc

Under the provisions of the LSA it will be entirely possible for a firm to float on the stock market as a plc, not necessarily under one of the consolidation-drive models but in order to finance organic and strategic growth. In the surveying world Savills plc is an example of a firm which has adopted this route, having floated in the mid-1980s, although some of its rivals, such as Knight Frank, have remained partnerships or LLPs. In order to provide sustainable attraction to the City, it would seem likely that only firms which are already market rulers, challengers, designer labels or bulk suppliers (as defined in Chapter 4) would be likely to attain successful flotation and many of those firms will not see the attractions of following such a route.

The integrated legal network

This model contemplates a network of mainly law firms operating under a hub and spoke structure. The hub would be a non-licensed holding company providing, for example, administration for central and back office services. The regulated law firm entities which make up the spokes would be subsidiaries of the holding company. Most of these entities would be legal firms under a national franchise or network arrangement but could well be other services (e.g., estate agency) in addition. Some variants of this arrangement are in force already, as many law firms have set up management companies to operate administrative management services for the law firm in return for a management fee. These are currently proving quite difficult for the SRA to approve and regulate and the new regulations will, it is hoped, ease this model.

In Australia a firm called Integrated Legal Holdings Ltd has already floated as a holding company for a number of law firms which can operate under an overall brand. Partners in the law firms which have joined Integrated Legal Holdings Ltd have an equity stake and are using employee share schemes to help increase staff retention and hiring. As a floated firm, they have the advantage of new capital injections. In addition to the regulatory requirements of the SRA or other licensing body, the firm would be also subject to stock market and corporate governance rules. Conflict of interest rules would come into play where the owning entity has more than one ring-fenced law firm, but the model can be designed so as to take conflict rules into account and to allow for some degree of separate branding.

The consolidation roll-up (externally driven)

The consolidator model of a law firm will usually happen in one of three ways. Model 4 envisages the first of such methods by which a larger firm sets out to acquire smaller competitors. The second is for a consolidation to be funded mainly or entirely by external investors – not necessarily lawyers – who start buying up small firms until they are large enough to launch or float as an initial public offering (IPO). The third method is what has come to be known as a 'roll-up IPO'. Roll-up IPOs are transactions in which a shell company goes public while simultaneously merging with or acquiring a number of law firms. This model does not require private investors to finance the transaction, nor does it necessarily require an established and well-positioned firm in the legal sector. This model first became popular in the mid-1990s as it allowed a firm to fund a huge level of growth over a very short-term period. It should be noted that potential financing for such transactions dried up in most sectors by the turn of the century largely because roll-ups performed poorly on average compared with the general market (see Brown, Dittmar and Servaes, 2004). There may, however, be some novelty value in the legal sector which might assist a selective number of roll-up IPOs in the early years of the LSA. Hence, consolidation is likely to start with the private acquisition of an existing law firm, followed by an IPO when sufficient firms have been acquired and integrated to demonstrate an established model which would be attractive in a public offering.

Online firms

In his recent book, Richard Susskind (2008) explores the current and likely impact on the legal profession of disruptive legal technologies. As he asserts: 'These systems might provide expert legal services, generate legal documents, assist in legal audits, or provide legal updates.' It is already possible to purchase or download legal documents on the internet from sites that specialise in offering legal document templates for consumers and commercial enterprises. Some of these sites are not currently regulated by the SRA and sometimes offer limited advice of a legal nature (see, e.g., **www.netlawman.co.uk**).

There is also a growth of law firms such as Linklaters and others providing online legal guidance, and in addition companies such as Epoq Group Ltd offer processes and online solutions on a retail basis through the internet, as well as on a wholesale basis via a network of subscribing law firms. Susskind also prophesies legal open-source solutions – rather like a legal version of the online encyclopaedia Wikipedia – fuelled by sustained online collaborators and volunteers.

Fringe models

Not for profit firms

This model envisages not for profit organisations providing legal services for low fees or within the publicly funded arena. In the United Kingdom there already are a number of charities, citizens' advice bureaux and not for profit firms which may make a charge for their services but only a charge which is sufficient to cover overheads.

In-house teams

This model anticipates some institutions which might plan to facilitate their in-house teams to offer legal services outside the institution. Many corporations and councils have quite large in-house legal departments and it might, in some cases, be attractive to them to be able to offer their services on the new open market to other companies outside their own conglomeration, or to consumers.

Governance requirements for firms practising as an ABS

It is absolutely clear that law firms will need to operate any ABS as a sound commercial business. Any investor in a traditional law firm will want to see the existence of sound management and stable cash flows within the firm before the investment is made. Investors will want to see both return on their investment and capital growth in the share value of the firm. Firms, therefore, will need to demonstrate strategies and a management regime that will add significant value and growth to the business. Whether or not the firm remains as a general partnership or becomes an LLP or a corporation, the governance model must, so far as possible, match that typically to be found in the corporate world. The board composition must be carefully considered to include outside directors, an external chairperson and decision-making processes which stick.

The introduction of external capital will be accompanied by a requirement on the part of the investor to have people within the business to support a management regime. They are likely to focus on board level appointments with knowledge about enhancing revenue, profits and cash flow, with financing and acquisition expertise and with skills in growing, upgrading and professionalising the firm. It is, therefore, vital for firms to improve their governance and the quality of their top management team so as to give them options for the future. The option may well be to remain a traditional law firm dominated by law firm partners rather than to seek external capital even if such external capital is readily available. This also impacts upon strategy. It is axiomatic that power is central to strategic choice. Strategies are not implemented so well in firms where there is no discipline, little accountability and no management power to enforce the decision-making.

The legal and compliance governance issues are in a way secondary to the primary need for there to be coherent governance structures, clear lines of accountability, a valid and compelling strategy and business recipe, and a culture and system for capable, efficient and progressive management.

The LSA provides a basic licensing framework for the ownership and management of ABSs. In brief, there will be a 'fit to own' test and a specific requirement for a licensed ABS to have a head of legal practice and a head of finance and administration, both of whom have to be approved by the licensing body. These heads are legally responsible for compliance with the terms of the ABS licence and will need to be approved by the licensing authority as fit and proper persons. Any ABS which is a limited company will also, of course, have to observe all the corporate governance requirements applicable to commercial entities. In general, even when a law firm becomes totally externally owned, investors favour a governance model which continues to involve the founder owners, whilst at the same time enforcing a regime that can actively manage future growth. The Brown, Dittmar and Servaes report (2004, p. 18) found evidence that continued involvement of the founders as shareholders and members of the board had a positive impact on the long-term performance of roll-up firms. One private equity house quoted in their study suggested that the founder management should be tied to a five-year contract with the new firm, that 75 per cent of the sale price should be in roll-up stock, and that the founders should have a majority of the seats on the board.

Good and sound management is necessary whether or not any law firm decides not to create or become part of an ABS. The changes to management required by external investors are to secure both a short-term return on investment and a longer term growth of capital invested. The requirement for strategies showing solid prospects of profitable growth and capable and efficient management is, therefore, common to all law firms. The need for consistency, for performance management and for enforcement of appropriate disciplines and behaviours is also starkly and clearly highlighted by the current and impending competitive pressures. Chapter 11 deals with the interrelationship between leadership, governance and management in more depth.

Endnote

1 MyLawyer is part of the Epoq Group which provides document assembly and legal workflow platforms as an outsourced solution for law firms.

7

Long-term funding of law firms

KEY POINTS

- The purposes and need for capital for long-term investment: the need for capital management and the link with growth
- What investors look for in a law firm
- Sources of capital: capital efficiency and balancing the sources of capital, debt, partners, outside investors, equity funding
- Conclusion

The purposes and need for capital for long-term investment

For many years, the financial drivers of law firms have been applied almost entirely to the maximisation of revenues and profit per partner. The attention of law firm financial managers has hence been heavily focused on the firm's profit and loss account and less focused on the firm's capitalisation. The balance sheet statements of most law firms are usually very straightforward as most of the firm's real and important assets are intangible. The areas of intellectual capital and resources and capabilities set out in Chapters 2 and 3 never appear on the firm's balance sheet but are the assets which make the firm competitive and profitable. They are, however, difficult to compute or value. Indeed, the balance sheet of a law firm often contains low levels of net tangible assets relative to the firm's revenues, and only moderate amounts of capital expenditure and depreciating assets. The most important issue for firms in relation to balance sheet management has been the ability of the firm to manage its working capital and hence its cash flows. For most professional service firms, work in progress is the equivalent of inventory in the industrial sector, and the firm's working capital requirement has been to generate sufficient cash in the relative short term to meet expenses as they arise. However, a firm's working capital requirement should be seen as a subset of the firm's overall capitalisation, addressing short-term (albeit consistently repetitive) cash flow needs rather than the longer term capital needs of the firm to fund investments and to support the firm's strategic objectives.

The growing need for capital management

It has also been traditionally quite easy for law firms until recently to fund their working capital needs. The banking institutions have for a long period been very ready to lend to the relatively safe law firm sector, and have been additionally enticed by the size and attraction of access to law firms' client accounts. Offset arrangements – whereby the interest payable by law firms to banks on their office account borrowings could be set off against interest receivable by firms on their client accounts – became seductive and popular. Easily borrowed money became cheaply borrowed money. Office equipment became easily leased rather than bought. The banks felt further comforted by the joint and several liabilities attached to the members of partnerships by which every partner became personally liable for their firm's indebtedness. In addition, firms generally found it possible to distribute earnings to partners without much need to require them to invest large amounts of capital in the firm. To this day, some firms still exist without partners' capital accounts, and have relied on partners leaving sufficient amounts in their current accounts to enable the firm's modest working capital needs to be met on an ongoing basis.

This traditional lack of attention to balance sheet management started to change during or as a result of the 1988–1991 recession. A relatively sudden decrease in the levels of transactional work put pressure on most firms' working capital requirements and challenged every law firm's ability to manage its cash and its creditors. Overdraft limits had to be negotiated against a less favourable trading environment. For the first time, cash flow forecasts became a necessary part of the law firm's financial management armoury.

The pressure on capital did not end with the upturn in the early 1990s. The last two decades have seen an increasing need for capital and balance sheet management. One example is that the advent of conditional and contingent fees has increased the working capital burden on law firms, particularly in the areas of long-running litigation (such as claimant personal injury) where work done by the firm can only be realised when the case is won or settled, sometimes more than a year after the work has been done. Furthermore, whilst it is also true that some firms have always invested in long-term assets such as freehold assets, in recent years the necessary investment in technology and expensive office fittings has also given rise to an expanding need to manage the firm's longer term capital expenditure needs. Tax burdens have also increased the need to manage cash flow as the previously favourable UK partnership taxation was steadily brought into line with the corporate sector. Historical unstructured borrowing patterns have further affected the balance sheet coherence of many firms, particularly smaller unsophisticated ones where capitalisation issues have not been adequately planned. Firms became used to regular and rather sporadic increases in their overdraft limits. If they needed to borrow a bit more, they would go and see their friendly bank manager who would usually look on their borrowing needs favourably. More stringent banking guidelines (to which we refer later in this chapter) have put such informal and casual arrangements firmly at an end.

The biggest change has, however, been brought about by law firm growth and the need for extra working capital which that growth has generated. As firms grew, it took them some time to realise that a firm's working capital requirement increased as it gained material amounts of new business. Even in the best run law firm, the extra working capital required can be approximately one-third of the annual fee revenue of the new work. This is because the work in progress and the amount of bills delivered but unpaid (accounts receivable) both have to be funded in order to meet the running expenses of the firm which will inevitably have increased as new staff members are introduced and additional office space is acquired. In one way, therefore, the level of the firm's investment in work in progress and uncollected fee invoices can be seen to represent the time lag between paying the firm's day-to-day overheads and the actual time of cash collection from clients. This time lag creates a funding gap. However, even in the case of the best managed firms, banks have always felt uneasy about funding the entire working capital needs of client firms, and have generally expected law firms to match the levels of working capital borrowings with their own introduced or retained funds. Many law firms consequently found their growth constrained by their inability to fund further expansion in offices and people even where new business was easy to find.

The link between growth and capital management

The initial, short-term answer to this dilemma of the growth-funding requirement became a long-term structural headache and illustrates the need for firms to consider their long-term funding plans more strategically. This longer term problem arose because, in looking around for new sources of capital, the attention of many firms was drawn to the possibility of promoting more and more young lawyers to equity partnership with a requirement on them to put in place a fixed capital contribution which could be readily borrowed by them outside the firm's balance sheet. In the short term, the gap in the firm's working capital contribution became suddenly and easily met and the firm could continue to expand. At the same time, this promotion strategy addressed difficulties in retaining senior lawyers, who might otherwise have left to join other firms where partnership looked easier to achieve.

In many but not all cases, this was an instinctive and short-term solution which caused three problems all of which had long-term, dramatic effects on the Holy Grail of law firm success measures – the much vaunted profit per equity partner (PEP) performance indicator. The first negative impact was the immediate effect on the firm's leverage structure. Part of the economic logic of law firms is that the firm's fee-earning pyramid structure contributes to profitability by allowing equity partners to take the profit generated by staff lawyers. The leverage ratio is therefore an important part of the profit structure of the firm. To maintain profitability, the firm needs to maintain its pyramid ratio and every time a staff lawyer is elevated to equity partnership, the leverage ratio becomes adversely affected. PEP becomes diluted as more partners are added and the firm will therefore tend to be compelled to grow further because, as it responds to the pressure to promote partners, it must recruit more assistants in order to maintain its leverage ratio and therefore its profitability. This in turn fuels a further need for more working capital which, ironically, was part of the main original justification for the partner to be promoted. In this way, firms entered a perpetual cycle in which they grew, hired, promoted and then hired again.

The second effect of growth on law firm's capital management and profitability was the Gadarene rush by large firms to relocate to bigger and more expensive new premises. With the benefit of hindsight, the decisions made by many law firms to burden themselves with additional fixed costs seem to have failed to take into proper account the risk of downturn. Whilst it is necessary to have extra space to house additional lawyers, the opulence and pretentious positioning of many such offices now seem unnecessarily self-indulgent. While property costs rarely exceed about eight to ten per cent of the firm's overall overheads, it is nevertheless a fixed cost which cannot be easily reduced in a downturn. In addition, the cost of expensive fixtures and fittings places more strain on law firm finances.

The third and possibly the greatest impact of many firms' decisions to promote partners and thereby introduce more capital was that it resulted in many firms becoming greatly over-partnered. This was in part because the growth-hire-promote leverage cycle became more and more difficult to maintain, particularly as the bargaining power of lawyers – one of the five competitive forces discussed in Chapter 1 – resulted in escalating staff costs and put pressure on both the leverage and the pricing models. Furthermore, the promotion of lawyers to partnership is a strategic mistake if the decisions are made mainly because of the need for capital as well as to ease retention worries. Not all lawyers are suited to the ownership and management demands of equity partnership, and many remain able technicians but poor managers. In short, many partners found it difficult to step up their fee-earning performance, management abilities and business-getting contributions to meet the expectations of partnership. As a result, many started to underperform.

Throughout the early part of this century, the better managed law firms started to address the over-partnering issue but it quickly placed a strain on partnership finances. As PriceWaterhouseCoopers (2004) noted in their 2004 report, 'the general trend towards a reduction in equity partner head-count has reduced the number of partners sharing the responsibility to cap-italise the firm without a corresponding reduction in the total level of capital required'. The natural response of most firms was then to increase the capital required of the remaining equity partners. By 2005, PriceWaterhouseCoopers (2005) noted that the fixed capital requirement of partners in the UK's top 25 firms had grown in two years from 30 per cent to 40 per cent of the total capital required, with current accounts hovering between 35 per cent and 40 per cent of total capital in addition. It was clear that well-managed large firms were deliberating hard on their optimal financing structures. By the time the 2007 recession came along, many large firms had worked out how to balance short- and long-term funding by an appropriate combination of equity partners' fixed capital, current account funding assisted by working capital controls, bank over-drafts, short-, medium-term and revolving loans, and leasing obligations.

However, during this 15-year growth period, from about 1992 through to 2007, many smaller and medium sized law firms had simply been unable to grow to the same extent as the firms in the top tiers of the posi-tioning diamond explored in Chapter 4 and thus were exempt from the dramatic scale of the growth-hire-promote leverage cycle in larger firms. Growth for them was constrained, in whole or in part, either by their inability to fund growth in their leverage structures or by the difficulties experienced in hiring good lawyers. Nevertheless, the buying power of lawyers which had led to salary escalation in larger firms cascaded down to all law firms and the need to grow to maintain and improve overall competitiveness – explored throughout this book – continued to be an imperative and brought about the same need actively and strategically to manage the firm's long-term capital and ownership structures.

Future needs for long-term capital

We therefore enter the second decade of the twenty-first century with many law firms at the limits of their ability to increase their capital base or actually under-capitalised. Most firms continue to be sufficiently well capitalised to remain liquid – in other words to convert their work into cash sufficiently quickly to cover current liabilities – and to fund partner drawings and distributions. They, however, lack the capital base to grow or, in some cases, to compete in the new world.

This will undoubtedly affect the ability of the majority of UK law firms both to continue to develop and compete as traditional law firms and to face or embrace the new competitive pressures and business models dis-cussed in Chapter 6. Growth throughout the sector is thus constrained by financing limitations. Firms increasingly find themselves at the limits of their borrowing capacities and unable or unwilling to introduce further partners' capital by capital calls or promotions. It is worth repeating at this stage three themes from other parts of this book. The first theme is that not all growth is good growth and that growth for growth's sake is ill-advised. Growth is only a valid choice if it is inextricably tied to a firm's vision and competitive strategic objectives and, in addition, if it can be carried out profitably. In other words, growth should be substantive rather than merely quantitative, providing depth and an increase in real competitive capabilities rather than just a growth in size. The second theme is that the assets which drive a firm's performance and contribute to its value – its value drivers – are the intangible assets discussed in Chapters 2 and 3 and not the tangible assets on the firm's balance sheet. The third theme is that – like other businesses – the critical element to achieve in law firms is free cash flow. In other words the ability of the firm efficiently to convert revenue into cash which can then be returned to its partners and shareholders is a vital competitive competence. PEP is merely one way of expressing and measuring the firm's free cash flow relative to the equity and capital invested in it (see Scott, 1998, p. 50).

Self-financed growth is also increasingly difficult to achieve. One really good way of strengthening the balance sheet is to grow the firm's profitability organically, but the ability of firms to achieve this by efficiency measures alone has a natural ceiling. It has often been pointed out that utilisation improvement is limited to the optimal productivity of the fee-earners. Once optimal productivity efficiency has been achieved, production capacity has to be improved (further hiring) or overall revenue per fee-earner has to improve (prices have to go up). As Chapter 4 suggests, prices in a static or highly competitive market can generally only increase by better positioning.

The two other general self-financed growth models are mergers discussed in Chapter 8 (which do give rise to real opportunities in the early years of the LSA), and the recruitment of the so-called 'lateral hire with a following'. The latter have proved easier to postulate than to implement. This is not just because lateral hires with any form of following are difficult to find, but also because on some measures the majority of lateral hire decisions turn out to be a disappointment either because of cultural difficulties or through over-optimism about the clients and business which the new partner proves ultimately able to introduce.

A further but perhaps more limited option for firms which have restructured into corporations is to self-finance the acquisitions of teams and firms through a combination of shares and paper in the home firm as well as deferred payments via earn-out structures. The problem here is that many such acquisitions will then have a pay-back period of several years and will not yield short-term additional profits or free cash flow during that period.

Growth is, however, not the only capital consideration. It is often forgotten that both foreseen and unforeseen events can have a catastrophic effect on the firm's financial base. It is easy to ignore the prospect that partners' capital needs to be repaid to those who retire, and the risk that the unforeseen departure of a key partner can cause loss of both capital and clients. Firms, therefore, need to have in place some form of capital cushion to protect against unforeseen contingencies and uninsured eventualities.

All of this points to the need for firms to consider carefully the capital and ownership requirements of their strategic options even in traditional law firms (Model 1 in Chapter 6). This period of reflection, if honestly and openly conducted, may well force some smaller firms to conclude that they do not have the capital capacity to grow – or even in some cases to survive – and that their strategies may be best served by consolidating with another firm or firms and thereby be part of a critically massed entity which is better able to finance the development of its capabilities and competitive positioning.

What is also clear is that many of the models of ABS set out in Chapter 6 will require injections of capital, sometimes of large proportions. If this looks impossible to achieve based on the firm's own capital structure and self-financing options, this then raises the possibility and problem of attracting further external investment.

What investors look for in a law firm

The investor proposition can be summed up in a few simple sentences. Investors of all types demand strong management and cash flow which is stable, predictable and growing. They will want to see both an income return on their investment and – a novel concept for law firms – the opportunity for capital growth and wealth creation. What is vital to recognise is that investors will not be willing to invest money in law firms just to enrich the partners. They will only invest if they are satisfied that their investment will lead to further growth.

To satisfy potential investors, firms will therefore need to demonstrate three main elements. The first element is essentially a strategic one. In short, firms will have to demonstrate compelling strategies and potential for fast and profitable growth. This strategic element contains essentially four sub-elements. First, the firm will have to have a vision and a set of achievable strategic goals that are coherent and action-based rather than merely hopeful or aspirational. Second, the firm will have to provide evidence that it thoroughly understands its competitive environment, the competitors and competitive forces which are likely particularly to affect it, and the competitive positioning which it has or needs to have to achieve its goals. These aspects are all addressed in Chapters 4 and 5. Third, the firm must be able to show that it enjoys or is actively developing the intellectual capital and capabilities which are both strategically important and capable of beating competitors. These factors are addressed in Chapters 2 and 3. The fourth and final strategic sub-element is that the firm should be able to show, through its business planning and execution actions and tactics, that it is actively implementing its strategies and has a compelling business recipe to fulfil the firm's strategic goals.

The second main element which investors will want to see is a track record of managing growth and cash over a sustained period. Firms will be able to evidence this track record not only by the production of trading records over time but also by demonstrating their performance and approach in client service and development, pricing strategies, process efficiencies, people management and the internal mix of sectors, services and practice areas. One issue here is that the revenues of many law firms are volatile rather than predictable. Firms with large numbers of client panel appointments or guaranteed streams of repetitive work will be attractive to investors because of the predictability of their income flows. On the other hand, transactional firms which rely on being able to attract a sufficiency of large deals in any year in order to make their targets have always found it difficult to predict or guarantee their revenue streams. For such firms, reputation, good positioning, a solid client base and a compelling history of success and increasing transactional revenues will all help to make an attractive case. Firms reliant on a very small number of large clients will, however, be seen as risky, as investors will want to see a track record of managing growth and balance in the client portfolio as well as overall firm growth.

The third main element that investors will want to see is a structure and a culture of capable, efficient and progressive management. It is this area where sceptical investors, mindful of the general record of law firm partners for bloody-mindedness, independence and inefficiency, will require a great deal of convincing. It will help if the governance structure of the firm is coherent, logical and approved by the whole firm. It will also help if the firm can show that it has agreed and implemented processes for partner performance, people performance generally, behaviours, accountabilities and discipline. It will also be helpful if the firm is able to identify and exemplify the positive and valuable cultural traits and attributes which can be directly related to the firm's effectiveness. The case will further be greatly supported by evidence that the firm is attuned to change and is able to show flexibility and embrace modifications in working practices. Finally, the case will be convincing if the firm has successfully introduced and embedded all those things which law firm partners tend to hate – systems, structures, processes, workflows, teamwork, accountability and project management.

In short, it is essential that investors see a complete firm rather than a loose group of individuals, where efforts are being made on a continuous basis to demonstrate consistency of service and a coherent and unified base of firm-specific intellectual capital (see Chapter 2).

Sources of capital

The sources of possible capital for law firms are in fact quite large. In addition to the self-evident contenders such as the existing equity partners and members, candidates include banks and lending institutions and, even, other law firms as merger partners or investors. There are some less obvious candidates. Future lawyer and non-lawyer partners may be obvious but, whilst many firms look for partnership qualities in recruitment selection processes, many employers would not have investment capability on their recruitment checklist as a desired attribute of a young lawyer. But, even despite the grow-hire-promote leverage cycle referred to earlier, future potential partners still represent a major part of any firm's succession and growth strategy. The LSA opens the list up still further. Other professionals (such as accountants, barristers or surveyors) may be prepared to invest in the firm by way of merger or minority stake or by diversifying into the legal sector through one of the ABS structures set out in Chapter 6. For smaller firms, family and friends are a possible source of investment by way of loan or equity stake. Furthermore there seems to be a growing set of business angels and private investors who might invest in a law firm if the case for investment is strong and compelling. Finally, there are the institutions, the venture capitalists and private equity houses as well as the market.

Attaining a level of capital efficiency and balancing the sources of capital

Institutional lenders are becoming increasingly wary of providing an unlimited supply of loan facilities to law firms even when they are satisfied about the security they are given. Banks will not normally expect to lend more than one-third of the firm's total financing requirement and prefer to see about one-fifth as a maximum, with three-quarters or more of the firm's capital funding contributed by the firm, in the form of undistributed free cash, and by the partners, in the form of fixed paid-in capital and current accounts. Banks will also often want to have the comfort of knowing that short-term borrowings are covered by the levels of accounts receivable and work in progress often on a 2:1 basis. It is also possible for firms to make an assessment of their capital efficiency by comparing and optimising the cost and risk of the various sources of capital used. One way of doing this – applicable mainly to large, sophisticated firms – is to calculate the weighted costs of the various sources of financing. The cost of each source of capital will vary and therefore has to be adjusted to enable a fair assessment to be made. A 'weighted average cost of capital' (WACC) calculation is a complex methodology used to assess the weighted average of the costs of each of the different sources of capital as one of many methods of establishing the right mix of capital sources as well as to see if the investment in each is worthwhile (see Arthur, 2009). Comparisons can then be made with peer firms and with industry benchmarks. The aim is to achieve an optimal balance between the various funding sources. At first sight it may, for instance, seem desirable to be entirely debt free. Yet, the cost of equity is clearly a lot higher than the cost of debt and therefore a debt free firm with partners and investors hungry for a high return may be less capital-efficient than a firm with a well-balanced debt profile. Equally, a firm with a high debt profile may be more capital-efficient in the short term but runs refinancing risks if the lender withdraws support.

Rules of thumb are also useful although these have to be used with caution. An often used rule of thumb in firms that are managing their working capital efficiently is that the amount of fixed capital supplied by each equity partner should be more or less equivalent to one year's profit share. For a firm with a net profit margin (distributable to its equity partners) of 30 per cent, for example, this means that the firm will then have an owner-provided capital base equivalent to 30 per cent of its annual revenues. In addition, many firms will often withhold the balance of partner distributions for the previous financial year for up to 12 months to assist with working capital and cash flow. A lot here depends on the firm's traditions and culture. We have seen possible mergers fall by the wayside simply because one party to the merger was financed to the hilt by debt whilst the other was virtually debt free and financed by high partners' capital and current accounts. Neither approach was either entirely right or entirely wrong, and it would have been perfectly possible to have charted a middle course to arrive at an optimal funding balance. However, the parties could not come to terms about what they clearly saw as the cultural aspects of departing from long cherished ways of doing things.

Few law firm partners, however, have traditionally looked on their financial input to a law firm as an investment which needs to be commercially assessed and verified by them for returns on capital. Partners will often assess the risk of equity partnership when invited to become a partner, but will rarely revisit the risk and return equation on a regular basis in the same way as they would consider their own personal portfolio of investments. It is worth remembering that business angels will expect at least a 60 per cent annual return on their investments and venture capitalists and private equity houses as much as 35 per cent to cover their equity risk: partners should assess their likely returns against those parameters.

Debt

Debt and partners' capital are the two most economical ways of financing a law firm but, as we have seen, both are limited in scope.

It is not just banks which will lend to a law firm. Leasing companies which provide financing for technology, and equipment suppliers which are prepared to extend payment terms (such as landlords of premises and even more recently Her Majesty's Revenue and Customs in the UK), and secondary lenders are all capable of supplying a line of credit which assists the firm in managing its cash flows and working capital requirements. Care also needs to be taken by firms in assessing the risk of borrowing, particularly in firms where the tradition has been to distribute as much as possible to partners as quickly as possible and to leave the bare minimum of working capital in the firm. As has been discovered during the 2007 recession, short-term borrowing enables banks quickly to reduce the amounts they are prepared to lend with little or no notice. In addition to bank borrowings both on a short-term and long-term basis, credit is sometimes available from leasing companies and on a trade/credit basis from long-term suppliers. Further and more innovative ways of managing debt capital are also possible. It is, for example, now several years since Clifford Chance raised a large sum by a private placement of part of their debt funding. This was done with bond issues of 10- and 20-year loan notes placed with institutional investors – a borrowing option which may only be available in a positive economic environment and even then only to large elite firms.

Partners' capital

Partners' capital in the form of both fixed and current accounts now forms the major part of most firms' funding structures. As noted above, it is not unusual to find up to three-quarters of a firm's overall capital funded in this way, especially if current year undistributed profits are included in the equation. Recent developments have also seen fixed share partners contributing modest amounts of capital, and some firms also link the level of individual fixed capital requirements to profit-sharing arrangements. In this way, the more highly paid partners end up contributing more than their lower paid counterparts. The level of monthly drawings distributed on account of the current year's profits is also a factor. A rough working average – which seems to have developed by custom – is to pay out up to half of each partner's expected profit entitlement by way of monthly drawings on account of the current year's profits. Conservative firms will pay less and more aggressive firms may pay more. The 2007 recession – as with previous downturns – has caused many firms to revise and reduce the levels of monthly drawings. Some firms have benefited from swift anticipatory action in their drawings policies whereas others have been caught out by poor planning carried out far too late. As with other overheads controls, it is absolutely vital for firms proactively to manage all aspects of both their working capital requirements and their overall capitalisation, of which partners' accounts form an important element. I am frequently surprised by the large number of firms which do not have rolling and regularly updated cash flow forecasts in place.

Some firms require new partners to make an upfront capital contribution, but few will have the financial resources available personally to achieve this. In response, many firms have credit arrangements in place with a lending institution to enable incoming partners to borrow their expected capital and invest in the firm. The firm will usually guarantee the loan or provide some comfort to the lending institution. Many firms also provide partners with an internal facility to allow partners to make a smaller initial capital contribution and then to build it up to par over a period of time.

Outside investors

Whilst many firms remain under-capitalised, the brutal truth is that the majority of firms are simply not profitable enough to attract outside investors. The first and most simple arithmetical test is to apply a basic living salary (for instance on a notional basis or on a market basis or on the basis of monthly drawings) and see how much profit is left over after making partners' salary deductions. In many smaller firms, such an exercise will absorb most of the firm's distributable net profit, and in some cases the whole of it. This savage test starts to bring home the unpalatable truth that many law firm partners are not gaining sufficient from their firms to compensate them for effort and risk, let alone to give them a modest or appropriate return on their capital invested.

Table 7.1 gives an illustrative and rough idea of the sort of annual returns on their investment which different classes of investors might well require. The point here is that there must be enough profit left over, after applying a living salary for partners, to encourage investors to invest. It is inevitable that venture capital funds and private equity funds will usually be interested only in the sector's creamy layer, i.e., firms in the upper tiers of the positioning diamond referred to in Chapter 4 (and see Figure 4.1), and bulk suppliers at the commodity end. The smaller scale of firm found in the lower half of the positioning diamond may well not be of much interest. This may leave only family, friends and possibly business angels available as potential outside investors to firms outside the UK top 50 and it remains to be seen whether the lower tiers of the UK top 100

Table 7.1   What investors might expect from investing in a law firm

Type of investor	Expected annual return on equity
Angel	60–70%
Venture capital	30–35%
Private equity	20%
Public company	12–20%

and below will prove to be of any external interest whatsoever. We rather doubt that – with the possible exception of smaller bulk suppliers and some designer label firms – there will be much of a market in such areas.

A further and more likely exception is the possibility of a trade sale. These are likely to form two broad types. The first type is the law firm or other professional service firm seeking to acquire and consolidate smaller firms (in line with ASB Models 4 and 12 in Chapter 6). Such firms will simply be in the market to acquire firms in much the same way as Vantis plc has done in the accountancy sector (see Chapter 6 and in particular the case study for examples of this approach). The second type is law firms which are prepared to invest a minority stake in other law firms. Trade buyers can often make very positive contributions. They may be able to offer referrals and access to networks to help the firm to grow. In return, they will often be looking to leverage the smaller firm's client relationships and intangible resources through their own networks. These minority positions, therefore, can serve a useful purpose in allowing two firms to work together more closely and to explore ways of creating further value. The minority investment possibility may also have some advantages for overseas firms seeking to get their feet into the UK market: the purchase of a minority stake in a UK law firm may be of greater appeal than the expense of opening a new office.

In general, minority stakes have to be viewed most carefully by law firms that seek to raise capital to fund growth or to develop an ABS. A minority stake usually comes with strings attached. Not only will the stakeholder require a degree of management input and control, the shareholding will also usually carry minority rights that may well enable the minority shareholder to block further takeover or merger. In addition, minority shareholdings are often acquired with the explicit intention of enabling the minority shareholder to extend its shareholding cheaply over time, either through share options and similar mechanisms or by the regular exercise of its minority rights.

Equity funding

Ever since Sir David Clementi published his review of legal services regulation (Clementi, 2004) and during the lead-up to the LSA, as well as after the Act was passed, the debate has raged over the possibility of raising funds on the open market for expansion. One model often talked about is that of the Australian firm, Slater & Gordon which offered around one-third of its shares on the open market and thereby successfully raised approximately £7.5 million for further acquisitions. The firm got its timing right by going to the market early in 2007 before the markets generally collapsed. It may be some years before the markets anywhere in the world will again be ready to give such favourable treatment to an initial public offering. Slater & Gordon was not a huge firm by UK standards: its turnover around the time of flotation was about £30 million, with a market capitalisation of around £70 million. A successful flotation in the UK might well require a firm to be twice the size of Slater & Gordon. However, there may be some attraction for firms prepared to make the first move, as a rare investment opportunity in a sector that has not yet fully adapted to the new environment and which may therefore carry some form of premium. Several UK firms have openly stated their intention to follow a strategy similar to that of Slater & Gordon. However, I do not expect to see very many firms gaining funding in this way. It is interesting to note that only one other Australian firm (Integrated Legal Holdings) has decided to float in the smaller Australian market and most firms in Australia have firmly declared that they do not intend to follow Slater & Gordon's example.

Conclusion

The major lesson for law firms is that – if they have not already done so – they should take immediate steps to consider their longer term capitalisation. This requires them to manage their cash flow budgets actively and to look beyond cash flows to their future needs and to match and balance the various sources of funds optimally. Firms should seek to build the intangible assets, which drive the firm's profitability and value, at the same time as seeking further efficiencies in their financial disciplines and cash collection processes. Above all, firms should start to impose on themselves the sort of management disciplines and accountabilities which an outside investor would demand to see, whether or not they have any intention of seeking outside investment. After all, law firm partners continue to be the primary investors in their firms and their shareholdings should be nurtured and cared for with the same attention that a lending institution or outside investor would demand.

8

Mergers and acquisitions

KEY POINTS

- The consolidation trend
- Rationale for mergers and acquisitions
- The ingredients for a successful merger or acquisition
- The possible impact of ABSs
- Equity funding
- Management buy-outs and leveraged finance

Introduction – the consolidation trend

Deregulation of professional services sectors has often heralded an unprecedented wave of mergers and acquisitions. As we saw in Chapter 6, the deregulation of the opticians industry in the 1980s transformed the market-place from being very fragmented – with the large majority of the market being served by small independent firms – into a highly concentrated and consolidated sector dominated by a few household names (Department of Trade and Industry, 2004). Deregulation, along with other economic drivers of sector integration, drove significant consolidation of European financial services firms between 1990 and 2000. As the Wharton Financial Institutions Center reported (Cummins and Weiss, 2004, p. 2), 'significant consolidation occurred both cross-border and within-border as financial services firms sought to consolidate their positions within national markets'. Economic and competitive forces can bring about industry concentration on their own, without deregulation acting as a catalyst. The advertising industry has seen a steady process of consolidation of major activities and entities into the hands of a small number of global players with more than half of the world's advertising spend concentrated in the hands of a very few players (Scott, 1998, p. 10). The accountancy profession is another sector where mergers and acquisitions have led to a concentration of revenue and market share at the top of the sector. The annual UK fee income of the 'Big Four' accountancy firms is now nearly three times the annual revenue of the remaining firms in the UK accountancy firms' league tables.[1] There is also a huge gap between firm number four (Ernst & Young with UK fee income of £1,282 million) and firm number five (Grant Thornton with UK fee income of £304.1 million). The lack of overall concentration in the global legal services sector means that the largest firm in the UK (currently a battle between Linklaters, Clifford Chance and Freshfields) has global revenues which are similar to the UK revenues of the fourth biggest accountancy firm. However, the top to bottom spread is far greater in the accountancy sector than in the legal sector, indicating a high level of market concentration at the top of the sector with a rapid fall-off in size below the top tier. In contrast, there are fewer huge law firms and a preponderance of law firms in roughly the same revenue range in the law firm sector. There are about 60 law firms in the UK with annual revenues in excess of £50 million. The lowest placed firms in the UK law firms' top 100 would be placed in the top 30 in the accountancy profession.

Every professional sector is, however, uniquely different, with diverse economic drivers and market conditions which will generally either speed up industry consolidation or slow it down. The strength of client relationships is a critical factor in the legal services sector as with some other areas of professional services. Hence, the consolidation of the accountancy sector closely tracked the globalisation of clients as rival accountancy firms competed for a finite number of global clients. In many sectors, the maximisation of shareholder value has been the main rationale for consolidation and this means concentrating on the resources which drive value creation and the extraction of that value in the form of profit. Production value in the manufacturing sectors, for example, is created by transforming raw materials into products which are valued by customers. In the professional services sectors – which are predominantly people businesses – the creation of value is directly related to client activities. It follows that the main opportunities for creating value from mergers arise in law firms from introducing existing services to each other's clients and from penetrating new markets through the development of new sources of expertise both in legal practice and service delivery (see Empson, 2000a). Hence, the economies of scale and scope, allied with increasing specialisation offered by the larger global firms, can go a long way in forming persuasive inducements to clients.

The rationale for mergers and acquisitions

It has frequently been observed that merger is not a strategy in itself but needs to be considered as a tool to implement or assist strategy. Equally, growth for growth's sake is not a strategy. There are, however, some compelling reasons for mergers and acquisitions. As we saw in Chapter 5, every firm needs to consider what is the minimum amount of growth necessary for the firm both to retain its existing market position and to keep its strength and ability to perform or survive. Clearly, all firms need to have a viable market standing. In a consolidating market, most firms therefore need a high minimum growth rate in order merely to stand still, survive or maintain existing competitive advantage and levels of profitability. The critical question then becomes whether the pursuit of growth is consistent with the search for profitability. Certainly, most firms which are seeking entry into commercial areas of work need a minimum size in each of the main heavy-lifting departments in order to compete. The issues of size, shape and growth are thus increasingly affecting the potential of all law firms to compete. Mergers and acquisitions need therefore to be considered against the background of the optimal size and shape of any law firm to maintain or improve its competitive capabilities.

First, mergers and acquisitions can help firms to change or consolidate their market position. There is no doubt that scale and size is becoming increasingly important for a law firm's positioning. I was talking some time ago with an environmental law partner from an 80-partner commercial law firm. He told me that he felt that his firm was just about the minimum size necessary to support a two-partner environmental team; for him, scale was definitely an issue. This conversation is similar to many which I have had with law firm partners over the last few years. Except for the perfectly formed specialist practices, the question of size is increasingly on the agenda. For clients, size is seen, amongst other things, as a safety or comfort factor. For law firm partners who wish to pursue better work (whatever that means for them), increased specialisation needs to take place in the context of a firm which is large enough to warrant deep teams across all the heavy-lifting core commercial areas. For the recruitment market, especially at senior level, the incoming lawyer wants to board a vessel which is capable of travelling safely but speedily through the water. Additionally, potential law firm investors will only be interested in firms which have strong track records in managing fast and sustainable growth over reasonable time frames.

The majority of law firm managing partners have appreciated for some years now that whilst mergers – or even growth generally – are not strategies on their own, they do nevertheless form the means to a strategic end. Size for size's sake is not the relevant point. The strategic question on the lips of many is: 'What might we need to look like in three to five years' time to attract and retain the best lawyers, to continue to serve our best clients and to attract both better clients and better work?' For some, the answer may be to continue steadily on the course which has already been chosen and is tried and tested. For many, however, profitable growth – carried out strategically in a consolidating market-place – will be an inevitable part of their plan. Such strategically directed growth needs to consider some size-related imperatives which are all closely linked with the firm's strategic positioning. The principal imperative is the growing, client-driven need for depth of expertise – smaller and more general practices with skin-deep expertise are finding themselves most exposed to the client-driven demand for greater specialisation and deeper levels of expertise. What is more, the more sophisticated clients also expect increased depth of service – the ability to progress larger matters quickly and efficiently with the work being done as a team effort and at the right level. Then there is the need to increase depth of resource – the increasing imperative for investment capacity and management capability to develop and maintain a supportive infrastructure. Finally, depth of brand is also important to give the profile and market perception necessary to provide a winning business recipe. In this context, many firms are striving to cast off their image as local utility firms in favour of a regional profile as a local hero. At the same time, regional firms are seeing the need to become national, whilst national firms are striving to extend their reach internationally as firms vie for the top tiers of market positioning set out in Chapter 4 – market rulers, designer labels and challengers.

The second main rationale for mergers and acquisitions is the pursuit of economies of scale. The argument here is less compelling than in the manufacturing sectors where the decreasing costs of production can bring about worthwhile reductions in unit costs. Even there, the costs of attrition and friction resulting from post-merger integration costs can outweigh the efficiency benefits. In the legal sector, the importance of economies of scale will vary depending on the positioning of the firm on the diamond matrix described in Chapter 4 (see Figure 4.1). Bulk suppliers will, for instance, derive great economies of scale in their advertising and branding expenditures as well as their investments in technology and process. Agglomerations and local heroes both find that their management infrastructures – from professional managers through to the operational efficiency of the post room – benefit through greatly increased quality or scale efficiencies. The improved use of knowledge management, technology investment and people leverage can all stem from sizing up the firm through merger and acquisition. At the bottom end of the diamond matrix, the minor league player simply does not have the investment capacity to improve marketing, to hire expensive lawyers and professionals or to invest in technology. In some cases, the merger itself can act as a catalyst for stronger and better management. One study of the banking industry, for example, found that, 'consolidations involving previously inefficient firms appeared to improve both cost and profit efficiency as the M&A event itself may have "woken up" management to the need for improvement or may have been used as an excuse to implement unpleasant restructuring' (Berger, Demsetz and Strahan, 1999, p. 164).

The third rationale for mergers and acquisitions is the achievement of related and unrelated diversification (see Chapter 5) which a merger or acquisition offers. This is the one-stop shop argument which relies on the obtaining of economies of scope. The argument here is that to offer a greater range and depth of services not only positively affects a firm's market positioning and its ability to differentiate, but also is more efficient in creating synergies between clients and the services they require as well as economies in the cost and delivery of marketing and client relationship management. The access that is given by the one-stop shop to an increased range of clients by aggressive cross-selling is a vital ingredient in the strategy for diversification.

The fourth rationale – particularly in a fragmented sector such as legal services – is that mergers and acquisitions help firms to achieve the necessary overall investment capacity and critical mass to give them competitive advantage against possible rivals. Whereas size matters in terms of positioning in order to enable firms to gain greater depth of service and expertise in their core practice areas, overall size also assists in a number of ways. Greater bulk gives firms the tangible financial resources and muscle to be able to invest in technology and people. The ability to field more lawyers in the market improves name recognition and branding. A bigger and better infrastructure of offices and back-up resources gives clients a feeling of safety. Additionally, size is often taken by clients as a proxy for excellence and quality even where the firm's bulk is spread quite thinly across offices and practice areas.

The fifth and final rationale for mergers and acquisitions is that they can improve market power, giving dominance in some cases and hugely increased market strength in others. As we saw in Chapter 5, dominant or monopoly positions enable firms to remove many of their competitors and – theoretically at least – increase cash flows by raising prices. Such positions of dominance or pre-eminence can be local (for example, a local hero firm as the most powerful firm in a geographical location), specialism- or sector-based (for example, a designer label firm as a leading specialist provider), or brand-based (for example a bulk supplier firm gaining a large market share in its given markets by virtue of its bulk marketing and branding power allied to lower costs).

Consistent with all these five rationales are the underlying dual needs of the firm to build a better base of clients and of stakeholders in the firm to see the creation of greater value. The linking of client bases from two constituent firms can, of course, provide the merged firm from the start with a better combined set of clients or synergies in sectors or client types which enable the merged firm to build further revenues. The main client base benefit is, however, more intangible and difficult to demonstrate empirically, in that it comprises the proposition that the combined firm is now able to win clients and work to which it was difficult or impossible for the previous entities to have aspired.

The other theme is the need for stakeholders to enjoy the advantages of the creation of greater value. In this context, the history of mergers in professional service firms is not impressive. There are three main problems. First, law firms have traditionally been seen as engines for short-term profits and not long-term growth. Mergers can, and usually will, take three years to show any profit improvement and, in the short term, profits can easily dip. Many law firms which are actively considering merger are daunted by the prospect of profit dilution in the early years of the merged firm, and are often horrified by the level of investment and effort required to make a merger or acquisition work. The second main problem is that law firms comprise sets of highly individual and independent practitioners who often enjoy considerable autonomy, and who have close personal relationships with key clients. These individuals can respond negatively both to the prospect of merger and to the requirements of the new firm for all its partners and members to share their technical knowledge and client relationships both within their own firm and with their new merger colleagues. A third problem is that professional services firms have not traditionally given as much attention to post-merger integration issues as to the selection and negotiation process which led to the merger. This is often because a degree of compromise has pervaded the choice of governance structure and the identity of the chosen leaders: the success of a merger depends at least in part on having the appropriate initial governance system and strong management. Another factor here is the speed (or lack of it) of integration. One set of studies of post-integration issues in merged professional service firms[2] found that true integration of the two firms often did not occur until the third year of the new firm onwards. Prior to that, at first, only the merger instigators and entrepreneurial individuals typically take the early opportunity to seek out like-minded colleagues in the partner firm to explore options for cooperation. Then, in the second and third years, a period of transition occurs as the more stubborn individuals either start to cooperate or leave the firm. For these reasons, most mergers can for a number of years be categorised as agglomerations on the diamond matrix (see Figure 4.1), during which time the benefits of size in competitive terms have not yet been realised.

The ingredients for a successful merger or acquisition

For any merger to be successful, six ingredients are needed which focus on a long-term vision, growing profitability and value creation and enhancement for the firm's stakeholders.

In the first place, and most important, there must be a strong and logical strategic case for the deal as a tool to aid the firm's positioning and competitive strategy. Box 8.1 gives a checklist of strategic issues to be considered.

Second, the choice of target or merger partner has to be made carefully and methodically against the background of the agreed strategy. Many mergers fail because of a poor strategic or cultural fit between the parties. In this context, it is helpful to prepare a list of the criteria and desirable attributes which the firm wants in its merger partner, in terms of the key strategic areas of positioning, size, geography, resources, specialisms and client types.

Third, it sounds obvious, but the merger rationale must be logical and compelling and free from personal considerations, greed or the lure of an exciting project. Subjective special pleading can take place at both ends of a personal risk/reward spectrum. At one end, mergers are rejected by a coalition of leading players within one or other firm because of the threat to job security or personal comfort zones, or because of the perceived loss of personal power that might ensue. At the other extreme, there may be partners – particularly in the case of the smaller firm in a merger – who find themselves personally motivated by a desire to maximise their personal fortunes. Equally, law firm leaders can become tempted to engage in merger and acquisition projects of questionable value but which promote their personal glory or position. There must be an honest appraisal of the total business case for the merger. It is not, for instance, sufficient to base a merger on the desirability of acquiring a particular individual or niche if all the other factors are negative.

Fourth, the firms must compile detailed and accurate inventories of each other's firms to ensure compatibility of client bases, accounting methodologies, cultures, systems and technical knowledge. Many of the steps which we have suggested in Chapter 2 need to be carried out to ensure that resources and capabilities are identified and stress-tested for strategic importance and relative strength.

Fifth, early financial analysis is vital to ensure that a logical merger case survives harsh economic scrutiny. Firms will differ not only in their profitability but also in relation to their profit drivers, their leverage or the economics of different offices and different practice areas. Early financial analysis can sometimes highlight fundamental cultural differences in the approach to debt, partners' capital and long-term investment. The firm's approach and attitude to work in progress and debtors can show discipline and accountability in one firm, or a cavalier attitude of poor controls and laziness in another. I have even found that different models and approaches to the funding of partners' cars can give cause for trouble at an early stage. In addition, the whole methodology for financing the firm's working capital and infrastructure can vary enormously. Some firms are convinced, for instance, that outright purchase of offices and equipment is the right approach whilst other firms are equally wedded to leases and hire agreements. Clearly, issues of profitability are also vital. Whilst it is possible to merge with significant differences in profits per equity partner, the existence of a large differential may reflect poor management, different business recipes, difference in quality of client bases or regional variations, all of which need careful handling.

Sixth, realistic implementation and integration plans should be developed as soon as possible. This is easier said than done. One problem, of course, is that of resources. Nobody wants to see either a merger or acquisition fail, but it is never easy to keep all the management plates spinning at the same time. The reality is that managing partners and their support teams usually have many more than enough projects to keep them constantly busy and continually shuffling their priorities. In these circumstances, it is all too tempting to declare victory prematurely or to assume that the partners will get on with the integration effort without constant nagging and reminders from above. Added to this, most lawyers are used to definable transactions and assignments in their working lives, which are at the 'hard' end of the project spectrum. It is the 'soft' projects (those involving people, teamwork, behaviours, values and culture) which time and time again have proved to be so much harder to implement. Such projects are important at all times, but particularly when new people are around. And, what is more, these projects need sustained and committed leadership from the top and much more than lip service from the partners at all levels. It is, therefore, important to work out an integration programme or project which is long-lasting and sustained, and which reaches team and individual level. Care must be taken to manage expectations from the very start, recognising that that there can be casualties and planning for that eventuality. All parties should be encouraged to spend as much time as possible getting to know each other, both formally and informally. Further, the leaders should form action plans to work out particular areas of cultural difference which need development.

BOX 8.1

Checklist for merger strategic planning

1. Improvement of competitive positioning.
2. Development of client service quality:

   - depth of specialisms;
   - range of services;
   - service delivery.

3. Improving quality and substance:

   - better knowledge management;
   - better management of risk;
   - better processes and systems.

4. Extension of market-place.
5. Increasing leveraging and improving the client base.
6. Improving the firm's resources.

7. Developing and enhancing human capital:

    - filling skills gaps;
    - improving recruitment/retention potential;
    - opportunities for further specialisation.

8. Developing value creation:

    - improving long-term profitability;
    - economies of scale and scope;
    - more efficient deployment and utilisation of lawyers;
    - better rates.

9. Positive effect on culture and behaviours:

    - clarity of roles and expectations;
    - improving discipline and accountability;
    - building entrepreneurship and dynamism.

10. Prioritisation of and plans to address structural, cultural and organisational impediments.

One of the key challenges for the new leadership is to decide who should be on board the new firm and who – put bluntly – needs to be moved out. The tone set by the new leadership in confronting performance (and underperformance) issues will define much of the ecology of the new firm. At the same time, a new firm – with a new profile and image – often finds that for a while it becomes an attractive recruitment option. If the merger can be regarded as merely the first step in a long journey, then some of the early steps must include the augmentation of the firm's skill base by hiring the best – individuals and teams. At the same time, many merged firms find that they are, in the short term, over-partnered and this can lead to two types of difficulties. In the first place, the firm may contain partners – and even teams – who have, in a sense, risen beyond their own level of ability and competence or will not fit the firm's new positioning. The rising tide engendered by the merger-induced growth of the firm will not in this case lift all boats. This issue will always need careful handling as it will often be politically difficult to hold a partner cull in the early months of the new firm. And yet, there is a great deal to be said for confronting such a disagreeable task at an early stage. The second issue is that over-partnering blocks the way for bright new talent, whether such talent already exists in the firm or is recruited laterally.

To deal with this, it is suggested that a comprehensive performance management and partner development programme should be agreed at an early stage.

In my view, every firm should define carefully the objectives which it has for introducing a performance management system for partners which can lead to the setting of goals and targets which can then be linked to profit sharing.

The possible impact of ABSs on the ability to execute merger and acquisition transactions

Given the drivers for mergers currently existing in the legal sector, it is a little surprising that mergers have not so far taken place at a greater rate. The difficulties of getting two sets of partners to agree the possible losses of personal position or to take a calculated strategic risk have meant that most merger discussions seem to end in failure. In the current economic climate of downturn and recession, firms which have taken painful steps to restructure and reduce costs will be reluctant to see their short-term profitability dip even further by merging with a firm which they perceive to have failed to address areas of weakness. At the same time, entrepreneurial firms have found that there are unique merger opportunities even in the worst of market conditions. The brutal truth is that partners in law firms remain likely to change only to the degree to which they are forced to transform rather than to the extent to which they ought to change. The fear of getting a merger wrong seems much stronger than the excitement of getting it right.

The advent of the LSA, however, is likely to have a growing effect on the attitude of firms towards merger, in providing both a stick and a carrot. The stick is the sudden increase of external and externally assisted new competitors which are contesting existing law firms with vibrant new offerings. The strength of these challenges may well persuade firms to enter the merger tournament in an effort to compete and defend. The carrot could well be the advent of some sort of market for law firm acquisitions. Since the days when goodwill disappeared from the balance sheets of most law firms, there has been little trading in law firms in the UK which has involved sale and purchase prices over and above the value of the net assets of the firm. Even now, the major claimant personal injury firms are acquiring smaller practices which include only a deferred payment for work in progress as it is realised. It is true that small solo practices do change hands on a reasonably regular basis for a consideration which includes some form of goodwill payment. There are also some small signs that goodwill or elements of value in the sale price may be starting to appear in larger merger and acquisition deals. As an example, in early 2009 the national defendant insurance firm, Beachcroft, acquired the insurance business of Welsh firm, Kingslegal and is rumoured to have paid a purchase price on an earn-out basis for the business.

I see the LSA, therefore, as being one of the consolidation catalysts kick-starting a period of consolidation and merger. Many of these mergers are likely initially to be of the traditional sort, two firms merging their practices without a purchase price and with the cost and expense of the merger self-financed out of earnings of the new firm. However, two of the ABS models explored in Chapter 6 – Model 4, the consolidated law firm roll-up and Model 12, the external consolidation roll-up – do require a level of investment in mergers and acquisitions which is likely to be beyond the pockets and borrowing capacity of the lead law firm. In addition, any law firm which decides to diversify horizontally to form a legal MDP (Model 6) may also need external finance to raise the necessary level of investment in order to acquire other professional service firms.

We also expect to see some barristers' chambers merging what essentially has been a set of sole practitioners into an integrated law firm chambers in an effort to compete against other models of law practice. Such mergers – along with consequential mergers between chambers – are likely to prove quite tricky, given the autonomous mindset of most barristers who will be even less accustomed than solicitors to the concepts of client- and knowledge-sharing, let alone inter-partner accountabilities, responsibilities and profit sharing.

Strategies for market repositioning which involve mergers and acquisitions are also likely to need injections of external capital in many cases. Law firms of every size may, for example, be anxious to acquire a number of smaller firms in order to make the leap from one tier to another on the diamond matrix. It is entirely possible in these cases that some firms may turn to larger law firms which can act as a financier for the smaller firm as a trade buyer of a minority stake. Such a stake will usually, however, carry minority rights which will enable the trade buyer both to block other potential acquirers and to extend their shareholding in the future at discounted prices. As we saw from Chapter 7, the sales of minority shareholdings carry with them the creeping risk of the minority shareholding gradually increasing its ownership stake. In addition, investors of equity require a return over time on their capital investment and will usually seek a harvest exit by floating the firm, so in many cases the sale of minority stakes becomes the prelude and intermediate step towards flotation or trade sale.

Equity funding to finance mergers and acquisition

As we saw from Chapter 7, the cost and danger of equity investment is higher than the risk and cost of borrowing. The need for growth capital needs to be balanced with the preservation of equity. In addition, investors in law firms will be fundamentally motivated by the ability of the merged law firm to drop cash to the bottom line. In other words, the attention will focus on the ability of the merged firm to increase operating profits over time. The raising of external finance is only therefore likely to be a successful solution for funding acquisitions if the potential benefits of the acquisition exceed the cost and burden of the capital required. It has to be remembered at all times that a strategy which involves the acquisition of more than one small firm with the aid of external funding relies extensively on the financial equation – the twin aim of achieving substantial market share and, therefore, economies of scope in revenue terms through the acquisitions, whilst at the same time realising significant economies of scale in cost reductions. The rigour and discipline of such a hard-headed approach will not appeal to all firms.

Many acquisition strategies will therefore rely – for a period at least – on the ability of the acquisitive law firm to start the consolidation process with its own funds or its own borrowing capacity. In Australia, for example, Slater & Gordon converted to a corporation in 2001, which was both a step towards going public in due course and an essential precursor to growth in that it gave the firm the ability to offer paper and earn-out solutions to the partners of acquired firms. For a period of five years, the firm acquired five smaller firms and a number of lateral hires which virtually doubled the firm in size from about 100 lawyers to over 200 lawyers. By 2006, the firm realised that its growth ambitions were limited without further equity funding and it ultimately decided to float on the Australian stock market. Interestingly, Slater & Gordon apparently considered selling a minority stake to a private equity house but rejected this strategy as the firm was apparently concerned about the amount of autonomy the firm would have to cede in return for a stake and how much of a contribution a private equity fund would actually make (see Lloyd, 2009). The Slater & Gordon example may well be repeated in the UK in one form or another.

Amalgamation models of ABS which involve partnerships and franchises – such as Model 2 (the marketing umbrella) and Model 3 (the law firm franchise) in Chapter 6 – may also emerge in the new world of legal services. Rather like the Specsavers example illustrated in Chapter 6, these models are not predicated on outright purchase but will involve the smaller firm retaining a level of its own equity, and hence the models are unlikely to require inputs of acquisition finance. Instead, external funding may be required for building, growing and branding the model.

Management buy-outs and leveraged finance

The management buy-out (MBO) is used in a law firm, typically, in two generic situations. The first is where a founder partner or partners obtain their retirement exit from the firm by 'selling' it to existing partners or – following the LSA – possibly to partners and key managers. The second situation is where a firm decides to dispose of a non-core or less profitable office or practice area to the practising partners in that part of the firm. If the business has both assets and a healthy cash flow, the financing can often be arranged via the banks and other lending institutions, particularly in the case of an MBO of an office or department where the purchasing equity partners or members have built up sufficient capital reserves.

There are both strategic and economic challenges to be overcome with the first generic situation where a retiring partner or partners sells to existing partners by way of an MBO. In the first place, partners who are approaching retirement are often not disposed to invest heavily in the firm in the years leading up to retirement and often organise the firm to obtain short-term profit-earning potential. It follows that partners in the run-up to retirement will often pay themselves as much of the available profit as they can, and will resist investing in people and assets which are unlikely to benefit them in the short term. Equity is often held very tightly in such firms so that the eventual MBO partners are often salaried or fixed share partners with little management and entrepreneurial expertise or experience. Indeed, many of the senior lawyers of firms where the equity is tightly held by one or a few founder partners were originally recruited and then retained predominantly for their technical ability and have little or no aptitude for equity partnership and display low management competencies. In the same way, such firms are also unattractive to high flyers if they are dominated by the iron grip of ageing founder partners.

The second challenge is that most non-equity partners or members who wish to engage in an MBO lack the capital to do so, even in those cases where the retiring partner or partners are being paid out based on net book value only, with no element of value for the 'goodwill' of the firm. MBOs typically require the seller to take a limited amount of cash on closure of the deal and to lend the balance of the purchase price back to the firm, to be repaid over a number of years. A loan-back has the advantage of simplicity and certainty but ties the new owners to an inflexible and fixed interest and repayment schedule. A more flexible method is to tie the purchase price in some way to the future profitability of the firm, but this places the selling partners somewhat at the mercy of the purchasers who can manipulate profitability or manage the firm incompetently unless the sellers retain some elements of control. Even an earn-out solution can be risky for the seller in an MBO solution, both because the sellers will often be of a retirement age where continued worthwhile involvement in the firm will be unattractive and because earn-outs can expose the sellers to the risk of downside exposure. In an earn-out, the deferred payments allow for some credit to the sellers for future growth in profitability which is often capped at an agreed amount. However, in a typical earn-out structure the risk to the sellers is that, if profits deteriorate, their deferred payments are exposed to possible reductions.

An MBO structured by way of leveraged finance is a possible alternative for cash-strapped MBO partners. The leveraged buy-out (LBO) focuses both the valuation and the payment methodology of an MBO on the maximum amount which can be borrowed by the new business in order to finance the purchase of the ownership interests of the retiring or selling partners. Here, the assets of the firm are used as collateral for the borrowed capital to enable the purchase to proceed. A heavily leveraged deal is one where the MBO partners have little or no financial resources of their own and become entirely or mainly reliant on the leveraged borrowings to complete the transaction. Until the 2007 recession, it was often possible to borrow up to 70 per cent of the purchase price in this manner. One advantage is that at least some of the risk is shifted to the third party financier. The financing party typically secures its position in two ways. First, it will demand high rates of interest secured on the assets of the firm. Second, it will enter into an agreement or pledge, exercisable on default under the loan, of sufficient shares in the MBO firm to give the financier not only a security interest on the firm but also, in most cases, a controlling interest. The availability of LBO solutions has recently slowed down in 2009 with the recession and in any event it appears that the number of LBOs taking place in the professional services sector is low compared with other sectors (Scott, 1998).

Conclusions

Further consolidation of the legal services sector by mergers and acquisitions seems inevitable. There are nearly 9,000 small firms of solicitors in England and Wales of four partners or fewer and around half of these are sole practitioners. One could hardly find a more fragmented profession in which the leading firms have such a relatively low share of the overall market,[3] and where the range of small entities makes up such a large proportion of the 10,000 law firms in existence. The forces of consolidation have for some time been applied to the profession and the LSA will act as a further impetus to more mergers and acquisitions.

Endnotes

1 *Accountancy Age* (2009) survey shows the top four firms with a combined annual revenue of £7,155 million, whilst the remaining 46 firms' combined income amounts to approximately £2,700 million.
2 See Empson (2000a) and Empson (2000b). These studies were carried out over a three- year period and covered six professional services firms.
3 The global income of Linklaters for 2008/09 is reported as outstripping Clifford Chance and Freshfields, at £1.298 billion. The UK legal market has an estimated turnover of £23.25 billion, which makes it likely that no firm has a UK market share of more than 5 per cent at most.

9

Law firm valuation

Michael Roch[1]

KEY POINTS

- Valuation in the legal services context
- Principles of valuation
- Valuation methods
- Adjustments
- Net book value and the valuation of individual practices
- Reality testing

Valuation in the legal services context

There is available a reasonable body of knowledge about how professional services firms and professional practices should be valued.[2] However, the practical intricacies of valuing legal practices and law firms in particular require special attention, both by the managing partner who is seeking to understand how much his firm is worth on the one hand, and also by a purchaser of a legal practice or a financial investor on the other. This chapter seeks to demystify, in plain language, some of the technical issues around law firm valuation and outlines some practical approaches.

It begins with basic valuation principles and explains the principal methods of valuation that we have found useful in the law firm context. This chapter seeks to pay particular attention to the impact on the firm's value of a firm's intellectual capital and intangible resources.

The reader should be clear that this chapter can cover only highlights and not serve as a comprehensive manual for valuation.

The business of valuation has become a great deal more professional during the last decade, fuelled by the significant volume of mergers and acquisition transactions that were a sign of the times in the early 2000s. A number of professional associations have produced standards around business valuation which attempt to apply uniform principles and approaches. The tax authorities of several countries have also sought to enforce consistent standards, particularly in the area of the estate tax valuation. None of these attempts to standardise valuation methodology has fully addressed the special nature of valuing professional firms and practices. A high degree of judgment continues to be required in this context.

Principles of valuation

We have chosen to highlight three principles that form an integral part of law firm valuation below. These are:

1. Understanding the valuation's purpose.
2. Understanding the basis of the firm's financial statements and making required adjustments.
3. Determining the key drivers of value (which, as we have seen throughout this book, are largely intangible).

These are considered in turn.

Understanding the purpose of the valuation

From the outset, it is important to understand that valuation approaches may differ depending on the purpose for which a valuation is sought. For instance, as we will see below, the approach to valuing the practice of a sole practitioner or a small partnership – where much of the revenue and profits depends solely on the capabilities and capacity of the firm's principal equity partners – will vary significantly from the approach used to value a highly leveraged firm that can rely much more on its internal processes, systems and structures as these are applied by several hundred fee-earners. The latter firm is also likely to be able to deliver more consistently and predictably and thus has a higher chance of future recurring revenue, a key driver of value performance. Also, value approaches may differ when one is seeking to value a partial ownership interest (for example for investment purposes) versus the business or law practice as a whole. Examples of rationale for a full business valuation include an acquisition by, for example, a consolidator of individual practices with the view to building a larger enterprise, or by the next generation of partners who are seeking to take over a law firm from its founder or senior partner. Admittedly, the latter case is rare in the United Kingdom as, in most cases, junior partners do not make an outright purchase of the interests of all of their senior partners; instead, they are brought on as partners early and take over the business, possibly paying a retirement fund or annuity to the senior or founding partner (see Chapter 8).

It is also important to understand that valuation principles of large industrial corporations will not be directly applicable to professional practices, and further that valuations of publicly traded equity, while based on similar fundamentals, will also require a significantly different approach from valuing privately held companies, including professional practices. One of the recurring themes of this book is that a great deal of the difference in approach has to do with the fact that much of the value that makes up a professional practice tends to be in the form of intangible, not tangible, assets. Dependence on individual professionals is high in professional practices and, as we have seen in Chapters 2 and 3, successful management of professionals in order to harness and develop the intellectual capital of their firm is a key driver of value for any law firm.

Last, a senior equity partner seeking to pass on his business to the next generation of partners also may view valuation from a different perspective from that of a large firm seeking to acquire a small one, or that of a financial investor seeking to make an investment.

Undoubtedly, there are many other reasons for seeking a valuation of a firm: the purpose for which a valuation is needed will drive the overall approach and the detail that needs to be applied.

Establishing a rational basis for financial statements and making required adjustments

Both 'published' accounts, for purposes of reporting to equity partners or banks, and management accounts form the initial basis of any law firm valuation. Practically speaking, no balance sheets and income statements of two law firms ever look the same, nor do they tend to be prepared on a comparable basis. The reason for this is not sinister, it is practical. Some firms essentially use tax compliance requirements as the basis for their management reporting and financial statement presentation. Some may use a simple cash basis of accounting, but most larger UK firms now use some form of accrual accounting. Irrespective of which basis of reporting a firm applies, both balance sheet and income statement require some adjustments before any valuation analysis of the firm can begin.

In particular, the global economic downturn during which this chapter was written has reminded all businesses, including professional practices, that cash is king. As a result, available cash, and the firm's ability to generate cash, must be reviewed closely. As was demonstrated in Chapter 7, it is vital to review the firm's cash management practices and the behaviour of its revenue cycles in order to get a wider sense of how this crucial element of the firm is managed. In particular in smaller practices, both how invoices are written and how cash is deposited are used to achieve certain income tax results, which may well skew any attempted cash flow analysis – which will form an important basis of valuation analysis as we will see below.

A thorough appreciation of the firm's management of accounts receivable and its work in progress is also important in reaching an understanding both of management efficiencies and of the factors which drive value. In many law firms we see, lock-up (i.e., the number of days in both work in progress and accounts receivable) is often above 150 or even 180 days – meaning that six months' revenue in working capital is required to keep the doors open and partners paid. We continue to be surprised by how little managing partners feel they are able to do in order to cause the firm to perform better on its cash receipts cycle. Close scrutiny of the ageing of accounts receivable (i.e. classification by customer and month due) at the beginning of a valuation process, and comparing this to the firm's actual payment history, will often set the stage for the 'cleanliness' with which a valuation can be carried out. It is not uncommon for accounts receivable to be adjusted by as much as 50 per cent, as firms are often reluctant to write down accounts receivable in the hope that the client will still pay even an account that is more than one or two years old. The reluctance in particular by legal practices to go after the client for collection continues to surprise us. Typically, larger firms have become more professional in their approaches to accounts receivable collection.

Work in progress deserves an equally hard look. All too often, the management of income tax effects will drive the year-end work in progress balance. A close look at the time recording, invoicing and collections cycle is important in order to understand how much of the firm's work in progress that is carried on the balance sheet will actually turn into receivables and then into cash. In particular, for small firms, it is often helpful to assume that work in progress for valuation purposes is zero and build the cash value of work in progress from the bottom up – make the firm prove that the cash will actually flow, with a presumption that it will not. This approach often causes resistance by either the seller or by senior equity partners when suggested by an outside investor or buyer; however this is often the only way to ensure that work in progress is rationally stated and is thus justified in being included. Often, we find that a detailed assessment is necessary on a matter by matter basis. The exception to this is any firm that is highly process driven and has – and enforces – internal audit controls. This bottom-up approach, of course, also runs into practical limitations for large practices. However, larger practices already have better procedures and controls in place than small ones in order to allow a more top-down approach; a review of only the large clients up to a contribution margin threshold and a sampling of the smaller clients provides for a rational balance in the scope of this analysis.

Other items on a law firm's balance sheet will include prepaid expenses, equipment and leasehold improvements. These are often less important.

Of significant importance, however, are intangible assets. As we have seen throughout this book, these often are not recorded on the balance sheet but contribute greatly to the earnings potential of the firm. Beyond the intellectual capital and resources and capabilities addressed in Chapters 2 and 3 and further detailed below, significant value can be derived from long-term client contracts (for instance, in the context of public sector practices), favourable leases, specially developed processes and know-how, management agreements and non-compete agreements with key personnel (to the extent that they are legally and practically enforceable), and none of these typically will be recorded in the balance sheet.

The liabilities side of the balance sheet tends to be more reliable than the assets side. The exceptions to this statement are contingent liabilities and potential claims, and a separate review of the firm's claims as well as forensic work to uncover contingent liabilities, for instance in the area of gender or age discrimination, are generally sound investments.

The income statement will need to be scrutinised in a similar way. Pricing policies (rate setting, fixed fee arrangements, contingent fee arrangements, and the like) deserve close scrutiny both in their current application and in relation to their sustainability in the market; simple comparisons to available benchmarks often yield interesting results about the sustainability of the firm's revenues in the future. Additionally, if an acquirer intends to change the target's pricing model so as to fit his own business model, care needs to be taken to ensure that revenue assumptions (see below) remain true.

Beyond pricing, the other drivers of gross profit – such as utilisation, staffing and revenue protection – will need to be reviewed closely to ensure that the firm has in place policies and procedures and comparative key performance indicators benchmarked to the market, and that they are being followed as implemented. As an aside, the choice of benchmarks is important: a mid-market firm that has a mix of practices (for example, corporate, real estate, dispute resolution, intellectual property) and a wide mix of services within these practices, will have a different revenue profile from that of a two-partner firm focusing on employment or personal injury claims.

Testing projected revenues (based on detailed partner interviews and, if necessary, interviews with major clients) forms an important part of this work, among other analytical reviews and benchmark testing. It is absolutely critical to hold several in-depth discussions with all the equity partners in the case of smaller firms (including those whom the managing partner does not want the investor to see!). In the case of larger firms, at minimum the practice head plus key equity partners should be interviewed. These interviews in part will serve the purpose of testing the veracity of past financial statements, which is important as they provide the basis for projections of future revenue and resultant cash flow.

Projections provided by law firm finance departments often need to be given a rigorous reality test. We often find that finance departments base their projections merely on fixed percentage increases from current revenue which, after a rigorous review and interviewing practice department leaders, can bear little resemblance to reality. Modelling different revenue and cost scenarios also provides important insights. Projections written before or at the beginning of the 2008/09 economic downturn have proved, six months later, to have been hopelessly optimistic. Long-running transactions must also be treated with some suspicion as they bear an increased risk of containing assumptions that go stale.

The cost side of the income statement is usually more straightforward. The exception typically tends to be equity partner remuneration. In the United Kingdom, it is customary for larger firms' equity partners to take a notional salary. Most smaller firms operate on a 'maximum distributable cash' basis without a notional salary. This becomes important both with respect to market benchmarking as well as in understanding the firm's profitability and distributable cash profile. Fringe benefits also play an important role in determining what cash remains in the end available to the equity owners (present and future). Costs also need to be sanitised of partner/family perks and other issues usually found in private company financial statements.

Understanding the elements that create intangible value

A good starting point is a review of the macroeconomic conditions and trends that affect the law firm. This begins with a review of the basic markets that a law firm seeks to serve and the general conditions surrounding it. For instance, in a recent valuation of a national firm, the international context and the national competitive context within which the firm operated played much more of a role than in the valuation of a smaller, local firm. In light of its market environment, it is then possible to evaluate its current competitive position and market trends that are specific to that firm's markets and clients, as well as its overall market share (usually by work type) and penetration of its major corporate clients.

First is the firm's competitive environment, its competitive position within that environment and its value-added strategy. At the level of the Magic Circle and upper mid-market firms – the higher tiers in the diamond matrix set out in Chapter 4 (see Figure 4.1) – the level and extent of competition is fairly clear. With respect to local practices – the high street and other firms described in Chapter 4 as utility firms and minor league firms, for example – the intensity and quality of competition is less determinable. Here, it is important to understand the success and model of the more sophisticated firms focusing on the same types of services in the area and what proportion of the population they share within that area. This picture – which is often time-consuming to develop – of the main sources of competition both in the area and nationally can have a significant impact on the value that, for instance, a consolidator looking to acquire practices would be willing to pay. The firm that has articulated and developed a rational value-added strategy to beat its competitive environment has a much better chance of attaining a high valuation than one that has not. The elements of a value-added strategy have been addressed in Chapters 4 and 5 and are not repeated here.

Many law firms still do not have a clearly articulated strategic approach, and often, in particular in Continental Europe, strategy remains defined by the strong will of individual partners. The absence of a clearly articulated strategy is highly negative in the context of valuation. This includes a strategy that seems incoherent or inappropriate given the external environment in which the firm operates (because it is either too ambitious or not sufficiently ambitious), or a strategy for which there is no record of effective execution: both such strategies will directly impact on the financial value of the firm.

The next step is to review the essential aspects of the firm's intellectual capital in the light of the firm's business strategy and competitive recipe and, in this context, to assess how the firm's intellectual capital supports effective strategy execution. By way of reminder of what was summarised in Chapter 2, a firm's intellectual capital has three essential components: human capital, relational capital and structural capital, and each impacts on the intangible value of the business. These are considered briefly in turn for their particular effect on valuation methodologies.

Human capital consists of two elements: the firm's professionals and its management. In the context of valuation, the skills and capabilities of all of the firm's professional complement should be subjected to close scrutiny. This includes both legal skills required to execute the work that the firm seeks to do and, as importantly, its lawyers' non-legal skills (e.g., commercial acumen, language capabilities, industry knowledge, client handling skills) that we feel are necessary for that particular firm's lawyers to service its desired clientele. We also spend significant effort understanding the skills and effectiveness of the managing partner, the management board and the senior partner in the context of strategy execution. The track record of the managing partner is given much more weight than his or her legal skills or accomplishments as a practising lawyer prior to becoming managing partner.

Relational capital consists of three elements: clients, brand and network. The firm's client base should be examined in detail to assess to what extent the firm is maximising the potential to generate cash flow from its client base. Depending on the type of firm, we may interview some clients to determine further the strengths and weaknesses of a particular law firm. Even if client interviews are not undertaken, it is vital to review very closely the longevity of the firm's client base, the firm's 'share of wallet' and other factors that indicate the quality of the client relationship. Brand recognition – both with clients and with talent – is tested, as is testing referral sources and other required parts of the firm's networks. For instance, a private client practice will typically rely heavily on chartered accountants and tax practitioners for its client base. The firm that is actively cultivating its referral base is likely to be more successful in the future than a firm that is not actively cultivating.

Structural capital consists of mainly three elements: the firm's service lines, its own processes and its culture. For instance, for a firm that primarily handles employment claims, we would expect to have processes and systems in place that allow the partners to do only that part of the work which truly requires partner involvement; we would expect that firm to have systems, i.e., technology, people and procedures, in place to execute all other parts of the work at the lowest cost possible. While many firms make much of their own unique culture, we test aspects of behaviour within the firm that make accomplishing common strategic goals easier or more difficult.

Chapter 2 sets out a methodology to assess the firm's components of intellectual capital, and its resources, investments, capabilities and limitations. Such an assessment is normally part of a firm's analysis of its strategy and competitive capabilities. The same assessment methodology is equally useful for the purpose of valuation. While these elements should be captured in a structured and objective way, in the end qualitative value judgments have to be applied. Armed with these qualitative value judgments, we then seek to understand how these value drivers will affect the firm's ability to execute on strategy, thus its ability to generate future cash flow and hence the firm's financial value.

How the firm invests in, continuously improves, and manages its risks around these components of intellectual capital also helps determine the firm's overall value. Although these components may appear abstract; there are many practical elements of intellectual capital that deserve a detailed consideration in the particular context of valuation.

First, a firm's 'network' consists primarily of its referral base. A firm where referrals come from a large number of clients will typically justify a higher value than a firm which relies on a fairly small referral pool or on referrals from other professionals. The value of the practice will increase significantly if existing referral relationships, and their success in generating revenue for the firm, are well documented and well managed. It is here where many law firms, both large and small, fail to realise their full value potential simply because referral relationships are handled much more casually than client relationships. Also, the dependency of the firm's referral base on one or a few equity partners, or whether the referral base is spread over a number of professionals, will have a significant impact on the firm's value.

Second, a firm's major client types are important. Most individuals tend to require legal services only once or twice in their lives, and in each case they will be significant events, either on the transactional/advisory side or on the litigation/dispute resolution side of the business. A firm that has a good number of large corporate clients will be able to rely upon a much higher stream of repeat business. When viewed at these extremes, this appears obvious; however, smaller firms in particular continue to view each client as having the same importance. For referral, revenue and profit generation, and thus valuation purposes, this assumption is not correct. In particular for high street firms, a practice with a large percentage of clients who pay their bills themselves will bear a higher overall value than clients who rely on public or private insurance to have their bills paid. In this regard, the public sector has become very aggressive in its procurement of legal services; clients who rely on the public sector tend to pay later and pay less per matter then the practice's standard hourly rate or fixed fee. This has an impact on the firm's potential to earn a profit. At another extreme, the risk of client attrition will negatively affect the valuation of a law firm which relies on a very few, highly concentrated and dominating clients for much of its revenue.

Third, the interplay between the firm's knowledge management, professional development and business development plays a crucial role in driving value. Many firms continue to view the above three areas as either information technology issues (particularly in the area of knowledge management) or as administrative tasks: professional development at many firms is ignored, left to individual equity partners, or treated as a 'nice-to-have' add-on to the firm's human resources function. In particular, smaller firms ignore the interplay between these three areas and tend to focus purely on business development. This is often pursued in an undifferentiated way or in a way that does not assist the firm in achieving its strategy – assuming it has a strategy. These key areas are best managed in an integrated way. Ironically, small firms, due to their owner-managed structure, can achieve this better than a firm of 25 or 50 fee-earners (which firm may have grown quickly but not have allowed its resources to catch up to match and support its new size). Because of this critical importance, a rigorous valuation methodology requires a significant amount of time to be spent in reaching a clear understanding of how well the firm manages these three areas, and in particular how well the firm integrates its approaches to these three issues in light of its strategy – again, assuming that there is a rational, value-added strategy.

Principles 1, 2 and 3 above form the context of the various valuation methods.

Valuation methods in the context of legal services

Valuing a publicly held company is fairly simple: at its most basic, one opens the daily newspaper, finds the appropriate stock quotation and multiplies the stock price by the number of shares outstanding to derive the current market value of the business. Current macroeconomic conditions aside, public company valuation rightly assumes that the collective market has perfect or near-perfect information and knows exactly the present value of future cash flows that a shareholder can expect.

When one seeks to value a private industrial company, things already become much more complicated. First, there is no readily determinable market for a privately held company. Second, a privately held company does not get bought and sold every day, and thus there is much less reliable information about the company than there is in the publicly held context. Third, valuation is as much a number-crunching exercise as it is a qualitative assessment of intangible factors that impact on the business's ability to generate future cash flow. Much depends on the company's ability to navigate its competitive environment, on the company's existing structures and systems and, most important, the skills and abilities of management to drive a strategically rational business model. While there are many common elements in how private company valuation can be approached, the plethora of books written on the subject leads to the conclusion that private company valuation is as much an art as it is a science.

Professional services firms – law firms included – provide a special, more difficult context of private company valuation. At first glance, many approaches and bases for an ordinary private company's valuation appear, at the very least, difficult to apply to law firms and, at the most, are simply inapposite. The ability of a law firm to generate future cash flow depends much more on the capacity of individual partners, and on the firm harnessing intangible value drivers developed by the firm as an institution; these are much more difficult to quantify than, for example, a private industrial company's ability to generate a return on assets.

While there are many valuation methods available for the valuation of professional services firms including law firms, each with its own nuances, advantages and disadvantages, for any firm of a substantial size we tend to favour methods that are based on the firm's ability to generate cash in the foreseeable future and that are easily communicated to many law firm partners who often bring to the table at best a basic understanding of finance and business valuation. As we have seen, the financial attention of most law firm partners is directed at past and current performance. Valuation principles acknowledge the evidence of the past as a predictor of future performance, but demand concentrated attention on the predictable and assured expectation of future earnings potential. In this chapter, we will focus on three principal methods – the discounted cash flow method, the multiple of earnings method, and the self-financed method. Each is considered in turn.

Discounted cash flow method

The discounted cash flow method requires two levels of analysis. First, it requires a reasonably accurate projection of the amount and timing of all cash flow that the firm is able to generate for its equity partners in the future; second, it requires the discounting of cash flow back to present value at a rate that reflects the chance of receiving that cash flow within the time required.

At the heart of an accurate projection of the amount and timing of cash flow available to the equity owners of the firm are the firm's historic income and cash flow statements, after any adjustment required to reflect economic reality (see above). On this basis, it is tempting merely to assume a percentage of growth and project cash flow forward. However, in particular during the economic crisis during which this chapter was written, simpleminded projections of this sort have not held up. As discussed above, they require in-depth discussion with practice group leaders and revenue carrying partners and are absolutely critical to understanding the firm's future ability to generate revenue. This is often a difficult and time-consuming task, requiring several iterations of discussion to smoke out both undue conservatism and undue optimism. We found that three iterations of both external and internal analysis, as well as partner interviews, provide a rational basis for determining the amount of projected cash flow. There is no right answer to the question of how long a projection should be carried into the future: the longer a rational, not emotional, projection is possible, the better.

Developing a defensible discount rate often is a difficult, but not impossible, endeavour. Conceptually, one begins with the risk-free rate – i.e., the interest rate on government bonds – and one then factors risk premiums as appropriate. In the professional services context, these include size (a larger firm is deemed less of a risk than a smaller firm), the degree of marketability (which in the private company context is often low), the degree of control (because risk increases as one takes a smaller minority interest with fewer rights of control), dependency on key client or key professionals and possibly some other factors. Where the value will be financed through a mix of debt and equity, the weighted average cost of capital is typically used to determine the discount rate (see Chapter 7 for an explanation of this methodology).

Taking the conceptual to the practical, such factors create large discounts, given that most law firms do not trade on a liquid stock market and that most firms are dependent on a few key equity partners and often on a few key clients. In this author's view, the discount rate will need to be at least twice the amount of the expected return that an investor will have in a publicly held company. Discount rates from between 18 to 40 per cent are not uncommon.

Conceptually, the discounted cash flows method is the most sound, but it has practical limitations: the risk-adjusted discount rate requires a plethora of assumptions which are difficult to establish in a volatile market environment. While the risk-free rate is easy enough to determine, both industry risk and company originated risk provide challenges. Understanding what return a willing investor might expect also is easier in a steady market than in a volatile one. In the current market environment, we suggest that several return scenarios should be structured and then stress-tested to determine a rational value under this method. Most will be surprised that the risk – and thus the expected return – will be much higher than in a publicly held company context – and this is especially true where the law firm is a 'motel' for lawyers instead of an integrated business with a collective proposition.

Multiple of earnings method

The best known, most discussed and simplest method of valuation is the multiple of earnings method whereby a chosen multiplier is applied to the firm's predicted profits. While the multiple of revenue method makes for a pleasant cocktail conversation, this measure should not be used alone. The multiple of earnings method is somewhat more reliable and conceptually easier to understand than the discounted cash flow method. Under this method, cash flow available to the equity owners is determined by a technique similar to that used for the discounted cash flow method.

The level of achievable earnings before interest, depreciation tax and amortisation (EBIDTA) is multiplied by a multiplication factor that a willing buyer would be prepared to pay. As a starting point for determining the multiple, we typically reference comparable publicly held firms. In the legal services context this is tricky because there are only a few publicly held legal services providers. Furthermore, the problem with using quoted multiples for private firms is that they can easily include a large premium for the firm being publicly listed. In our view, other publicly held professional services businesses (for example accounting firms, management consultancies and recruiting firms) do, however, provide a rational starting point, provided one makes adjustments for the different business model under which these other professional services firms operate. For example, an accounting firm with a 20:1 leverage of staff to equity partner is likely to yield a lower net profit margin but may yield a higher multiple. In addition, the qualitative analysis of value drivers as described above then serves to adjust (usually downward) the price-earnings comparable derived from the publicly held firms. It is also worth repeating that the key is not the most recent financial results, but the sustainability of performance in the future.

Various attempts have been published to derive an earnings multiple scientifically, taking into account factors such as net profit margin and size of EBIDTA (see, e.g., Mayson, 2007, in particular Chapter 10). What goes into determining the earnings multiple in the end depends a great deal on the nature and structure of the firm as well as the judgment applied by the valuation professional.

Self-financed method

While this method seems somewhat backward at first, it provides a good reality test of whether the other methods yield a rational result. This method determines the maximum value that the firm could sustain if it had to pay for its own shares and it was briefly touched on in Chapter 8. It is based on the classic leveraged buy-out model for which private equity has become famous during the last boom. While highly leveraged acquisition transactions are out of fashion at the time this chapter was written, leverage and acquisition finance will always remain an integral part of acquisition transactions irrespective of the then current economic environment. Accordingly, this method retains its validity despite a reduced availability of credit.

On the basis of future cash flow, one determines the maximum amount that could be available for debt service. Based on financing available in the market, the maximum loan amount available (plus the down payment required to get the loan approved) at then current interest rates and terms determines the value of the firm. The value drivers analysed above inform the firm's ability to generate the cash necessary for debt service and also the interest rate and terms that a financier would be willing to offer. Note that the results of this method may differ depending on the identity of the lender: where loan funds are available only through private equity or through special funds, the terms may well be significantly less favourable than if a local bank were willing to lend funds.

Adjustments

As we have noted, various adjustments are often appropriate, whatever valuation method or combination of valuation methods are used. These include adjustments for excess cash in the business (excess cash being defined as more cash than required to continue reasonably operating the firm so as to generate the return that has been projected), assets and liabilities (including contingent liabilities), as well as special arrangements with the current equity owners. Real estate owned by the firm also invariably requires an adjustment to the value of the firm. In addition, exceptional items such as the impending costs of moving to a new building may have to be factored in.

Discounts for lack of marketability and lack of control also are commonly deducted from the value which is determined via the above methods. For the valuation of partial interests, control premiums and minority discounts also need to be addressed.

The key issue is that the above methodologies only work for integrated law firms. At a minimum, a firm would have to have developed a cohesive business model that values the objectives of the firm above and beyond the contributions of individual partners; it is quite difficult to find this cohesive business model in firms that are 'motels' for lawyers. However, the above approach to valuation should be applied so as to allow the use of specialist market knowledge to look deeply behind the numbers. This way, it is possible to understand what has to happen for financial performance presented by the firm to be sustained, to be expanded and also how additional capital will increase future cash flows and thus support long-term value generation.

Net book value and the valuation of individual practices

The above assumes that an entire firm is being acquired or at least a substantial, integrated part of a firm. The above methods do not serve well for the acquisition and valuation of sole proprietors or small partnerships. The reason for this is simple: the dependence on these individuals to generate future revenue is so great that without them the organisation would not generate any revenue and profit. High street firms and motels for lawyers are at particular risk of being worth very little more than the current income generating capacity of its equity owners. In these instances, the above valuation methods will be far too complicated to apply and also are not likely to yield a rational economic result.

Because of the lack of predictability of the firm to generate a profit without the active involvement of the equity owner, one returns to the balance sheet. In small practices in particular, the net book value method will be applied. Under this straightforward method, the balance sheet is reviewed and adjusted as per the above (paying due attention in particular to claims and contingent liabilities); the difference between assets and liabilities becomes the adjusted net book value of the business. If there are intangible assets that create a residual revenue stream (e.g., through an online client tool for employment compliance), the income generating ability of this asset would need to be reviewed separately or within the context of the above methods.

In the absence of residual income generating assets, the more likely scenario for an individual practitioner is that he or she will receive an amount equal to cash, collectible accounts receivable, and a percentage of work in progress, plus a small amount for (usually fully depreciated) tangible assets as the 'value' of the business, as well as an employment contract with the acquiring firm (representing the goodwill).

We understand that the foregoing paragraph may be a harsh message to those practitioners who may have expected an easy golden parachute once the LSA is fully implemented. The savvy practitioner will undertake steps several years before putting his or her practice up for sale to ensure that the business runs as independently of the practitioner as possible: this is achievable through ensuring that other professionals within the firm maintain key client relationships, ensuring that professional staff are developed in a structured and consistent way (also by others), ensuring that intellectual capital is managed according to the value-added strategy that has been carefully developed and operations that run, managed by someone other than the owner, as efficiently and effectively as possible.

Reality testing

Finally, any valuation will have to be tested for reality. We have seen numerous valuations prepared by valuation professionals where the valuation seemed instinctively to veer towards the higher or lower end of the comfort zone of both parties to the transaction.

At the same time, we caution against using rules of thumb (e.g., '1 × revenue') as the sole basis for valuing any practice. While rules of thumb may provide for some reality testing, they are no substitute for a careful analysis of all of the method and relevant factors, especially with respect to a law firm's intellectual capital and resulting intangible assets.

A final word on the presentation of valuation results

We have reviewed a number of highly technical valuation reports for professional services firms in various contexts and with various objectives. All of them were well done to the extent they understood the special nature of intangible assets and value drivers within professional services firms, and law firms in particular.

However, it is important to understand that a valuation report of a law firm is not presented to a board of directors of a corporation that is well used to acquisitions and sales of businesses. When the report is presented to the managing board of law firm partners, it is important that difficult concepts are explained clearly and that they are broken down so that they can be understood, questioned and challenged.

A high-level executive summary will do wonders, assuming that it is backed up with sufficient detail so that the partners can reconcile their perceived reality with the work of the professional adviser. In larger partnerships, workshops with no more than 10 to 12 partners at a time to review these results will achieve a greater understanding than a presentation at a large partners' meeting.

Endnote

1 Michael Roch advises law, accounting and other professional services firms on competitive positioning, strategy, structure and finance, for management consultancy KermaPartners.
2 See, e.g., Koller, Goedhart and Wessels (2005) and Frykman and Tolleryd (2003) both for a general introduction; Mayson (2007) for a solid conceptual approach to law from valuation; Pratt, Reilly and Schweihs (1998) for an excellent comprehensive reference work; Arnold (2005) for valuation in the public equity markets context; and Lake and Lake (2000) for the financial investor's perspective.

10

Remuneration revisited

KEY POINTS

- Managing expectations
- Choosing a profit-sharing system
- Lockstep and other systems
- Aligning with a corporate model

As the legal profession attempts to respond to recessionary and competitive pressures as well as the opportunities and threats offered by ABSs, some firms are altering their business models towards strategies and structures aimed towards both longer term growth and sustained expansion. Inevitably, therefore, survival and expansion will have to rely more on a combination of clever strategic thinking and entrepreneurial efforts and contributions. In turn this may redirect law firms more and more towards performance related systems of rewarding partners who contribute well. In addition, as more firms become corporate in style or structure, there is likely to be a trend towards more corporate models of senior executive remuneration.

Clarifying and defining expectations

Before deciding the best method of compensation and profit sharing in law firms, it is important to be clear about what the firm expects of its partners and what roles and responsibilities it needs them to perform. Partners equally need to be clear how they are to discharge their various roles as owners, managers and producers. The current trend away from the more revenue and formulaic systems is no accident. Firms are increasingly responding to the growing realisation that such revenue-driven systems reward only a very restrictive set of behaviours and at times actually serve to penalise longer term entrepreneurial activities.

Law firms have, at last, therefore accepted the importance of developing management and leadership skills in their partners. This recognition is somewhat patchy and inconsistent and there is often a mismatch between what law firms say they value in their partners (in terms of the competencies and characteristics) and what they actually reward (often by recognising and rewarding billing efforts mainly or exclusively). Additionally, there is a reluctant but growing appreciation that skills and competencies can be developed across the management/leadership spectrum, from a base level through an intermediate level to an advanced state of leadership.

Significant time input is required across the world for partners in all law firms. On top of time spent on client work, I am seeing partners being budgeted to spend marketing and business development time in the range of 300 to 500 hours a year and other non-chargeable time depending on factors such as the size of team and type of client. Non-chargeable efforts also need to be made in respect of client relationship management, team and human capital management and the partner's contribution to the firm as an institution. This results in many firms expecting partners to spend (and record) a minimum total of 2,300 hours a year on the business of the partnership. Within this time frame it should be possible for the non-chargeable activities to be carried out, even within the context of a large client portfolio.

In general, as the firm continues to grow, partners will need steadily to become managers of others as their main activity; they will need to reduce the time spent on files and matters, and to increase aspects such as delegation and supervision. In addition they will need to build capability and competence in four or five key areas.

Choosing a profit-sharing system

Methods of profit sharing in law firms have traditionally differed greatly between North America and Europe. In Europe, the majority of UK law firms have historically operated against a background of 'true partnership', with equal sharing for all partners after a period of progression in lockstep up the ladder. In smaller law firms, the progression of an incoming partner towards equality tends to have proceeded by negotiation, or as a result of senior partners 'giving up' part of their profit-sharing entitlement on an ad hoc basis. In larger European firms, the tendency has historically been for the firm to have a formal progression arrangement. In contrast, many North American firms have tended to operate on more meritocratic principles based on individual performance of partners as originating and working attorneys, which finds its most extreme model in the 'eat what you kill' principle.

What is interesting, however, is the extent to which we see a growing trend on both sides of the Atlantic towards performance related systems based on a wider managerial and business role for partners. In general terms, external investors and new models of ABSs will also confirm the trend towards performance related systems. There is now broad recognition that partners in successful law firms must – as their firms grow – develop their roles as managers of people, developers of business, leaders of teams, builders of 'thought-ware' and nurturers of client relationships. This immediately raises a difficulty in that success in many dimensions of these roles can only be considered qualitatively rather than quantitatively. The identification of winners and losers (and those in between) therefore contains many subjective elements.

The two simplest models of profit sharing lie at each end of a wide extreme. At one end, we find the egalitarian, equal sharing model with the seniority progression known as lockstep. At the other extreme is a formulaic, performance based system founded on the principle that every partner's profit share or compensation is inextricably linked with the revenue introduced to the firm by him or her – sometimes known as the 'eat-what-you-kill' system. These two simple but very different systems may continue to work for an ever dwindling number of law firms, but have – in their pure forms – already become less common and I dare say they will become even rarer. As firms make changes to their system to recognise and reward the differing roles and contributions of partners, it is inevitable that some features of the previous system will remain, if only in terms of nomenclature. Traces of the old ways will also remain deeply embedded in the psyche or culture of the firm. As an example, many firms in the United Kingdom continue to refer to their system as 'modified lockstep' long after all recognisable elements of a pure lockstep have disappeared. What they mean by this description is that their system is now heavily performance related but that seniority continues to be an element. There is a further example of adjustments at the other extreme of the reward system – the heavily formulaic extreme. Here, some firms are fond of saying that they have 'stopped looking at the numbers'. What they mean is that partners' compensation or profit shares are no longer entirely driven by the numbers, but that the firm will look behind the financial data to consider total contribution. But, as we will see later, financial and economic performance continues to be a critically important area.

The big decision, therefore, is where firms will choose to lie on the spectrum between the two extremes of pure lockstep and pure eat-what-you-kill. There is no one right answer. History will be an element, as it is clearly easier to move along the spectrum by incremental steps than it is to lurch from one extreme to the other.

For start-up firms, or for firms which want to expand quickly, an eat-what-you-kill system continues to have great attractions, as both the overall need for working capital and the fixed-cost elements of overhead are quite significantly diminished in comparison with firms whose compensation model obliges them to pay market rates for all their professionals. However, significant recruitment constraints also apply, as they are in a position to attract only those lawyers who are prepared to take a business risk in joining or starting a firm in which there are few compensation guarantees. In order to lure the best talent from other firms, it is often necessary to offer a compensation package which is sufficiently high and secure to seduce the partner into leaving his or her existing – and probably quite comfortable – position at a rival firm. In the face of this, we will see a number of established firms and new organisations which are prepared to take significant financial risk – by incurring debt or inviting external finance – in order to fuel profitable long-term growth. For such firms, a performance related system of compensation for their partners is usually essential, but there will also be a reasonably high fixed element to partner packages.

As the legal profession attempts to respond to recessionary pressures, some firms are altering their business model towards a model aimed at both longer term growth and sustained expansion. Inevitably, therefore, expansion will have to rely more on a combination of clever strategic thinking and entrepreneurial efforts and contributions. In turn this may redirect law firms more and more towards performance related systems of rewarding partners who contribute well.

Lockstep and its variants

In the UK, Europe and Australia, more than half of partner remuneration (see Wesemann and Jarrett-Kerr, 2008) is still largely based to some extent on a lockstep system, but the use of pure unadjusted lockstep continues to fall steadily in these jurisdictions. Instead, hybrid forms of lockstep are slowly growing in which performance related adjustments of some kind are made based on qualitative criteria.

Not many firms in North America have ever used lockstep and most which have used the system have now abandoned it. Partners in North America seem more willing to place their compensation in the judgment of others, while UK, European and Australian law firm partners prefer a more predictable and pre-established set of criteria.

Under a lockstep or seniority based system, an individual partner, upon admission to the partnership, is exchanging his own individual earning power and his own intellectual capital for participation in a 'mutual fund' of other partners. Through this, he is able to share in the joint future incomes of his partners, some of whom will be his contemporaries and some of whom will offer differing levels of expertise and experience gained through the years.

The main benefits of a sharing or lockstep system of profit sharing

For a firm with a large element of firm-specific intellectual capital, the sharing or lockstep system of profit sharing has some important potential advantages. The main benefit is to provide outstanding diversification and to reinforce a culture in which clients are viewed as firm clients and in which efficient teamwork is encouraged.

In the case of many lockstep firms the client is regarded as central to their whole ethos, and for such a firm a culture of 'firm before self' is entirely consistent with a sharing, lockstep model of profit sharing. What is also clear is that the presence and level of firm-specific capital is so marked in such firms that they are potentially much more profitable for individual partners than alternatives outside the firm.

The drawbacks of lockstep

Lockstep or the sharing system of profit sharing does, however, have the following disadvantages:

- it does not deal explicitly with the issue of underperformers or shirkers;
- it does not deal with the issue of exceptional high flyers;
- it does not reward, sufficiently quickly, superior young partners;
- it can reward moderate partners to a greater extent than they deserve;
- even if underperformance is not a problem, nevertheless, in the world of professional services there is a fine line between the good partner and the excellent one;
- it can prove difficult to find the right place on the equity ladder for lateral hires.

In the lockstep firm, the problem of underperformers is seen as more of a management and development problem than a problem of reward. Firms with a lockstep or sharing system of profit sharing tend to be less tolerant of poor or mediocre performance than firms which make extensive use of individual, performance based rewards. The attitude can be very much one of 'shape up or ship out'. The problem is that not every issue of underperformance results from laziness or lack of intellect.

The experience of a number of firms is that a reduction in profit share to cope with underperformance can tend to demotivate the partner still further with the result that performance levels drop even more.

How lockstep works

Lockstep works by providing for a progression for incoming partners from a starting allocation of a profit share until he or she reaches parity with the other partners; this parity is often known as 'the plateau'. The most common way of expressing this formula is by a points or units formula, and this generally works in one of two ways. The first and most common method is for the distributable profit to be divided by the aggregate amount of points allocated to partners, to arrive at a points value which will of course vary from year to year as profits (and the number of points in play), go up and down in each accounting year. The second method, which is less common, is to attribute a fixed value to each point. This is sometimes useful in order to provide a differential points value when the firm has different offices operating under wholly different market and profitability conditions.

Trends for firms retaining 'pure' lockstep

We see many firms across the world that are wedded to the concepts and values of 'true partnership' and equal sharing which finds their expression in the lockstep principle. However, many such firms are tending to sand down the edges of pure lockstep in order to maintain flexibility and to improve the firm's ability to manage performance.

As a partner moves up the ladder and grows within the partnership, firms generally expect his or her contribution to increase. This development does not relate just to the overall hours spent on firm business or the degree of collaboration, but relates more to the value that the partner brings to the firm. Firms very often, therefore, provide benchmarks and criteria which they wish to see partners attain as they develop through the partnership. These benchmarks are supported by training and coaching, and are monitored via appraisals.

At the same time, these benchmarks and criteria will often provide the minimum acceptable standards for partners of the firm, protracted or persistent under-shooting of which will result in the partner being asked to leave. The more caring firms will sweeten this frightening prospect by providing for a period of intensive care and coaching to allow the partner to address his or her perceived shortcomings.

Variations of lockstep (hybrid lockstep)

More radical solutions have also made their way into the structures of many firms. In the United Kingdom and in Europe, two-thirds of firms now report (Wesemann and Jarrett-Kerr, 2008) that they have some form of lockstep. Only 13 per cent of firms surveyed regarded themselves as using pure lockstep, whereas 30 per cent described their lockstep as modified by performance factors.

A further 22 per cent of firms had 'managed' locksteps where gateways exist at which the case for upwards progression is evaluated.

There is growing evidence that firms are reluctant to admit new partners if those partners are going to progress automatically to parity. Equally, many firms are reluctant to go the whole way into a pure performance related system, but wish to retain the flexibility to even out elements of unfairness and to make some measure of alignment between individual contribution and individual rewards. Many of these 'hybrid' systems seek to give partners two things. First, they give certainty in that partners will know in advance the level of their guaranteed minimum income, assuming the firm meets its financial targets. Second, partners know that they will also be rewarded for performance in due course. What is important always to bear in mind is that the system must support the firm in its growth and in the attainment of its objectives.

We have seen many such modifications but there tend to be five main types:

1. **Managed lockstep.** A managed lockstep is one where the progression up the ladder is assumed but not presumed. The firm will preserve the right in exceptional circumstances to hold a partner at his or her current position in the lockstep, or even to reduce points, if that partner's performance does not warrant progression. In addition, there will often be a 'gateway' at one or two places in the lockstep through which a partner can and will pass only if the firm agrees that he or she should progress further. Some firms also retain the right to advance a partner through the lockstep faster than the standard progression and in some cases to reduce a partner's share. A common provision is to provide that a partner can advance by up to two steps each year, but that no partner can be reduced by more than one step in any one year in the case of underperformance.

2. **Lockstep plus discretionary, performance related element.** Another variation provides for some form of seniority-based progression to apply to the major part of the firm's distributable profit pool, but further provides for the remaining part of a partner's profit share to be performance or merit related. There are three main methodologies currently in play. The first methodology divides the profit pool into two parts, with one part allocated to the lockstep and the other part reserved for performance related 'bonus' allocations. The bonuses are usually quite small – 10 per cent being quite typical. In some cases, however, we have seen firms allocate as much as 40 per cent of the firm's profit for distribution on a performance related basis and this trend may increase over time. The advantage of this methodology is that partners can often be persuaded to feel that, unless they are perceived to be underperforming, all partners will receive something from this part of the profit pool.

   The second methodology provides for additional merit points to reward retroactively for superior or exceptional performance, but with a re-base to 100 points each year. Some such systems seek to restrict the effect of such a provision by providing that points for superior or exceptional performance are unlikely to be awarded to more than a fairly small percentage of partners.

   The third methodology – occasionally used – is one which provides for the allocation of additional, pre-determined points for partners with a defined management role, such as senior and managing partners, and divisional or practice area heads. The issue here is that the points entitlement is tied to the role and does not necessarily reflect adequate, exceptional or ineffective performance of the role. However, in effect, this methodology can be used to reward performance on a prospective basis, on the basis that inadequate performance will quickly result in a role adjustment.

3. **The super plateau.** The super plateau system is a managed lockstep under which, having reached, say,100 points (which would be the points plateau for a firm operating with a lockstep to 100 points), an exceptional partner can then progress further to a super plateau which is reserved for a very few, star partners. This super plateau generally operates prospectively in that partners are moved on to the super plateau on the assumption that future performance will match or exceed past performance.

4. **Lockstep plus formula bonus.** A further variation gives a partner a formula bonus in addition to his or her points based, lockstepped profit share. This bonus generally operates as a first slice of profits and is based on a percentage of the partner's realised billings and possibly a percentage of revenues of clients introduced or cared for by the partner. It has the advantage of incentivising and helping to drive individual revenue performance where it is appropriate and necessary to do so. However, it also carries the disadvantage of focusing partners away from non-revenue producing management activities and can also reinforce tendencies to hog work and to be anti-collaborative.

5. **Exceptional bonuses for extreme high flyers.** Some firms also provide for the ability to award an individual payment in order to reward a 'one-off instance' of exceptional performance. Unless the exceptional performance is widely perceived to be exceptional and head and shoulders above the performance of other partners, these bonuses can cause bad feeling, particularly if the partners benefiting have a tendency (often associated with high revenue producers) to act like badly behaved prima donnas.

Other systems

It is widely thought that most large firms – particularly in the USA – operate on a highly objective, numbers-driven individualistic or pure formulaic system, often labelled 'eat-what-you-kill'. Around two-thirds of US firms are now thought to base substantial parts of their compensation packages on 'subjective' considerations which may include statistical data. Only about 10 per cent of large firms use a strict formula.

'Eat-what-you-kill'

Typically, in a system based on eat-what-you-kill, performance as a practising lawyer is objectively measured by examining a combination of originations and the value of work performed or for which the lawyer is the responsible attorney. Although this approach is usually modified to include a few other performance criteria besides only billing, it still means that the lawyers in the firm who produce high levels of revenue are rewarded commensurately, while those who do not are penalised. The advantages of this system are that the firm can pay the premium salaries that the very top talent demands, and that the system self-corrects for lawyers who want to reduce their workloads, perhaps for lifestyle reasons. For middle sized and emerging firms, a highly incentivised system such as this may be the only way to attract top talent.

Under the extreme form of this system each partner in effect becomes a profit centre island. He or she bears a share of firm overhead, but is responsible for his or her direct costs such as the salary of his or her secretary or assistant. Also, individual marketing, continuing education, personal technology and membership costs remain the responsibility of the individual partner. The time of junior lawyers can be purchased from the firm at set rates but charged out to clients at whatever billing rate the partner thinks is appropriate. Partners can also sell an interest in a particular file to another partner at a negotiated rate. Typically, the client-originating partner will get 10 per cent of whatever is billed by the other partner. Having dealt with all of the costs, the partners then retain 100 per cent of all receipts.

Even the extreme version of the system does have some strengths. As every partner has total responsibility for his or her income and clients, partners know exactly what they must do to achieve the income levels they desire. The system provides incentives at various levels. First, some partners and shareholders like retaining control and a measure of independence over their own affairs. Systems where partners share the overheads proportionately but keep their own revenues are not, after all, far off franchise-style businesses and have their attractions for some entrepreneurial lawyers and business people. Second, the partners will see the benefit of bringing in business for others because they get a percentage of the billing when they 'sell' the file to another partner or when they get a junior to manage the file. Internal billing rates are fixed to make the internal transfer of work easy, but internal bargaining still occurs and partners will always tend to work on matters which are more profitable for them. Third, the system encourages efficient and lean operations. There is, for instance, a real incentive to hire and retain only profitable, hard working juniors so that partners can maximise their own incomes. Partners are also strongly motivated to collect their receivables because it is their own money. Fourth, the system allows for the introduction of new partners and offices at less financial risk to the firm than with a more sharing style of compensation system. If partners are expected to fill their own case load and are compensated accordingly, much of the investment risk stays with them. Fifth, partners in eat-what-you-kill systems usually offer a great deal of care for their clients, as they have a lot to lose if lack of efficient client service prompts the client to go elsewhere.

There are also institutional benefits to what are essentially cost sharing systems as opposed to profit-sharing ones. Such systems can promote fast investment in growth, as much of the risk stays with the individual partners or the local office and not the whole firm. The system will automatically cope with the otherwise sensitive problem of unequal earnings and profits from offices and practices in less profitable work types and geographical areas. Furthermore, the firm's central management and overhead will remain lean and mean. The firm is discouraged from creating an overly cumbersome set of central systems and bureaucratic rules, and will maintain tight controls on central spending because partners will not tolerate too large a central overhead allocation. In addition, partners will not waste valuable time in low level office administration but will focus maximum efforts on profitable work. There is another institutional benefit for international firms which often have to observe 'local' regulations which militate against sharing profits with 'foreign' partners, and therefore have organised their international agreements through cost sharing arrangements rather than profit-sharing schemes.

There are, however, huge problems with eat-what-you-kill. It is no accident that firms in the USA are modifying their systems or moving away from them. In the first place, the building of teams, departments and specialisations can all be somewhat impeded. Second, there is little or no recognition for efforts and contributions made towards firm management and institution building. Indeed, the system does little to encourage partners to work on creating efficiencies in work processes. Third, such a system can affect the firm's ability to act in the best interests of its clients, as partners may hog work for which they are not properly qualified, or favour using staff on the basis of the potential profitability to the partner rather than on the basis of who will do the best job for the client. Furthermore, partners could theoretically be inhibited from giving advice to their clients in the clients' long-term interests if such advice could affect the partners' short-term revenue stream.

Formula systems

A system which historically has been in common use particularly in North America is a formula system but, again, this seems to be making way for systems which are more flexible, holistic and discretionary. Under a formula system, a formula is set up which typically centres around objective criteria including each partner's revenues, collections, originations and the like. The most usual of these credit partners with differing amounts of points both for the fees for clients whom they have originated and for the value of work which they have billed.

This then becomes easy to measure – you simply calculate the volume of work introduced or originated, the volume for which the partner is responsible in terms of being a team manager. Additionally, the firm would measure the volume of revenue which the partner actually generates from his own efforts. Overhead factors then need to be taken into account and a formula then applies to work out each partner's compensation. The system clearly is designed to encourage the building of individual practices and rapidly to reward rainmakers and partners who have developed substantial books of business.

There are, however, many problems with such systems. First, tracking and then rewarding originations can produce difficulties and scope for argument. The second problem is that almost all formula systems, in looking at 'objective' financial data alone, fail to recognise or reward all the criteria necessary for a firm's success. The argument is that the partners with large books of business, who devote time and care to their team and issues such as service quality, will find their revenues and compensation statistics becoming more and more favourable. The third problem is that formula systems have been proved to be easy to manipulate. Playing the numbers game can mean that partners and shareholders concentrate more on efforts which will directly enhance their compensation rather than efforts needed for the firm. The fourth problem is that formula systems are highly inflexible unless they are used as a guide only and not as an automatic entitlement. There is no automatic credit for partners working on emerging areas or new specialisations which will not produce profit for a while. Despite the discouragement of an inflexible compensation system, many partners are still prepared to invest their own time (and see their short-term compensation suffer) on long-term business or niche building, but one cannot help feeling that firms which recognise long-term effort will do better in the long run.

Performance related (or 'subjective' based) systems

There is a discernible global trend away from both pure lockstep and the more individual and statistics based systems such as eat-what-you-kill and formulaic systems. Firms moving towards performance related systems will usually keep some vestiges of their historical or formula based systems, and many provide some certainty and security for their partners by fixing base salary or compensation tiers for their partners. Some large international firms have moved on to compensation and rewards systems which are wholly performance based. Such firms often have as many as nine to twelve bands and partners are allocated into bands on an assessment of the sustained value which they have brought to the firm. In other words, the firm tries to look not just at one year's performance but for long-term contribution. Some such firms will look two years back and one year forward to arrive at a view.

The bands themselves are arranged so as to have significant gaps between them – £50,000 (US$100,000) or more is a popular band interval between each tier. Structurally, the firm will – as with performance criteria – tend to fix the highest and lowest bands first. The highest band will represent what the firm feels it must pay (assuming it is affordable) to the firm's star performer or performers, whilst the lowest band will represent a fair market package for an incoming equity partner. The other bands will be arranged with suitable intervening gaps between top and bottom.

Although this methodology can theoretically lead to huge uncertainty (as partners have no assurance or guarantee of what band they might be in next year), firms will often provide that partners can move up no more than two bands in any one year and partners can have the certainty of knowing that they can only be demoted by one band in any one year. I have also seen some partnership provisions which provide for almost automatic expulsion if a partner is demoted more than once in a reasonable period of time.

The point should be clear by now that movement either wholly or in part on to performance related (or subjective based) compensation should not be attempted until and unless all the partners are crystal clear as to what the firm expects its partners to do and how it needs them to behave. However small the firm decides that the performance related part of the overall compensation should be, and whatever the balance between client work production and other more 'subjective' areas, the firm has to decide the areas in which it wants its partners to perform, as well as the criteria for success – those behaviours and outcomes which the firm will value and reward. In addition, it has to form a view as to how the 'subjective' factors are going to be assessed, scored or judged.

Equal sharing

The most collegial and purest form of partnership is one where all the partners decide to share both risk and reward equally. Lockstep is, after all, a variation of the equal sharing model aimed at providing a stepped progression to equality rather than immediate entry to equity ownership on equal terms. Many, admittedly smaller, law firms continue to be totally dedicated to the concept and practice of equal sharing. For such firms, all the institutional and collaborative opportunities set out in this chapter as advantages of a lockstep system apply in even greater fashion to firms where equal profit sharing is the norm. The disadvantages, however, also apply – there is, for example, no recognition for inequality of performance and contribution.

Ad hoc systems

Although we have no explicit survey evidence to prove it, there are a great many law firms throughout the world which have historically allocated their profits and partner compensation on a fairly informal basis, and continue to do so. I have, however, noticed that this exercise becomes more difficult and contentious once the firm grows to about 15 or so equity partners, members or shareholders. Above 20 or so partners, formal systems and structures generally become necessary.

Many firms employing ad hoc compensation systems started as family or sole proprietor firms, where the founder partner or partners set all the rules and provided all of the leadership and partnership control. As partners came in, they were allocated profit-sharing and compensation packages by the controlling partner or coalition of partners, and their shares tended to increase over time only if the firm leaders so decided or where the firm was faced with defections. Firms with strong and controlling leadership, whether or not from a founding partner, have much to commend them. The famous 'herding of cats' problems do not apply to firms where partners have to do what they are told. Such firms, however, usually find that both a spirit of entrepreneurship and continuing profitable growth of the firm will eventually become stifled, unless heavy central control and dictatorship develops into a more sustainable institutional model. This generally leads to the formalisation of the rules for equity membership, progression and compensation.

Other firms have continued to adopt an annual negotiation where profit-sharing allocations are discussed or fought over by the entire partnership. In some firms, each partner fills out an anonymous slip of paper with his or her compensation proposals and these are then aggregated. Occasionally, a remuneration or compensation committee is appointed to apply rough justice, without any detailed rules of engagement or criteria being agreed.

Ad hoc systems therefore can range from a heavily autocratic extreme to a predominantly democratic model where every partner is allowed an equal say in compensation setting discussions. They can work well or badly depending on the level of trust and the culture of collegiality within the firm. Partners generally need to have the comfort of knowing that their overall contribution to the firm is both known and being fairly taken into account. Systems which are perceived to favour the popular partners and those who are best at selling themselves and their accomplishments within the partnership often act to disconcert those who prefer to keep themselves to themselves, or work in more humdrum areas of practice.

Aligning with a corporate model

It is becoming fairly common for law firms to try to align with more corporate models of salary and compensation structures, especially as jurisdictions such as Australia and the United Kingdom start to embrace deregulation for the legal profession. However, the world of corporate business has no easy formula for resolving salary and compensation issues for its senior staff. For senior executives at the same level as equity partners in a law firm, the salary package in most corporations will combine a fixed salary with bonuses, some of which will be payable in cash and some in longer term stock options. In contrast, the traditional partnership model has historically operated on the basis of the partners allocating to themselves the whole of each year's profit; indeed most partnerships are taxed on the whole of their income each year. The main change for law firms which embrace full corporate structures would therefore be the concept of deferred compensation – not all of the firm's income would be on the table for allocation and distribution each year. Apart from that fundamental change, the main compensation and reward challenges currently facing law firms would continue to apply whether the setting is a corporate one or the firm uses the more traditional partnership model.

Many professional services firms, from investment banks to surveying firms, have for some time abandoned a partnership structure in favour of a corporate model. In the last decade of the twentieth century, firms such as investment banks used long-term guaranteed contracts and bonuses to attract and retain staff. This was soon abandoned in favour of more flexible systems, with performance related bonuses structured to include a greater proportion of restricted stock which is released over a number of years. These base compensation structures are supplemented by a menu of signing and year-end bonuses, pension provisions and other perks and reimbursements.

The banks also instituted salary targets to align with revenue, in pursuance of strategies to reduce fixed costs and to increase the proportion of variable overheads. Such fixed targets are often around 50 per cent of revenue. Typically, therefore, fixed salaries became capped at what is considered in the industry a relatively low level (£125,000 being fairly common). The problem, however, arose that although many of the bonuses remain theoretically discretionary, some bonuses have to be paid in order to retain the best talent even in a downturn.

Further considerations have affected the mergers and acquisitions market. In a consolidating market, acquisition strategies have driven those financing deals to devise compensation plans which provide incentives for the current management to stay and to build up the value of their equity within the consolidated entity. Hence, a substantial part of the purchase price usually gets paid in stock, notes and other forms of paper in the purchasing company. Typically, the deals depend on several years of growth to make the finances work for all parties, and many deals are therefore structured to pay one-third of the purchase price in each of cash, equity (in the new firm) and loan notes.

With new competition, new models and mergers and acquisitions increasing in pace and scale, we are likely to see a growing movement towards more corporate remuneration structures. These trends, combined with the ability to convert many law firms into corporations, will see partners' salary and compensation packages become combinations of fixed base salary, performance related flexible elements and some elements of deferred compensation tied to long-term growth. The assessment of total contribution over a balanced scorecard or a number of critical areas of performance will, therefore, be increasingly important.

Setting base partner salaries or base level compensation

As has been seen, many firms are starting to introduce the concept of a base salary or base level compensation for the equity partners and members. From the individual partner's point of view, this gives the security of a fixed level of reward which is not subject to the tides of personal good or bad fortune within the firm. Partners know that this fixed base will allow them to pay their mortgages and living expenses. It is very important to fix these salaries at the appropriate level. If it is fixed too high, the fixed base element may give partners too much security and may also become a disproportionately high focus of attention in the compensation setting round. If fixed too low, it can become somewhat meaningless. The experience of a number of firms is that the aggregate level of such base salaries should be targeted to be around half of the total compensation package, thus leaving a realistic proportion of total compensation subject to both performance related and proprietorship aligned factors.

A number of different models can be employed to arrive at the appropriate amount for these base fixed salaries, although many firms do not have any systematic methodology in place, and some firms will consider combining a number of these methods to arrive at an overall result. Once these base levels have been set, there is a trend not to reconsider them not but regularly to apply an inflation element to them.

Method 1 – conversion of drawings

The first method in common use is to convert existing monthly drawings levels into a 'salary', sometimes grossed up for tax purposes (although only the net sum would, of course, be paid). This has the advantage of providing only a minimal change but, depending on the firm's drawings policy, may not necessarily make fair distinctions between partners. Some firms have a flat drawings policy under which all partners receive an equal monthly sum irrespective of seniority or performance, whilst others adopt a very conservative monthly drawings policy which bears no relation at all to the sort of fixed or flat base sum upon which partners would expect to rely for their basic needs.

Method 2 – converting part of compensation package

Another method sometimes used is to convert a part of the overall compensation package from the previous year into a fixed base salary for the current year. This has the advantage of preserving the existing differentials between partners and also forms a small and therefore uncontroversial change.

Method 3 – salaried partner plus

Another method is to look at the market salaries and compensation packages currently paid to very senior lawyers and attorneys below equity partner level. New incoming equity partners or members would start at a base salary level, around the same level as a salaried partner, and the base levels would rise proportionately from there for all other equity partners.

Method 4 – market salaries

This method is not dissimilar to Method 3 in that the firm makes an attempt to fix market salaries for all its equity partners or members, having regard to salary levels both in the private firm market and for in-house lawyers and general counsel. In theory, this sounds sensible and logical, but it can be quite difficult sometimes to obtain meaningful benchmark salary levels and even more difficult to set a level for, say, a generalist partner in his or her 50s. It is, however, an attractive way of differentiating between partners in high cost and low cost offices, particularly in a firm with international offices.

Lateral hires

Base level salary or compensation packages are brought into stark relief when considering the introduction of lateral hires, whether at shareholder or equity level or as a non-equity partner. Firms will want to draw an appropriate balance between offering a seductive package (which therefore will often contain a high fixed element) and the creation of flexible compensation which is tied to the performance and success of the laterally hired partner. The overall package needs to be sufficiently attractive to persuade the partner to leave his or her current firm, but the hiring should never be carried out without reference to those who – perhaps as a remuneration or compensation committee – have the responsibility for the firm's partner remuneration and compensation setting for the whole of the firm. It is worth noting that the level of fixed or base salary set for the new laterally hired partner will ultimately affect the base salary structure for the rest of the partners – too high an introductory package can destabilise the firm and lead to key existing partners leaving the firm.

Furthermore, the possible introduction of a lateral hire can usefully test the viability and purity of the firm's compensation system. If the system is quirky, inexplicable, over-complex or thoroughly outdated, it is unlikely to be attractive to a new joiner.

Paying and protecting those who manage

In order to attract the best internal candidates for positions of management, firms are finding that they have at least to match the compensation of top equity partners and in some cases to supplement it.

The financial cost of losing a partner from fee-earning can be extremely high. In addition to the direct financial replacement costs, such as recruitment fees, the intangible costs at partner level should not be underestimated. Core skills, knowledge and experience can be difficult to replace, and the extraction of a key partner from a team can threaten stability, morale and growth internally. Externally, key client relationships can also be put at risk. In addition, the loss of team or departmental management or leadership skills can create long-term problems.

Against all these expenses, the huge advantages of an internal appointment have to be weighed. The risk to the business in appointing an unknown outsider is, after all, considerable. Unlike an internal appointee, the external appointee will need to take time to understand the firm's culture and behavioural characteristics. He or she will have to gain intimate knowledge of the dynamics of the business, its history, and its strengths and weaknesses. Whilst the external appointee will bring objectivity, lateral thinking and advanced management competencies, he or she will have to earn the respect of the partnership, particularly after the honeymoon period is over. In contrast and from day one, the internal appointee will understand intimately the dynamics and politics of the partnership, and will have detailed industry, market-place and competitor knowledge. The internal appointee will also know the firm's strengths and the opportunities to be exploited, as well as being acutely aware of the firm's weaknesses and the threats and challenges which need to be addressed.

It is somewhat easier to gain a balance between all these factors, both culturally and economically, in firms which have a lockstep background than in firms which have relied on individual fee-earning performance. Having said that, many firms are managing to provide fair packages for their managing partners and group heads, that combine personal, measurable, performance related objectives with the attainment of group and firm objectives. It is, however, sometimes difficult to reward (or at least protect from penalty) the managing partner whose excellent work is let down by the rest of the firm, or a group of underperforming teams and partners, over whom the managing partner's impact will be seen in the long term rather than in the current year's profits.

The ultimate cost of reintegrating the managing partner at the end of his or her term of office must also be factored in, and some security has to be given, as otherwise partners will not be attracted to take up the role of managing partner. This will involve retraining and the rebuilding of a client base, and the ex-managing partner's remuneration and compensation arrangements should be protected for a reasonable period whilst this takes place. The ultimate cost of this should be taken into account from the outset of the appointment. Many firms are allowing at least a two- or three-year period for this protected reintegration. The exit package should also recognise the possibility that the ex-managing partner may no longer wish to return to full-time fee-earning at the end of his or her term of office, and provision should be made for the possibility of an alternative career plan.

11

Governance, leadership and management in the changing law firm environment

KEY POINTS

- Management of 'traditional' law firms
- Governance, leadership and management challenges
- The need for better organised management structures and the purpose of governance
- ABS governance: partnership board or council, executive board, departments and 'C-suite' of executive officers
- Partner adaptation as the governance structure develops

Management of 'traditional' law firms

Partnerships are not what they used to be. Over the last 20 years law firms have changed and grown out of all recognition. And with those changes, coupled with the possibly dramatic effects of deregulation, the tectonic plates that underpin partnership structures are shifting permanently. The fact is that – with the exception perhaps of very small partnerships – it is just not possible to get by any longer without some proper leadership and a coherent governance model.

BOX 11.1

Seven habitual failures of law firm managers

1. Inconsistent standards.
2. Short-term thinking.
3. Failure to follow through.
4. Weak communications.
5. Poor prioritisation.
6. Controlling behaviour.
7. Ineffective decision-making.

When you look at the governance and leadership record in many law firms, you do not have to look very hard or long to see that backbench partners are probably right to be sceptical of management or to distrust their leaders. What we see in many firms on the part of their leaders is a management shambles exemplified by seven habitual management behaviours which – even when briefly suppressed under new management – tend to resurface under stress and can become chronic. These 'default' behaviours can be described as belonging to one of seven categories:

1. **Inconsistent standards.** Standards are agreed and set, but are not applied by partners in management positions for several reasons. First, a degree of favouritism is often shown to cronies and power partners, particularly partners who are responsible for a large book of business. Second, many managing partners prefer to avoid confrontation where they can. Third, the standards are vague and leave much room for debate and varying interpretations. Managing partners can easily find themselves undermined by the unpleasant behaviour of one or just a few partners who are hugely powerful figures in the firm. Such prima donnas amongst partners are often poor managers of people, poor communicators and unreliable and unsupportive on internal projects. It is difficult for any partner to have the courage to stand up and confront disruptive but powerful partners, unless they enjoy active support for a showdown from the senior tier of partners within the firm. The point is that if you fail to enforce the rules against even the most powerful and senior of partners, it becomes consistently more difficult to enforce them against anyone else.
2. **Short-term thinking.** This is usually exemplified by a focus on fees and hours and practically nothing else. Many firms appear to be focused on short-term profit to the detriment of long-term investment. Additionally, we live in an instant world, where emails appear to demand instant response, where short-term crises (partner and client defections, cash flow problems, and bickering within the partnership) seem to happen with increasing frequency and demand fire-fighting attention. In the face of this, it is somewhat hard for the law firm leader to rise above the tide of the short-term, urgent issues to deal with the long-term, important priorities.
3. **Failure to follow through.** We have lost count of the number of incomplete management projects and failed initiatives which we have seen in law firms. The problem is that if partners see a history of half-finished undertakings, they will quickly become cynical about the next project and any form of change becomes more difficult.

4. **Weak communications.** Managers so often fail to communicate adequately, consistently or even at all. The preference of some managing partners is to communicate by email, if at all.
5. **Poor prioritisation.** In addition to the problems of short-term fire-fighting, we find managing partners often get bogged down in trivial administration and miss out on the important task of interacting with their people. Such managing partners probably manage a few minutes a month on long-term planning. Practice area heads are often as bad: by spending a disproportionately large amount of time on client work, they succeed in losing precious management nurturing and further devaluation of the management currency.
6. **Controlling behaviour.** Open and empowering management is not easy, but there are some law firm leaders who only seem to be able to manage by the imposition of heavy controls. Thankfully, complete control freaks rarely last long in law firms, but I see much evidence of unnecessarily controlling and directive behaviours amongst law firm leaders.
7. **Ineffective decision-making.** Getting a decision made in some law firms is a tortuous and slow business. It is not unusual to see a leadership group suffering paralysis by analysis or – at the other extreme – making a kneejerk reaction with hasty and ill-considered decisions in a misguided attempt to appear decisive.

In the face of all this, it is not surprising that backbench partners can be bloody-minded, grudging, untrusting and sceptical about the way in which a sorry mixture of poorly structured partnership governance, badly drafted partnership agreements or rules, and pathetic leadership skills is letting them down. In short, I blame the leaders, not the followers, for the lamentable management morass into which many law firms have fallen. Conversely, there are a few firms around the globe led by a leadership group which enjoys a great deal of trust and in whom the partners repose the utmost confidence. These firms achieved their leadership model not by luck but by getting their leadership recipe right.

The kneejerk reaction of many firms in a management mess is to appoint a new leadership group or a new managing partner, often without much thought for the underlying governance and structural issues within the firm, or the malaise and general partner cynicism into which the firm may have lapsed as a result of previously poor management and leadership. Nevertheless, a new appointment and a set of fresh faces may work well for a short period, while the new leadership group addresses all the short-term problems which the firm is facing. We have, however, noticed that many managing partners feel that they have been appointed with a specific mandate – to sort out profitability issues or underperforming teams, for example. Such managing partners then get down to their initial responsibilities with enthusiasm, and the freshness of their appointment often gives a honeymoon period which enables some early successes to be achieved. There are then typically three problems. First, the early, short-term issues usually demand capable administrative skills rather than advanced leadership capabilities. Getting out of the administration rut to become a true leader is somewhat difficult. The short-term game plan can inexorably become the long-term management recipe. This state often coincides with the end of the managing partner's first term. The easy problems have by then usually been addressed, but the underlying and more intractable issues remain. So, the issue for any managing partner to face towards the end of his or her first term is to recognise that the skills and attributes which led to his or her initial appointment (and which have enabled early successes to be achieved) are not necessarily the right skills and attributes to lead to success in the second term.

The second of the three problems faced at the end of the honeymoon period is that the underlying infrastructure often does not exist for the firm to be run properly, as a well-coordinated business offering a 'one-firm' consistent approach to its clients. What then happens is that some or all of the underlying leadership and infrastructure issues, which may have become latent during the new leadership's honeymoon period, become blatant at the end of that period.

The third problem faced at the end of the honeymoon period is that, being confronted with more difficult and intractable issues, the dormant management behaviours – 'the way management is usually done round here' – can again become the 'default' standards and the vicious management cycle starts all over again.

The governance, leadership and management challenges

At the risk of repetition, we are witnessing right across the globe a trend towards firms that attempt to be well coordinated rather than just loose groups of individuals. Partners in more firms are beginning to work more closely in teams.

We have observed four essential elements which successful firms consider in order to provide the right environment for the long-term success of their firm and also to provide the right foundations for their leaders to prosper. Somewhat magically, addressing these four issues becomes a virtuous cycle. To achieve success, the leadership group must move out of its administrative comfort zone by exercising leadership skills. Correspondingly, by introducing new ground rules, the exercise of leadership skills becomes easier for the purposes of running the firm in a more businesslike manner.

> **BOX 11.2**
>
> ## Four essential requirements for running the firm as a business
>
> 1. Clarity of rules.
> 2. Coalition of leaders and managers.
> 3. Collegiality not control.
> 4. Consistency.

The first step is to clarify the rules of engagement for partners. It is well worth persevering with efforts to agree some essential and clear disciplines and accountabilities. Real agreement, with head and heart, is needed for a shared vision and agreed values. This requires a healthy debate in the firm with a view to agreeing and introducing the right level of management intervention in partner activities. The discussions should focus on what is needed to ratchet up partner ambition and performance. But the leadership of the firm should be extremely careful not to introduce disciplines and rules unless they are committed to carrying them through without fear or favour. What is more, the agreed rules should be clear and unambiguous. It is, for example, much easier for a policeman to enforce a 30 mile an hour speed limit, than to try to enforce a law to drive carefully. Equally, a rule that requires team meetings once a month or staff appraisals twice a year is much easier to monitor and enforce than a general requirement to treat staff fairly.

Second, the leaders of the firm should achieve unanimity about both the enactment and the enforcement of partnership disciplines. There should be a coalition of cohesiveness between senior partner or chairperson and the managing partner which should also extend to the rest of the board or management committee.

Third, it ought to be clear from the start that the leaders will exercise their power and authority in a spirit of collegiality rather than as control freaks. Here, there are two extremes of fears and concerns to be addressed amongst the backbench partners. One extreme is the issue of trust – it is important at the rule-setting phase to ensure that all the partners are satisfied that the rules will be enforced fairly, as otherwise they are unlikely to ratify them. At the other extreme is the issue of inertia and apathy. Many partners will feel safe in voting for something in the perhaps mistaken belief that what they are voting for is a transient whim on the part of the management which they may indulge at the voting stage for a quiet life, but which will never in fact be enforced. A balance is not easy to strike here. The leaders must work hard to gain credibility. They should also, wherever possible, take time to speak to all the partners on an individual basis, both to discover their fears and anxieties and to persuade them that it is safe to agree to what is suggested. In other words, the leaders should display leadership skills at the rule-setting stage as well as the enforcement phase.

The fourth element is the issue of consistency, which clients complain is so often lacking in law firms. Traditionally, lawyers often practised more as individuals than as part of a team. Although things have changed, some of these historical patterns remain. Junior lawyers are still faced with the mystery of adapting to very different working methods and practices employed by partners in the same practice area. Different practice areas sometimes now operate under independent rules and systems, with even some of the basics, such as document house styles and storage, operating diversely. Clients still complain of patchy service and dissimilar operating methodologies, systems and quality standards between offices and departments of the same firm. The achievement of a one-firm, consistent approach is in itself a huge project not least because partners are resistant to change, particularly when changes are demanded of them in their day-to-day working practices.

The need for better organised management structures in a changing world

Traditionally, many law firms have come from a background of independent sole practitioners operating under a single name or under one office roof. Within this model, each lawyer practises in his or her own way for his or her own clients using systems, processes, templates and documents which have been well tried and tested by the lawyer over the years. As we will see later, this model is changing fast and as it transforms, many firms are struggling with the issue of partner independence versus organisational efficiency, as well as the challenge of working out the optimal governance for capable, efficient and progressive management. Sveiby and Lloyd (1987, pp. 62–3) describe the four categories of personnel in know-how companies. The professionals are the lawyers who form the firm's source of revenue and the lawyers are supported by the clerical staff. There is then a managerial category whose members lack legal skills and lawyerly know-how but who are strong on management skills and administering and managing the business. The leader is seen as the prime mover combining both professional and managerial skills. As they note: 'The balance between professionalism and leadership is crucial. Since the professionals are the core of the company, leaders need their full support to be effective.' This balance of professional, support, management and leadership skills will be necessary in every firm – whether a traditional law firm or an ABS.

The role of the modern firm has changed from the 'chambers' model to one where the firm aims to provide the necessary structure for highly talented individuals to collaborate in a way that makes the best use of their talent and the existing market opportunities. The lawyers have to be formally managed in a way that allows them to develop their core know-how but only in line with the strategic objectives of the firm.

Small firms often seem to survive without much by the way of governance or organisation, but as they grow they tend to find that further systems and processes are necessary. Firms in a heavy growth phase tend to be organised around people rather than tasks and policies. They usually focus on what people must not do rather than what they should do. The firm, in short, is driven by its opportunities and people are assigned tasks by virtue of their availability rather than necessarily by their competence. Full freedom is given to individuals to develop their skills irrespective of their value to the firm. The lawyers with the highest billing rates hold too much power but are often reluctant to take on too many management tasks because it keeps them away from their clients.

For many firms stagnation can then ensue. The ruling coalition of partners only wants the firm to make the decisions that those partners would have made themselves. Such partners strangle or stifle continued growth by their insistence upon involvement at every stage. In some firms where there has been a heavy influence of a founder partner, paralysis can occur when the founder leaves the scene even temporarily. The recognition that some systems and processes are necessary comes to many firms at a stage of their growth when they realise that tightly controlled, centralised decision-making by a single partner or all the partners no longer works.

What we often see at that point is some controlled decentralisation of authority and decision-making from those partners to committees and boards. We also tend to witness changes in leadership and the advent of professional management.

However, this leaves few partners and managers in the firm who have the skills, experience or aptitude to become capable professional managers. No governance structure can entirely prevent problems caused by weak and ineffectual management, the general muddle which accompanies management vacuums, or long-term disasters caused by petty tyrants. However, a coherent and balanced management structure clearly helps. This is particularly true of a governance structure which is aligned to the strategic and business needs of the firm and which contains the appropriate provisions for mature and sensible accountability. There is, of course, no shrink-wrapped governance solution which will suit every firm at every stage in its development. It is, however, important to understand both the reasons for governance difficulties and also the principles which can assist firms to discover sensible recipes to suit their particular circumstances. This chapter provides a framework for firms to consider when thinking about their governance. It explains the transition points at or around which firms may need to consider changing their structural model, and looks at some of the typical problem areas encountered as firms grow. The chapter also outlines a typical structure for professional partnerships with 50 to 75 partners or more and in excess of 200 professionals – what might be described as medium sized firms.

Understanding the fault lines in the firm's structure

The problem is typically historical. In many cases the management arrangements, which may have suited the partnership in the past, have just ceased to function adequately as the firm has moved on. As firms grow, it is no longer practicable to involve every partner in every decision. Equally, it becomes difficult for the managing partner in a fast growing firm to consult with all partners or even connect with them in a meaningful way. At the same time, growing firms have usually not yet developed a sensible hierarchy of accountability. Combined with an absence of role definition at the level of department or divisional head, this can lead general partners to feel disenfranchised and uninvolved in major decision-making, and – even worse – to become disengaged from the strategic planning and business direction of the firm. One example is the annual budget. Tablets of stone delivered from a mountain top do not seem to work well in partnerships. A budget which is prepared and delivered top down to uninvolved partners does little to engage and motivate partners to stretch for an uncomfortable target. What happens usually is that subversion and inertia take over. Partners simply ignore the loftily delivered edicts and the firm's financial performance meanders or deteriorates.

The problem then is that firms, unless well advised, can often tend to lurch from a previously extreme consensus model of governance to an equally extreme autocratic model, spurred on by calls for 'strong management'. In the extreme version of the autocratic model, consultation and partner involvement disappear out of the window and partners find themselves bullied into meeting performance targets. Consensus freaks get replaced by control freaks.

There is also no greater example of management muddle than the tangle in which many firms find themselves over management elections. Typical examples of weird election provisions include:

- partners in a department or practice area having the entrenched right to vote for their practice area head who then automatically has a seat on the management board or executive committee;
- the partnership as a whole voting for board members who then divide up the jobs of managing partner and departmental heads between them;
- in one firm, it is reported that the managing partner is elected by a board of advisers. The board of advisers is appointed by the managing partner;

- in another law firm, the partners in each practice group elect the practice group leaders. If partners are in more than one practice group, they get half a vote for each group they are in (a partner in three groups gets one and a half votes whereas a partner in one group gets one vote). The chairman of the corporate department is by definition chairman of the firm and the chairman of the litigation department is by definition the managing partner. If the chairman or managing partner retires or resigns, an election is called and all practice group chairs stand for election.

Such bizarre practices may be designed to act as a check and balance on management, but tend to produce governance systems which are inflexible and slow to change and in which partners gain election success through politics rather than management competence. Equally, peculiar voting processes will not hold much appeal for external investors. The structure should support methods of selection which give the best chance of appointing the best managers rather than those who are most senior, the most popular or the most politically savvy.

Recognising the transition points

It is critical to recognise, as early as possible, the growing need for a change in governance structure, and to anticipate the transition points at which the previous arrangements for managing and governing the affairs of the firm can become ineffective. I have noticed some typical transition points in the growth of many partnerships (see Box 11.3). Just as milk can go sour seemingly within minutes, the transition point from effectiveness to ineffectiveness can happen within a very short time.

BOX 11.3

Typical transition triggers for changes in governance

- Size.
- Mergers.
- Changing to become an ASB.
- Significant changes in leadership group.
- Sudden change in profitability.
- Onset of crisis.
- Increase in numbers of offices.

One such transition point occurs when a firm reaches about 20 partners. Until that point a large measure of informality can be seen in many partnership arrangements including partnership reward systems. Often, of course, such smaller firms are heavily influenced or led by a strong or idiosyncratic founder – or set of founding partners – and can falter quite markedly in the classic founders' trap if the firm fails to appreciate the need for change as it develops. At around the 20-partner point, however, informality of management tends to stop working and needs to be replaced with something a bit more formal. Partners usually have a growing appreciation that not every decision can made in partners' meetings and become ready to embrace a structure in which decision-making is filtered and refined, provided that they continue to be consulted by someone they know and trust and that consensus is somehow achieved on most decisions. In this phase, a simple management structure is usually enough. Accordingly, many firms will simply have a management committee presided over by the managing partner and reporting to the partnership on a regular basis.

The next stage of development is trickier. There is a governance transition point when the small to medium size firm becomes too large for management by consensus. Although this point is reached by firms at varying sizes, this transition point often (but not always) occurs when the firm reaches between 50 and 75 partners and more than 200 professionals. But there are two problems. First, change in size of itself may not always bring about the need for change and is not the only transition trigger. The need for revisions to the governance structure can also be brought about by mergers, significant changes in the leadership group, sudden changes in profitability, the onset of a crisis of some sort, and even an increase in the number of offices or jurisdictions. In addition, a change of structure to an ABS (even if dominated by lawyers) will give rise to the need to conduct a governance review.

The second problem is that some firms continue with their existing management structures long after changes ought to have been made. After all, the development of appropriate governance arrangements (particularly in medium sized professional services firms) tends to lag way behind the development of the firm's strategy and growth, and varies somewhat according to how democratic or autocratic the firm has previously been. In many firms partners, accustomed to consultation and even control in the context of a small firm, are reluctant to cede their authority as the firm changes. This means that many firms carry on growing far beyond the normal transition point without any change in structure; the growing pains become more acute as they struggle to continue to accommodate extreme consensus (or indeed extreme autocracy). Accordingly, the trick is for the leadership team to look ahead for anticipated transition points and to be aware of what triggers those transition points. The team can then take steps to work out what governance structure is needed and work on the partnership to educate the partners and begin to soften them up for the unpleasant reality that the firm needs to make changes which are likely to lead to the twin displeasures of decreased autonomy on the one hand and increased accountability on the other.

The purpose of governance

Whether you are a partner, a client, a lender (or even an investor), there are certain things which all parties want to see in a vibrant and progressive professional services firm. They want to see a well-coordinated firm rather than just a loose group of individuals. Clients are also interested in a firm's governance structure which might, on the face of it, seem odd. Their main interest, however, is in the ability of the firm to manage and deliver a consistent and ordered service. As noted previously (p. 14), all external parties want to see a 'one-firm' approach.

The governance structure can assist with all of these desirable features. The ten propositions set out in Box 11.4 highlight the areas where a properly constructed governance and management structure can help support the overall objectives of the firm. One such aim of any governance structure is to achieve alignment with the formulation and implementation of strategy. This balance between strategy and structure takes two main forms. First, it is critically important to ensure that the way the firm internally operates and manages itself matches the way the firm operates externally, both currently and in the future. If the firm's objectives include

---

BOX 11.4

The purpose of governance – ten principles

1. Strategy creation for committed, competitive and profitable businesses.
2. Alignment of internal operations with external service.
3. Cash control and financial overview.
4. Progressive, coordinated and consistent working practices.
5. Flexible and efficient decision-making.
6. Architecture of business units.
7. Formulation of plans for business units to match overall firm strategy.
8. Clarity of rules and accountabilities.
9. Provision of resources.
10. Risk management, regulatory compliance and succession planning.

growth objectives, for instance, the firm needs to be sure that the governance structure will be fit for the purpose as the firm grows. It is not always possible to get this adjustment right. The point, however, remains that partners' meetings can fairly quickly become too large for sensible decision-making, and management committees can also become too big or too unrepresentative. The same is true of the issues which are often described as 'reserved matters'. These comprise areas of decision-making which have to be put to the vote of the general partnership, rather than being delegated to the managing partner or some board or committee with executive authority. These reserved matters usually shrink to a few important issues over time and it is vital that they should be kept as minimal as possible. I have, for example, seen in some partnership agreements provisions that prohibit the spending of more than a fairly small amount of money without the partnership's approval – and usually that financial limit has not changed for many years. Ultimately, there are only a few key decisions over which partners as shareholders should retain a vote. These are all in the area of major changes – changes to the firm's constitution or entity status, mergers and acquisitions, major changes in policy or strategic direction and major changes in capital or debt structure. In practice, whilst many partnerships reserve the right to vote on new partners, the admission of new partners can quickly become a nominal ratification process.

The second balancing act between strategy and structure concerns the creation of the firm's ongoing strategy. It is clear is that getting the strategic choices correct for any firm is not an ivory tower exercise during which the managing partner and a few others closet themselves in great secrecy before unveiling a new strategy to their admiring partners. Rather it is often an emerging and evolving exercise which requires input at all levels. Nevertheless, there is a top level need for a selective group of partners to filter ideas, analyse situations and issues, and generally oversee the whole process of strategy formulation. The task here is to conduct a bench test of the emerging plan for clarity and reality and to ensure communication. In the smaller firms, partners can be highly involved in this process, but as the firm grows, the business needs to find the right formula and structure to enable this overseer task to be done effectively.

Another main aim of any governance structure is to ensure overall coordination and firm cohesiveness. The brutal truth is that many firms completely fail to achieve any sense of assimilation. A multitude of firms remain loose associations of solo practitioners even as they grow. Some firms achieve cohesiveness at office or practice area level, but do not transfer that cohesiveness to the whole firm – and a silo culture is spawned. Other firms seem to enter a phase where the top level management becomes remote and aloof – uninvolved and disconnected from the areas of fee generation. One managing partner was fairly recently described to me as 'never seen round the offices, managing by diktat and email'.

In another firm, the management committee was made up of the managing partner and senior professional managers in charge of the support function – with no representation at practice group level.

The trend towards corporate structures – governance of an ABS

In the face of law sector consolidation and deregulation, the increasing trend towards a more corporate style of governance seems inevitable. The imperatives for this trend are clear. Firms need to drive business performance, and the overriding priorities of the management structures of the firm must be directed towards this imperative as well as strategy implementation. At the same time, the role of the managing partner or chief executive officer (CEO) is becoming much more 'executive' – with greater authority and less need to obtain endless consensus. The authority of the management boards and bodies is also increasing, as the interests of partners as shareholders steadily become separated from the management and operational decisions of the organisation. In some progressive firms, we are seeing the introduction of external, non-executive directors at board level, whilst line management is being strengthened with beefed-up-roles – and accountabilities – for group and divisional heads.

These trends will become stronger as the new era of the LSA takes effect, not just because of the regulatory requirements imposed by the new regime but because of the need both for traditional law firms and ABSs to reconsider their governance models.

Regulatory compliance is only one of the governance principles set out in Box 11.4, but the LSA does contains some governance and management provisions – that an ABS appoints a head of legal practice (HOLP) and a head of finance and administration (HOFA). This separation of the professional know-how and the managerial know-how is thought not only to provide a good check and balance but also to make it easy both to identify and perform the roles.

Clearly, there is no one-size-fits-all governance structure for any firm. However, medium size, traditional law firms should consider making a clear distinction between the interests of partners as proprietors on the one hand and those of the firm as a business on the other. There are many ways of achieving this; one is by changing the structure to a three-layered model as illustrated in Figure 11.1. The three layers in this model would be the partnership board (mainly oriented towards the partners as owners), the executive board (mainly oriented towards the firm as a business – the managerial know-how) and the divisions, practice areas or groups (mainly oriented towards the delivery of client services – the professional know-how).

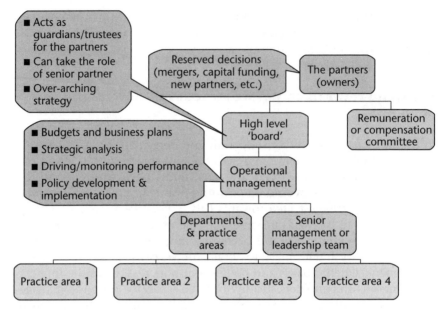

Figure 11.1   Typical governance model for medium sized firms

The partnership board or council

This elected body would in effect act as the guardian or trustee for the partners. It would consist of the senior partner or chairman, the managing partner or CEO, and a number of directly elected members which might include representation from fixed share or salaried partners. Among its duties would be to undertake an overseer role for the firm's over-arching strategy and, in most cases, strategy formulation would start in this forum. It could, absent a separate compensation or remuneration committee, be responsible for partner remuneration and discipline. The partnership board or council should also be responsible for the principles behind all the big decisions which are likely to affect the partners in their capacity of owners. Its responsibilities should include recommendations to the partners on all reserved matters – matters such as the opening and closing of offices, mergers, and partner promotions. One concern of any partnership is that there should be some checks and balances, hence some of the bizarre election processes referred to earlier in this chapter. It would therefore be a primary purpose of the board or council to act as the firm's moderating and monitoring control on the operations of the executive board and the leadership team.

The executive board

This board would typically comprise the managing partner or CEO, and the senior management team (comprising the chief operations officer (COO) – if there is one – and the heads of professional functions such as finance, HR, and marketing). This group is often known as the 'C-suite'. For many medium sized firms these people make up the leadership team. Additionally, a small selection of partners (who would usually be the group or divisional heads) should be members of the board, together with a non-executive external board member in some cases. The executive board's responsibilities would include the formulation and implementation of annual budgets and business plans. This board would have a big role in the context of the development of strategy and the detailed analysis which accompanies strategic planning. This work would be done in conjunction with the partnership council or under its overseeing eye. Strategy formulation and strategic positioning for some firms may be straightforward in concept terms but strategy implementation is never easy – the executive board has important executive duties here. Other responsibilities would include:

- driving and monitoring economic and business performance, including the performance, both financial and operational, of each practice group and team, and the improvement of profitability;
- the development and implementation of policies for the improvement of the firm's intellectual capital, including risk management, quality, client care, human resources, IT and marketing.

It may be controversial for some firms, but we believe that the partners with principal executive responsibility – those who will have a seat on the executive board – should be selected by the managing partner who needs to be free to choose and balance his or her management team. In many firms, there is a trend for the managing partner to be selected by a selection committee rather than by a direct election.

The divisions, practice areas, and departments

There are many operations within a professional services firm that can only be done at a practitioner level. These are familiar to most firms and will not change much as the governance structure develops. The main responsibilities at this level include the apportionment of work between partners and teams and the setting of team/individual targets within the context of the overall budget and business plan. Consistent services must be delivered and knowledge management, workflows and precedents have to be developed. The division or practice area also needs to be accountable to the managing partner, and ultimately the partnership, for its performance, its quality of work and the development of expertise.

Although such responsibilities may be familiar, what is often missing on a day-to-day basis is appropriate implementation. Governance structures can only supply a framework in which accountability can happen, follow-up occur, and the principles of active management be adhered to.

The managing partner, chair and 'C-suite' of executive officers: agreeing and clarifying management roles

Law firms have historically underinvested in their management teams, and as a result have been undermanaged. For many firms, there traditionally may have been a managing partner, who may also have been assisted by a variety of other partners – typically a finance partner, a marketing partner, a staff partner and an IT partner. There may also have been a senior partner or chair.

Some firms have preferred to appoint either a practice manager or, in the case of larger firms, an array of professional managers. Hence, there has been the steady development in law firms of the so-called C-suite – chief executive officer (CEO), chief operations officer (COO), chief finance officer (CFO), chief marketing officer (CMO), chief information officer (CIO) and chief human resources officer (CHRO). As we will see later, a new role of chief legal services officer (CLSO) may also emerge because of the requirements of the LSA.

In all cases, law firm partners have been quick to question the cost or benefit of external appointments, and somewhat slow to adapt to an era of professional management. The cost of internal partner appointments to key management positions can seem a viable and cheaper alternative, but the hidden costs can make even a partial diversion from fee-earning an expensive luxury. Against all this, the advantages of internal appointments to key management positions have to be weighed. The risk to the business in appointing unknown outsiders is, after all, considerable. Unlike an internal appointee, any external appointee will need to take time to understand the partnership culture and behavioural characteristics. He or she will have to gain intimate knowledge of the dynamics of the business, its history, and its strengths and weaknesses. Whilst external appointees can bring the considerable advantages of objectivity, lateral thinking and advanced management competences, they will have to earn the respect of the partnership, particularly after the honeymoon period is over. In contrast, and from day one, partners in management positions will understand intimately the dynamics and politics of the partnership, and will have detailed industry, market-place and competitor knowledge. Such partners will also know the firm's strengths and the opportunities to be exploited, as well as being acutely aware of the firm's weaknesses and the threats and challenges which need to be addressed.

Clearly an affordability balance has to be achieved. Whilst only the very largest firms can afford a full team of professional managers, even the smallest firms are finding great benefits can be achieved and huge value can be added by the appointment of a practice manager, operations director or finance manager. Such firms have proved that the expense of these appointments is more than made up for by a combination of added value by the appointee and extra fee-earning capability for partners who are able to divert more time to client work.

Any commercial organisation needs to have complete clarity over its leadership roles and it is easier to see clear lines of accountability in a corporate environment than in a professional services firm partnership structure. In the law firm context, it is particularly important to understand where the real power lies in any firm and to harness it – the power to direct or materially affect the strategic direction of the firm, to gain the firm's commitment to that direction and to ensure that it is executed. In addition, those who hold the real power in any firm are almost always the ones with the highest level of credibility. As the law firm governance model has developed, the leadership roles have become clearer.

Thomas Delong, John Gabarro and Robert Lees (2007) in their review of professional firm leadership emphasise four sets of vital leadership activities – setting direction, gaining commitment to direction, execution, and setting an example – and place them in what they describe as an 'integrated leadership model'. Tony Angel, former managing partner of Linklaters, stresses also the importance of providing the infrastructure and support that enables the firm to achieve its goals and objectives (see Empson, 2007). Chapter 12 highlights what I consider to be the three main leadership challenges for law firms – creating vision and direction, building trust, and realising the potential in the firm.

As roles become clearer and better defined, there is also a risk of the overall leadership responsibilities becoming confused by role ambiguities and lack of boundary identification unless a coherent and integrated governance model is adopted. The LSA model, for example, envisages the top leadership roles being split between the head of legal practice and the head of finance and administration. The former might be a managing partner or could be a chief legal services officer (CLSO) under a 'C-suite' structure, with the role of the HOFA being taken by the CFO. Under the regulatory requirement for an ABS, the HOLP should be the 'leader' of the professional part of the firm, with the HOFA being responsible for the environment and infrastructure. The HOLP will be the channel of intellect and has to win the trust and respect of the lawyers, by being in touch with the development of the core know-how and maintaining its quality. The HOLP must also be able to use the informal network that exists in all firms. As such, he or she should be a mentor and tutor for the firm's professionals and will have an important monitoring role. For these reasons he or she most likely has to be a lawyer by training. By removing many of the administrative functions from this role it should be more attractive to the professionals. The HOLP will develop ideas about the work environment to suit the delivery of the know-how to the firm's clients but hand over the delivery of that work environment to the HOFA.

The HOFA should be responsible for providing the work environment, and has the difficult task of driving through the one-firm approach and providing the infrastructure and mechanisms to make it happen.

Whilst it is clear that neither the HOLP nor the HOFA can work without one other, we think there is a danger of the left hand of the law firm not knowing what the right hand is doing unless properly coordinated and accountable to an overall leader or leadership group, although there is no particular reason[1] why the HOLP role should not be taken by the managing partner, leaving the HOFA role to be taken by the COO or CFO. Indeed, the model suggested by Sveiby and Lloyd (1987) for know-how businesses would suggest that the top leader of a law firm should have an appropriate combination of legal and leadership skills. The balance of power between the two roles of HOLP and HOFA will also shift depending on the incumbents and stage of tenure. The strategy and overall direction of the firm may also help to determine the exact role definitions. Thus, for example, in a firm that adopts a strategy of volume business as a bulk provider, the role of the HOFA will increase in power in order to provide an infrastructure, work environment and systems to deliver standard service at low cost. The HOLP will reduce in power as the core know-how will become narrow and relatively static and the balance of employees will shift to lower grade and non-legal employees.

The two key leadership roles which firms therefore need to consider are, first, the role of the senior partner or chair and, second, that of the managing partner or CEO and these roles will vary a bit from firm to firm.

Senior partner or chair

In most publicly traded corporations in the USA, the chair of the board of directors is usually also the CEO, whereas in Europe, the chair is not an executive officer at all but is usually an externally appointed, non-executive overseer (see Finkelstein, Hambrick and Cannella, 2009). The role of the senior partner in a traditional law firm also varies – occasionally externally appointed and often a non-executive, ambassadorial role.

In some firms, the role of this senior person is, jointly with the managing partner, to set and lead the firm's vision, strategy and direction, although there is a tendency in other firms to leave matters of strategy to be driven by the managing partner. What is often found, however, is that the senior partner is responsible for inter-partner relationships, the chairing of partners' meetings and for acting as a link and a moderating influence between the executive teams and the professionals. The senior partner or chair should also have an oversight role over the executive teams to ensure that those who are responsible for operational management are both operating within their terms of reference and taking care of the overall health of the partnership. There is also a further useful role for a senior partner – in addition to the figurehead and external ambassadorial role – which is to assume the role of protector of the firm's values and culture.

Managing partner or CEO

The main responsibility of the managing partner or CEO is for the effective management of the firm, the implementation of the firm's strategy and, in particular, executive responsibility for the economic and operational performance of the firm. For this purpose, the managing partner or CEO should be afforded a wide range of executive powers to enable him or her to lead, manage and remain in overall control of the firm on an executive operational basis and to deliver the objectives of the firm. This will include powers to manage and remain in overall control of such matters as:

- the management of the firm (and each office) within it on an operational basis;
- the execution of the firm's management policy as determined by the management board, management committee or the partnership;
- the provision of comprehensive and efficient support, administrative, facility and accountancy services;
- the performance management systems necessary to ensure that the partners and fee-earners are effective in the delivery of the firm's services to its clients and do so profitably;
- the leadership and line management responsibility for the firm's senior management team in developing, for approval by the partners at appropriate times, the firm's business and operational plan, including budgets, so as to achieve maximum profitability.

The senior management team – the 'C-suite'

The need for professional management within the legal profession is growing all the time. Banks, incoming partners and clients all take comfort from knowing that the firm has a well-organised and highly professional senior management team. Moreover, any external investor in a law firm will demand a high degree of board-level expertise. The composition and degree of expertise and experience of the professional members of the senior management team are clearly contextual and will differ widely from firm to firm, and from ABS model to ABS model (ABS models are identified in Chapter 6). The functional heterogeneity which is necessary to provide specialist skills across a variety of management disciplines can supply innovation by giving a wider set of perspectives and information sources, but can also give rise to conflict and dissensus. Careful team composition, identification of boundaries and consideration of interactive processes are all important here.

It has often been noted that members of the senior management teams in law firms generally have a tough time in getting partners to accept their decisions. It is usually not long before they find that the partners are not prepared to give them very much respect or authority: they may be allowed to manage subordinates, but the partners often consider themselves above the law and beyond the rules.

Against this sort of background, it is hardly surprising that management careers in law firms, and for that matter the job of managing partner, have traditionally been seen as a dead end. For these appointments to work, therefore, certain conditions must apply. First, the roles and jobs must be valued, not just by lip service but also by a supportive and enabling environment. Second, the partnership must be prepared to put its money where its mouth is and invest in appropriate development and training. Third, those who manage the practice must be allowed to manage, with the ability and facility to enforce decisions within an agreed framework.

Partner adaptation as the governance structure develops

In order to achieve the objectives of any new governance structure, partners need to recognise that the changes will not just be theoretical but that the whole mode of operation will alter. Whilst there will, of course, be consultation, there will no longer be consensus on many areas of decision-making. The leadership team must be allowed to get on and make decisions which would then be reported to the partnership. Additionally, those board members who are partners will not just be representing their office or division but will need to understand that their role will be executive and decisive. They will be part of a leadership team which is responsible for driving the firm forward. We come across many firms where the partners who are members of either of the main boards continue to regard attendance as both optional and secondary to their client work. For any vibrant business, meetings just have to take precedence over client work and should be run on a tighter, corporate-type model with properly prepared papers and focused discussion, and a minimum of 'house-keeping' and circular discussion.

Partners do not always respond well to such changes in management structures. At times, they will protest vocally, but often their protests are seen silently in undermining, backsliding, and even subversion. Partners may simply ignore edicts which they dislike and, if they get away with it once, will try the same trick again. At one firm, many major decisions of the board until quite recently were invariably reversed as a result of partner protests. Other decisions were frequently made by the board as a result of political pressure rather than business need.

Before making any changes, the firm leaders need to achieve three things. First, they must communicate a compelling view of the horizon which they visualise for the firm, and the structure which needs to be in place to enable the firm to move successfully towards that vision. Second, they need to anticipate the likely obstacles to sensible and disciplined governance at an emotional level within the partnership, bearing in mind the loss of influence which many partners will feel that a new structure will entail. Third, they must work to build up trust and confidence amongst partners. This is why it is important for partners to discuss structural issues openly and maturely, recognising that if the firm is to progress, the implementation of strong but sensible management needs to be accompanied by responsible and accountable partner behaviour.

It is often correctly said that structure should follow strategy, but in our view it should not lag far behind. As firms consolidate and grow, there is a constant need to keep a watchful eye on the management and decision-making processes in any firm, and the likely transition points when changes need to be made. The design of the changed structure is critical – it needs to be fit for current and future purposes – but how those modifications are proposed and steered through the partnership requires a deft touch.

Endnote

1 Unless detailed regulations (as yet to be introduced) forbid this.

12

Summary and prospects – the imperative for action and implementation

KEY POINTS

- Four predictions
- How to take advantage of this book
- Summary

Four predictions

I make four predictions for the future of law firms.

Prediction 1 – the law firm market will see further and possibly dramatic consolidation

As I have noted throughout this book, and particularly in Chapter 8, all industry sectors consolidate over time, and the legal sector will not form an exception to the rule. The LSA provides a further catalyst to what I see as an inexorable process. I expect to see the larger firms continuing to grow by acquisition and merger, and medium sized firms striving to reposition through merger and amalgamation to provide critical mass and deeper resources and capabilities over time. I expect to see smaller firms still finding it difficult to recruit and retain the best people and the resulting lack of succession resilience will force them to link up with other firms. Additionally, we will witness smaller law firms struggling to maintain both their existing market shares and their established client bases and becoming marginalised. Smaller firms will also find their lack of critical mass hurting them in other ways. The increasing cost of professional indemnity cover will force some sole practitioners into subsuming themselves into larger firms. The advent of the LSB will, in my view, increase both the cost and the general burden of regulatory compliance. The steady contraction of publicly funded work will continue to erode much of the work which is open to high street firms, and increasing commoditisation and competition will make small offices unviable. I do not expect to see as many law firms in ten years' time as there are now, and a 25 per cent reduction in the number of firms in the UK is highly possible over the next five to ten years.

Prediction 2 – law firm flotation will not define the market

It is clear from the experience of other jurisdictions, notably Australia, that some law firms will undoubtedly float under one or other of the ABS models set out in Chapter 6. Both these firms, and others, will also use the avenues of finance set out in Chapters 7 and 8 to enable growth. However, I do not expect to see these flotations defining the market, except in the context of the bulk providers where the provision of low priced, heavily packaged work may well become dominated by a few, very large, publicly owned entities. If my prediction is correct, then I think many firms may breathe an entirely premature sigh of relief that the fear of publicly quoted juggernaut firms seems to have receded. However, I predict that it is not the floated firms which traditional law firms should necessarily fear but general market consolidation, pressures on margins and the growth of novel forms of competition that are more likely to form substantial threats.

Prediction 3 – pressure on margins will intensify

Over the last two decades or so, rates in most law firms practising commercial law have climbed exponentially. Law firms at the higher end of the positioning diamond have been able to improve and maintain their margins and levels of profitability by increasing their charge-out rates year by year. The same ability to increase price has not been experienced at the bottom of the diamond, where increasing consumer pressure and the existence of alternative providers has squeezed both rates and margins. I predict that client pressure on a global basis will cause rates actually to start to contract over the next decade and that this will, in turn, lead to a contraction in the larger firms' margins, placing some restraint on their growth. The exception to this may be the designer label firms which may find it easier to maintain their premium rates in areas of special demand. This increasing price sensitivity will lead to the emergence of new and improved pricing models, with firms using technology, systems and workflow streamlining to make improved profits on fixed price work. An additional pricing pressure may become apparent to global firms which operate a dual pricing model as between their expensive capital cities and homelands on the one hand, and their less expensive operations in parts of the world such as Asia and Africa on the other hand. It is, in my view, difficult to maintain a dual pricing model for the same type of work and it is entirely feasible that, as global clients experience the lower rates (but similar service) to be found in low cost offices of the same firm, they will resist paying the premium prices being demanded at the more expensive locations.

I also expect to see an intensification of outsourcing and offshoring of back and middle office work, as well as some types of legal work, both in anticipation of increasing fee sensitivity and to buttress margins by achieving lower overheads.

Prediction 4 – new forms and types of competition will change the game

I have highlighted throughout this book the likely game-changing business models and technological advances which present a huge threat to any law firm which fails to take account of the dangers ahead and to provide for them. Some of these changes are dealt with in Richard Susskind's book (Susskind, 2008) to which I have frequently referred. The use of the internet and the emergence of specialist entities will increase to take advantage of new ways for clients and lawyers to communicate through social, collaborative services, information sharing, webinars, podcasts, and video technologies. The different types of ABS which I identified in Chapter 6 provide both opportunities and huge threats as entrepreneurial companies muscle in on the traditional law firm domains. Many law firms have been seen as their locality's 'best kept secret' with excellent skills and experience and yet an inability to make their services widely known to potential clients. The new forms of competition will therefore have the opportunity of a twin-headed attack. Their superior ability to advertise and conduct marketing campaigns and their preparedness to invest will enable them to bring their services to market and 'outpunch' established but lower profile law firms. The second type of attack will come from their ability to change the way legal services are carried out – largely by means of technology, workflow management and the deployment of less qualified lawyers.

How to take advantage of this book

These threats are real and menacing. Many firms will not survive. As we have seen throughout this book, there are only a very few firms for whom an optimal strategy is to change little or nothing but rather to rely for future prosperity on existing strategies, an organically growing intellectual capital, well-organised sets of resources and capabilities and an established market position. For the vast majority of firms throughout the world, the future will undoubtedly entail fundamental change. Strategically directed change is far from easy in law firms. It requires the partners or owners to have a compelling vision of what they would like the firm to be. It requires a culture which embraces a shared commitment to life-long learning and new ways of doing things. It requires discipline and courage to work out what needs to be done and then to implement what has been agreed, and a degree of resilience to cope with difficulties, setbacks and uncertainty. It also demands that the owners or partners are unified as team players in driving the firm forward in accordance with some agreed values, and that they are prepared to make long-term investments in resources, capabilities and people. Finally, it calls upon learned professionals – adept in technical, analytical and linear skills and thinking – to move from left-brain activities to the right-brain attributes of creative, entrepreneurial and lateral thinking.

What law firms require above all is collective and responsible leadership and the ability of the firms' leaders to introduce and implement effective winning strategies.

Improving leadership in law firms

Partners in law firms dislike change and are difficult to lead. They may be content to transfer a great many management and administrative tasks to a management team, but there is a raft of sensitive subjects which remains close to partners' hearts. In these areas, they often consider intervention by professional managers to be unwarranted interference. Additionally, partners remain anxious to assert and protect their independence from further erosion as and when they can. The leadership roles of the managing and senior partner become critical in tackling sensitive, close-to-the-heart issues. Anything which threatens a partner's comfort zone or is likely to have real implications for him or her is likely to cause problems. The issue of partner remuneration is another such sensitive subject. Indeed, I cannot think of any thorny subjects about which partners consistently feel more strongly than how partnership profits are distributed.

Before tackling any leadership topic or challenge, it is important to prepare the ground thoroughly and there are at least three leadership challenges which have a significant impact on the direction and strategy of the firm. The first leadership issue is the visionary task – to find an agreed and common sense of purpose and direction for the firm. The second leadership issue is the issue of trust – the important challenge of building trust and reducing paranoia. The third leadership issue is to clarify the expectations of partners so that they spend time on and devote energy to their career, skills development and behaviours, thus working to improve their overall contribution to the firm.

Creating vision and direction

It is part of the leadership day job to establish the firm's overall strategic goals. In achieving the firm's overall objectives, it is also important to ensure that the systems and management processes within the firm support those goals. This can sometimes be difficult if the firm does not have a clear view of its overall direction and destination. Lawyers' eyes start to glaze over when the subject of vision is raised. It can seem like meaningless waffle. What is more, a lot of firms have found that having a 'vision' or a 'mission statement' means little and changes absolutely nothing. However, it is clearly vital for all partners to have a common understanding of the hopeful and attractive future and desirable state for the firm which they can all work towards – a sense of purpose which unites the partners.

As Mike Pedler, John Burgoyne and Tom Boydell (2004, p. 51) put it in their excellent book on leadership: 'A sense of purpose runs deeper than the popular notion of vision. It builds on the foundation of established values and thereby honours the past in looking to future aspirations. A key element in purpose is the sheer force of will, the determination and persistence without which visions are mere dreams.' Hence, the systems for partner progression, compensation and rewards, as well as partner performance management, become an essential part of the credibility and realisation of the firm's vision. In short, the firm's systems must be able to support, encourage, value and reward the commitment of partners to work towards the firm's vision. Visions are meaningless concepts unless they are linked to action. The firm's systems for partner performance management should become part of the foundation which helps to turn concepts into reality. The key visionary propositions are answers to questions like 'Where are we going? What do we most desire? What is our common dream?'. The key implementation action points then in turn need to be answers to questions such as 'How do we get there? What are our core competences and how can we improve them? What objectives and action points can we establish? How do our partners need to behave in order for us to succeed? How do we think that our partners should be held to account and managed?'.

There is another important point here which concerns change. As has often been said, there are really only two things which motivate change in law firm partners – fear and conviction. Partners will only modify their attitudes and behaviour if they really have no viable alternative or if there is something in it for them. Whilst it is no doubt possible to impose a partner performance system on a firm by an exercise of dictatorship or martial law, it is clearly better for the firm to reach a common view of what is best for the firm – and for the leaders to persuade and convince partners of this. There needs here to be clear dialogue within the firm, but not necessarily a mediocre compromise of views which can result from attempts to achieve consensus. Rather than wishy-washy compromise, what should be sought is an informed, sophisticated and educated structure affected and influenced by the inputs of the whole partnership.

Building trust and reducing paranoia

The dynamics of any people business are both complex and fragile. Law firms, more than most, can be hotbeds of insecurity, paranoia and mutual distrust. Part of the reason for this stems from the lawyers' training – analytical, suspicious, testy, sceptical and cautious.

Lawyers are used to evidence-based decision-making and shrink from conclusions which are based on balancing probabilities or result from subjective opinions or qualitative assessments. Whilst many partnership dealings can survive and even prosper on an arm's-length clinical and formal basis, issues such as partner progression, promotions, compensation and rewards are all areas where trust and good faith between partners need to be at a premium. As David Maister (2008, p. 229) points out: 'The ways of thinking and behaving that help lawyers excel in their profession may be the very things that limit what they can achieve as firms.'

Partners in law firms also love their independence and react against any measures which they perceive might jeopardise their autonomies. Maister goes on: 'Committees proliferate to address all topics, large and small. They are designed not only to ensure extensive participation, but also to put in place checks and balances intended to circumscribe the ability of any individual (or group) to decide anything on behalf of the firm.'

Management issues can seem somewhat easier at larger firms, where there is a greater acceptance of the need for formal decision-making processes and where the remoteness and perceived objectivity of a senior management team helps to imbue a sense of confidence. Problems can, however, exist in larger firms, where partners sometimes feel they have to walk a political tightrope and conform to corporate guidelines. I was disheartened, for instance, to talk quite recently to a partner at a major UK law firm who told me that he takes great care to keep all his communications and emails anodyne and inoffensive, to ensure that he is seen to be doing the right things and obeying the rules at all times. What is more, another partner at an international firm recently told me that he felt more and more like an employee and less and less like a partner as time went by.

It follows, therefore, that law firm leaders and all partners should contribute towards 'making the firm a better place', where people are valued and there is a true spirit of collegiality and shared identity. A firm with high mutual levels of trust can be both creative and effective. At the same time, the leaders must have the ability to take tough decisions early and to maintain levels of trust by acting as role models, by calm and rational decision-making and by transparency and integrity in their communications.

Realising the potential in the firm

When clarifying the overall strategy and direction of the firm, it is important to understand the potential of the partners to implement and realise the firm's strategic objectives. The research and analysis of the firm's intangible resources outlined in earlier chapters will help in this. It is, however, also vital to be clear about what the firm expects of its partners and what roles and responsibilities it needs them to undertake. Corporate goals drill down to individual goals. Partners equally need to be clear how they are to discharge their various roles as owners, managers and producers. The current trend away from the more revenue and formulaic systems of profit sharing and reward is no accident. Firms are increasingly responding to the growing realisation that such revenue-driven systems reward only a very restrictive set of behaviours and, at times, actually serve to penalise longer term entrepreneurial activities.

As we discussed in Chapter 11, law firms have at last accepted the importance of developing management and leadership skills in their partners. This recognition is somewhat patchy and inconsistent, and there is often a mismatch between what law firms say they value in their partners (in terms of the competences and characteristics) and what they actually reward (often by recognising and rewarding billing efforts mainly or exclusively).

If growing law firms are to be run as well-coordinated and properly managed businesses, then partners must be prepared to develop their roles from legal technical professionals into business people. They need to be active contributors in various critical or key performance areas which are crucial to their firm's strategy.

It is, therefore, vital to focus on the changing roles and responsibilities of the modern law firm partner or member, and how such new roles and responsibilities are demonstrated by partners' day-to-day expected behaviours. Not only is this topic an extremely important one for the ongoing strategy and governance of the law firm, but it is also critical that every firm should decide and define its expectations of partners before contemplating any changes to the firm's compensation and reward system.

The leadership and management challenge is to put in place the systems, processes and disciplines which are necessary or appropriate to achieve a consistent and coordinated firm. But, even with all the best systems in the world, it takes leadership to bring about changes in the way partners behave from day to day.

Implicitly or explicitly, partners understand the behaviours and attitudes which actually count and do not count in their firm. When partners start to make themselves absent from team meetings, for instance, it will be clear that they do not feel that their absence will be noticed or penalised. The unwritten rules of behaviour at any firm can only be learned by working at the firm or studying it from inside. They illustrate the way things are actually done in the firm, and include the underlying assumptions, behaviours and attitudes which in reality drive the way the firm operates. To bring about changes in the way partners are valued and rewarded, leaders have to set about creating some forces and influences which will gradually affect partners' experiences and then their attitudes and behaviour. For this, firms need three things. First, a set of performance criteria or a 'balanced scorecard' approach encourages partners to believe that there are other things which the firm values in addition to financial performance. Second, the firm must have in place the policies and procedures which will help to give partners the comfort they need to be able to trust in the new arrangements. Third, the firm must work hard on the firm's climate and environment to ensure that a supportive culture exists.

All these issues require leaders to work effectively in orchestrating and inspiring the firm's partners towards the firm's overall objectives, and to define very clearly what behaviours and contributions the firm requires of its partners. Then the firm must ensure that those expected behaviours are reinforced, valued and ultimately rewarded. In addition, the firm must take care to ensure that the fine words of both leaders and partners then match the music of everyday behaviour.

The thrust, therefore, is for leaders to devote time, energy, skill and focus to achieving the difficult but not impossible challenge of developing a firm with a shared sense of direction and destiny, where an atmosphere and environment of trust exists and where partners know what is expected of them, both in terms of their contributions and their day-to-day behaviours. If the leaders succeed in this, there is every chance that partners will clearly know what they have to do to be personally and individually successful in their partnership careers and this will lead to the firm's overall success in agreeing and implementing its chosen strategy.

Creating the prospects for a successful future

There are many ways of approaching the topics dealt with in this book and it is not necessary to think of the process as being prescriptive or linear. In cases where the time is not yet right to undertake a full strategic review, we nevertheless strongly recommend a realistic appraisal of the firm's intellectual capital and its resources and capabilities: this appraisal forms an essential part of or is even a precursor to any strategic planning process. It would, however, be most unwise, in our view, to lurch straight into dramatic or radical action – such as a merger or acquisition, opening a new office (or disposing of a superfluous one), or the use of an ABS without first considering the strategic implications of any bold and far-reaching actions.

We therefore suggest that firms should at the very least test and assess their existing strategy. In most cases, this assessment will reveal a need to review the strategy and we set out the steps which they should take to achieve this.

Step 1 – testing or reviewing the firm's existing strategy – the seven stress tests

When we look at the strategic documents of law firms it is often evident they are a patchwork of many separate plans and business recipes – sometimes as many as there are partners in the firm. It is probably no surprise then that the summary statement of a firm's purpose and direction (sometimes known as the firm's 'mission statement') can often appear very bland, resulting – as such statements often do – from much internal debate, negotiation and compromise. After all, a statement which is too overtly global can upset partners who practise only locally. Descriptions which are explicitly corporate can alienate lawyers who do not do corporate law, whilst litigation lawyers may not resonate with a focus which looks too transactional. Hence law firms gravitate towards the meaningless and the anodyne in their quest for words which sum up the firm, resulting in phrases such as 'the pre-eminent firm in our region', 'a top 50 law firm' or 'a leading national firm', adorned with descriptive but largely empty adjectives such as 'client-focused', 'energetic', 'dynamic', and 'innovative'.

The problem is that none of these statements ends up meaning much either to clients or to partners. It is true, of course, that what matters is not the mission statement but the detailed strategic plan. However, if the mission statement is bland and meaningless, there is every chance that the strategic plan will lose its impact; if, for example, a newspaper article has a weak headline, the reader will usually turn the page leaving the article unread. What is more, without a compelling sense of destiny, a strategy plan can easily default into yet another operational improvement plan – the pursuit of high quality, excellent client service, effective people management, hygienic finances and outstanding profitability.

At the opposite end of the spectrum, we have come across a number of firms which have worked out a compelling and inspirational sense of their vision, purpose and direction and which then assume that they have a strategy – when in fact all they have is an ambition with no real idea of how to attain it. The starting point, therefore, is to consider whether the firm's strategy – however recently adopted and whether or not it is captured in a neat written plan or is simply in the minds of the partners – passes seven tests. If the strategy fails to score well on any one of those tests, then the firm needs to move to Step 2.

1. **The strategy must be futuristic.** It should look at the future rather than summarise the past. It should take account of trends and developments which may affect the firm for better or worse. To be able to compete in the future, the firm is going to have to make an assessment of the opportunities and threats outside. This analysis ought to be radical and forward thinking, but is more than just a brain storming item at a partners' retreat – there needs to be careful and painstaking

research and information gathering. It ought to be a mixture of blue-sky thinking and visioning – daring to dream, if you like – and thorough research into markets and trends. And the firm needs to look at what others are doing both in the legal profession and outside it, in this country and further afield. I would go so far as to say that more than 50 per cent of what law firms are going to have to learn in order to face the future will have to come from outside our own profession – other service industries, high tech, manufacturing and so on.

Finally, so many strategies talk about moving from where we currently are to a place where we might be in the future – 'from here to there' philosophy. I believe this to be the wrong way round. We should try to stand at some point in the future and work backwards from there. If, for instance, we had known in, say 1999, what we now know about the market-place and working practices, how would we have changed our attitudes, actions and the way we practise? The sorts of questions to be asked will include: 'Do we have to practise in that way?' 'Is there a different way of doing things?' and 'What demands can we contemplate from our clients – present and future – arising out of changes in the way they will be doing business?'

2. **Review of successful areas.** To be of any practical use, the review of the firm's current strategy must assess what the firm is currently doing to be successful, and the areas where it is likely to be successful in the future. When a client is choosing a single law firm, there are no prizes for coming second. A good starting point is to make a reality

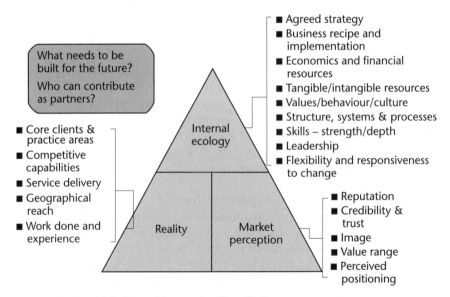

Figure 12.1   The balanced firm – a reality check

check of the firm's strengths and weaknesses, particularly in connection with the firm's resources and capabilities as set out in Chapter 2, and the other facets of intellectual capital studied in Chapter 3. This assessment should help to gauge the areas of strategic importance where the firm needs to improve in order to win, as well as the areas where there is a chance of adding value to clients.

The triangle or pyramid, as shown in Figure 12.1, can be helpful as an assessment tool. The three dimensions outline the internal 'ecology' of the firm and its infrastructure, then the market perception – what the clients, the referrers and the market think of it – and finally the reality of the firm's situation.

All the reality checks should be internal and external. The internal examination may entail a certain amount of navel gazing but it is important to keep this within limits. What sort of firm is it? What is the culture? How does the firm both do things and measure its accomplishments? What structures and systems does the firm have and what are its skills, resources and capabilities? What are the noticeable and acceptable behaviours? How is the firm financed? The answers to these questions will help identify how (internally) the firm may be different from the other firms round and about.

Next, how does the market really see the firm now? What is the firm's reputation? Is the firm trusted? Does it have credibility? Is it seen as cheap or expensive? Does the firm seem to have a strong brand? What do the firm's clients say about the firm? Who would the market say are the firm's competitors and what are its natural boundaries?

Finally, what is the reality? What is the firm's list of core clients? In what practice areas can the firm really claim to be strong and where is it weak? Whom do the firm members regard as their natural competitors? How does the firm deliver its services – in person, on the telephone, electronically and so on? And where does the firm deliver its services – what is the firm's geographical reach? Does the firm rely extensively on partners to do the work, or does it have an engine room of other fee-earners with case management systems who do most of the work?

The point about the pyramid or triangle is to assess whether or not all three areas are balanced or aligned. If, for instance, the perception of the firm in the market-place is better than the reality of its clients and service quality, then the firm can be said to be 'punching above its weight'. Very often it is the other way round and then the firm knows that some of its objectives and goals need to be centred upon the improvement of market perception.

3. **Goals and objectives.** Does the firm's existing strategy include a set of goals and objectives which are still relevant? Unless the firm's strategy is firmly rooted in action, it will be ineffective. And the objectives must be action-based too. Consider, for example, an objective such as

'we must win better clients' or 'we aim to continuously improve profitability' – unless these can be refined down into a task or series of tasks, these are meaningless aspirations. One very important feature of an effective strategy for a law firm is that there should be a clear line of sight for every partner between his or her day-to-day operations and the firm's overall strategic goals. In short, partners must be capable of identifying how their work, career aspirations, specialisations and capabilities fit in with and contribute to the firm's overall strategy. It is difficult to achieve this line of sight when the firm's stated but vague objective is just to get bigger, to become generally famous, or to improve its profitability. It is therefore very worthwhile to take a look at every partner to see if his or her contribution works towards the overall good of the firm and whether or not there is a clear link between the plans of the individuals and the firm's plan. It is worth considering whether or not the strengths, capabilities and experience of each and every individual partner are strategically important to the achievements of the firm's strategic objectives and relevant to the firm's success. For the firm to succeed, each partner needs to help the firm stand out from the crowd in a manner which supports the firm's strategy and in ways which are meaningful to the generality of the firm's clients and referrers.

4. **Sharing, ownership and commitment.** The plan delivered from on high just does not work. To stand any chance of success, the strategy must be contributed to and owned by the partners. Much of the work will, of course, be done at a high level, and leadership, inspiration and vision need to be evident from the firm's leaders. But the strategy of the firm should be an iterative, ongoing process involving all partners, who should have a clear understanding about where and how their day-to-day work fits in with the firm's overall objectives.

    If involvement and engagement have been achieved throughout the firm, then the task of implementation and follow-through becomes easier.

5. **Competitive challenges.** Assess realistically the firm's competitive positioning within its current strategy and the realistic chances of success for the firm with its present plans. Chapter 1 introduced many of the increased competitive challenges law firms face both currently and in the future. Chapter 4 set out a methodology by which firms can assess or decide how they are seen (or want to be seen) in their market-place, how they are currently positioned in the markets they wish to occupy and what type of client will provide the firm's core business as it goes forward. It needs to consider its resources and capabilities in order to service the clients for whom it aspires to act, and the required depth in each practice area.

    In short, the firm needs to decide and define how it is going to compete and what it wishes clients to perceive as its competitive edge.

Chapter 6 added an extra dimension to the assessment of competitive challenges by setting out both the opportunities and threats likely to take place from the various types of ABS which are steadily emerging as the LSA takes effect.

6. **Profitable growth.** The firm's strategy must focus on profitable growth, rather than growth for growth's sake. To gain growth in profit, four key levers have to be methodically applied – margins, leverage, utilisation and realisation – and technological solutions are key to all these, if integrated with the overall strategy for the business. The majority of law firms still have a lot to do to clean up their financial disciplines. There are very few firms which can claim to be working with maximum efficiency and full productivity. Productivity and utilisation is still lacklustre. Write-offs and leakage occur all too frequently. Billing disciplines almost everywhere can be improved. Lock-up in debtors and work in progress are still too high in most firms. Overheads and budgetary controls are often not rigorously in place. What is more, issues of underperformance, both at partner level and below that, are tolerated and not confronted.

A successful strategy for a law firm always includes some measures for better financial disciplines, firmer accountability and stronger management of the key performance indicators.

A greater focus on leverage is also essential. It is worth remembering that leverage can be defined as 'any measure which gets things done at lower aggregate cost' – through technology, 'packaging', or people, with less partner time on matters and more time at a non-partner level.

7. **Adding value.** The last and perhaps the most important element is that the strategy should add value to clients, be aimed firmly at the fulfilment of their latent and blatant needs, and provide the necessary resources and capabilities to enable the firm to obtain the most lucrative work possible during the lifetime of the plan.

Step 2 – undertaking or renewing the strategic planning process

The seven-point reality check at Step 1 may convince the firm's leaders that the firm's existing strategy, perhaps with a few modifications, is sufficiently robust to lead the firm to a successful future. In many cases, however, a brutal and frank reappraisal of the firm's existing resources and capabilities, the threats it faces and the risk of remaining or becoming uncompetitive, will persuade the firm to undertake a deeper strategic planning process.

Chapter 5 suggested that the likely increase in competitive pressures requires law firms to address three burning issues. Unless the strategic planning of law firms enables them to face the future with clarity of purpose and direction, they are likely to meander. Unless firms have an external focus on the likely demands of clients and on how they are going to fulfil their clients' needs with excellent service, their strategies are likely to become inward looking and irrelevant to the external market-place. If firms do little or nothing to make some deliberate and perhaps radical strategic choices, their strategies are likely to remain at best as worthy improvement plans and at worst as do-nothing policies leading to inevitable decline

I see four planning phases to address those burning issues.

1. **Information gathering and research.** It can be seen from the previous chapters of this book that a great deal of internal and external information gathering and analysis has to take place in framing a successful strategy. In this first phase of information gathering, efforts should be made to analyse both the markets and the environment in which the firm is operating. A market analysis will typically examine the variety of industry, practice, service and pricing strategies available to the law firm, the location of the firm's practice of law together with the geographic market, and comparisons with neighbouring markets which may assist in seeking economic opportunities in the legal market-place. The possible impact of political, economic, social and technological trends will need to be considered. Additionally, as Chapter 2 demonstrated, a great deal of analysis of the firm's resources and capabilities needs to take place – tangible resources and intangible elements of intellectual capital broken down into human capital, relational capital, and structural capital. This research will inevitably involve information gathering from people inside the firm (including partners), as well as from clients, referrers and institutions. The analysis can then conveniently be broken down into the three areas of market analysis, practice area analysis and financial analysis. Areas of strategic importance to the firm should be assessed for their strengths and weaknesses relative to the firm's competitors. The sub-areas of specialisation that provide the greatest opportunity for profitable growth should be established, along with an identification of industries where each group has a particular expertise and experience. Areas of possible diversification (as outlined in Chapter 5) should also be considered.

2. **Identification of main issues, vision and options.** When all the information has been gathered and all the data and trends have been analysed, the firm ought to be able to list the spectrum of conditions and opportunities available to it and to identify where it is best positioned to focus its attention and resources in order to develop its strategy and competitive positioning, new clients, new markets and new revenue streams.

   To accomplish this, firms should review, discuss and digest the information and then develop observations about the firm and its environment. The result will be a variety of different pathways for the firm's future which can be developed into strategic options. Essentially, the work at this phase needs to reduce all of the Phase 1 research and analysis into one or two pages of conclusions.

Using this information, the firm can create a vision for the future. This vision is really a statement of objectives to describe the end result which the firm is trying to achieve. Typically, the vision describes the firm's practice mix, areas of focus and any constraining features. This brief statement – the simpler and shorter the better – is used to develop a shared commitment by the partners to a desired goal.

3. **Strategy formulation and testing.** Using the conclusions drawn and the vision expressed in Phase 2, the firm can now start to determine the strategies it intends to pursue in order to achieve the vision. Typically, this means the conditions which must be present to achieve the vision and normally involves a series of specific, prioritised strategies, usually six to eight in number. The result of this session will be a strategic planning document which can then be tested to ensure both that it matches the seven stress test elements listed above, and that it is also sufficiently resilient to enable the firm to survive and prosper in worst case scenarios as well as the most optimal environment. This can then be presented to the partnership.

4. **Business planning and implementation.** The business plan has a dual function. It is the implementation arm of the strategy process, designating the specific actions which must be taken to implement the strategies, the partners that will be accountable for making sure the action occurs and fatal dates for execution. At the same time, it integrates the specific action plans necessary to implement the firm's strategies with the operational support required. This involves such aspects as budgetary cost impact, recruiting priorities, technology requirements, necessary training and development of attorneys and staff, required marketing support and similar logistical issues.

During the course of Phases 1 to 3, a number of issues will surface regarding operational efficiencies, market opportunities, technology needs and other considerations that do not directly involve the firm's strategy for positioning itself in the market-place. The business plan provides an effective means of harnessing those issues.

True advancement of a business strategy occurs through the successful completion of an incremental series of actions, rather than the creation of a grand plan that ends up relegated to a bookshelf.

Implementation is a day-to-day process of ensuring that actions occur and deadlines are met.

Summary

All is not lost. The end of the world for lawyers is not imminent. There will be winners as well as losers. However, this is not a period where any firm can afford either to put its head in the sand or to assume that no change is necessary. Not every firm will want or need to become an ABS, but every firm does need to look very closely at the competitive pressures it will face and figure out its own answers to the key question 'Why should clients choose our firm?'. The various exercises I have suggested should help the firm to face its future through a deeper understanding of the firm's intangible and tangible assets – its resources and capabilities and its intellectual capital – by taking deep stock of its competitive positioning, by looking at its strategies for both attack and defence and by considering ABSs. The possible provision of external funding, the use of mergers and acquisitions and the augmentation of the firm's intrinsic value all have their place in the strategic toolkit as well. In addition, the structure of the firm, from the way partners are remunerated to the firm's governance models, needs to be examined and the key question needs to be answered: 'How should we be best organised to make profit and fulfil our strategy?'

Fortune will favour those firms which make their strategic choices wisely and boldly and then implement them rigorously and with commitment.

Bibliography

Arnold, G. (2005) *Handbook of Corporate Finance*, Prentice Hall.

Arthur, W. (2009) 'Capitalization and working capital: is your house in order?' (2009) 1 *Kerma Partners Quarterly*, available at **www.kermapartners.com**.

Berger, A. N., Demsetz, R. S. and Strahan, P. E. (1999) 'The consolidation of the financial services industry', 23 *Journal of Banking and Finance*.

Bowman, C. (1998) *Strategy in Practice*, Prentice Hall.

Brown, C., Dittmar, A. and Servaes, C. (2004) *Corporate Governance, Incentives and Industry Consolidations*, Society for Financial Studies.

Clementi, D. (2004) 'Review of the regulatory framework for legal services in England and Wales', 15 December, available at **www.legal-services-review.org.uk**.

Cummins, J. D. and Weiss, M. A. (2004) *Consolidation in the European Insurance Industry: Do Mergers and Acquisitions Create Value for Shareholders?* Wharton Financial Institutions Center.

Delong, D. J., Gabarro, J. J. and Lees, R. J. (2007) *When Professionals Have to Lead*, Harvard Business School Press.

Department of Trade and Industry. (2004) *The Benefits from Competition: Some Illustrative UK Cases* (Economics Paper No. 9).

Edvinsson, L. and Malone, L. S. (1997) *Intellectual Capital*, Harper Business.

Empson, L. (2000a) 'Merging professional services firms'. 11(2) *Business Strategy Review*.

Empson, L. (2000b) 'Mergers between professional service firms: exploring an undirected process of integration', in A. Gregory and C. Cooper (eds.), *Advances in Mergers and Acquisitions*, vol. 1, pp. 205–37, Elsevier.

Empson, L. (ed.) (2007) *Managing the Modern Law Firm*, Oxford University Press.

Finkelstein, S., Hambrick, D. C. and Cannella, A. A. (2009) *Strategic Leadership – Theory and Research on Executives, Top Management Teams and Boards*, Oxford University Press.

Forsyth, P. (2003) *Marketing and Selling Professional Services*, 3rd edn, Kogan Page.

Frykman, D. and Tolleryd, J. (2003) *A Corporate Valuation*, Prentice Hall.

Gilson, R. and Mnookin, R. (1985) 'Sharing among the human capitalists: an economic inquiry into the corporate law firm and how partners split profits', 37 *Stanford Law Review*, 313–92.

Grant, R. M. (2008) *Contemporary Strategy Analysis*, Blackwell.

Gratton, L. (2000) *Living Strategy – Putting People at the Heart of Corporate Purpose*, Prentice Hall.

Koller, T., Goedhart, M. and Wessels, D. (2005) *Valuation*, 4th edn, Wiley.

Kotler, P. and others. (2002) *Marketing Professional Services*, 2nd edn, Prentice Hall.

Lake, R. and Lake, R. (2000) *Private Equity and Venture Capital: a Practical Guide for Investors and Practitioners*, Euromoney Books.

Legal Services Board (2009a) *Business Plan 2009/10,* January, available at **www.legalservicesboard.org.uk/news_publications/publications/pdf/ business_plan_2009_10.pdf.**

Legal Services Board (2009b) 'Wider access, better value, strong protection', May.

LegallyBetter.com (2008) 'How the internet is transforming user behaviour and legal services marketing', unpublished White Paper.

Lloyd, R. (2009) 'Market forces', *Legal Week*, January.

Maister, D. (1993) *Managing the Professional Service Firm*, Free Press.

Maister, D. (1997) *True Professionalism*, Free Press.

Maister, D. (2008) *Strategy and the Fat Smoker*, Spangle Press.

Mayson, S. (2007) *Law Firm Strategy: Competitive Advantage and Valuation*, Oxford University Press.

Mintzberg, H. (1994) *The Rise and Fall of Strategic Planning*, Prentice Hall.

Moss Kanter, R. (2001) *Evolve! Succeeding in the Digital Culture of Tomorrow*, Harvard Business School Press.

Office for National Statistics (2006) *Annual Business Enquiry, figures for 2006*.

Pedler, M., Burgoyne, J. and Boydell, T. (2004) *A Manager's Guide to Leadership*, McGraw-Hill.

Peters, T. (2003) *Re-Imagine*, Dorling Kindersley.

Peters, T. and Waterman, R. (2004) *In Search of Excellence: Lessons from America's Best-Run Companies*, 2nd edn, Profile Business.

Porter, M. E. (1980) *Competitive Strategy*, Free Press.

Pratt, S., Reilly, R. and Schweihs, R. (1998) *Valuing Small Businesses and Professional Practices*, 3rd edn, McGraw-Hill.

PriceWaterhouseCoopers (2004) *Financial Management in Law Firms Survey*.

PriceWaterhouseCoopers (2005) *Financial Management in Law Firms Survey*.

Ridderstrale, J. and Nordstromm, K. (2004) *Karaoke Capitalism*, Prentice Hall.

Rosenweig, P. (2007) *The Halo Effect*, Free Press.

Schein, E. H. (1999) *The Corporate Culture Survival Guide*, Jossey-Bass.

Scott, M. C. (1998) *The Professional Service Firm*, Wiley.

Solicitors Regulation Authority (2009) 'Regulating alternative business structures' (consultation paper 18).

Susskind, R. (2008) *The End of Lawyers? Rethinking the Nature of Legal Services*, Oxford University Press.

Sveiby, K. E. and Lloyd, T. (1987) *Managing Knowhow*, Bloomsbury.

UK Treasury (2009) *Professional Services Competitive Group Report*, March.

Wesemann, H. E. (2005) *Creating Dominance – Winning Strategies for Law Firms*, Authorhouse.

Wesemann, H. E. and Jarrett-Kerr, N. (2008) *A Global Survey of Large Law Firm Compensation Practices*, Kerma Partners, available at **www.kermapartners.com**.

Index